Judith Overmier
Rhonda Harris Taylor
Editors

Managing the Mystery Collection: From Creation to Consumption

Managing the Mystery Collection: From Creation to Consumption has been co-published simultaneously as *Collection Management*, Volume 29, Numbers 3/4 2004.

Pre-publication REVIEWS, COMMENTARIES, EVALUATIONS . . .

"IF ONLY THE READINGS IN MY COLLECTION DEVELOPMENT CLASS BACK IN LIBRARY SCHOOL HAD BEEN SO INTERESTING AND READABLE. . . . Potential readers should not be fooled by the apparent genre-specificity of this title. This is in many ways a primer for how library collections can be built, utilized, and promoted. Fifteen estimable writers guide us through a series of separate yet ultimately connected topics, such as how authors make use of libraries; specific audiences, writers, or subgenres; review and acquisition resources; collection descriptions; establishing publicity/support activities such as discussion groups; and examining the scholarly study of a popular genre."

Allen Ellis, MLS
Professor of Library Services
W. Frank Steely Library
Northern Kentucky University

More Pre-publication
REVIEWS, COMMENTARIES, EVALUATIONS . . .

"INVALUABLE. . . . A MUST, NOT ONLY FOR LIBRARIANS, BUT ALSO FOR EVERY SERIOUS MYSTERY READER, WRITER, COLLECTOR, OR SCHOLAR. The lively, well-selected, crisply written contributions represent a comprehensive resource for librarians, whether at small public libraries or large research universities. From providing research services for mystery writers, to building collections and special collections, to accessing print and online resources on the mystery genre, to programming for mystery readers, this book recounts the illuminating experiences of individual libraries and librarians, and INCLUDES A WEALTH OF RESOURCES. Now, in one volume, I can find bibliographies of African American and Native American mystery writers, lists of mystery publications and Web sites, the locations of special collections on Sherlock Holmes and popular culture and law, and advice on acquiring hard-to-find mysteries."

Marty S. Knepper, PhD
Professor and Chair
English Department
Morningside College
Past President
Popular Culture Association

The Haworth Information Press
An Imprint of The Haworth Press, Inc.

Managing the Mystery Collection: From Creation to Consumption

Managing the Mystery Collection: From Creation to Consumption has been co-published simultaneously as *Collection Management*, Volume 29, Numbers 3/4 2004.

Monographic Separates from *Collection Management*™

For additional information on these and other Haworth Press titles, including descriptions, tables of contents, reviews, and prices, use the QuickSearch catalog at http://www.HaworthPress.com.

Managing the Mystery Collection: From Creation to Consumption, edited by Judith Overmier and Rhonda Harris Taylor (Vol. 29, No. 3/4, 2004). *A unique collection of essays from mystery authors, readers, critics, scholars, and librarians examining the progression of the mystery story from the author's creation through its inclusion on library shelves on to its consumption by readers.*

The New Dynamics and Economics of Cooperative Collection Development, edited by Edward Shreeves (Vol. 28, No. (1/2)(3), 2003). *Explores state-of-the-art techniques and new possibilities for cooperative collection development.*

Electronic Collection Management, edited by Suzan D. McGinnis (Vol. 25, No. 1/2, 2000). *A practical guide to the art and science of acquiring and organizing electronic resources.*

Creating New Strategies for Cooperative Collection Development, edited by Milton T. Wolf and Marjorie E. Bloss (Vol. 24, No. (1/2)(3/4), 2000). *Discusses current initiatives in cooperative collection development and points the way to expanding the scope of this activity in the future.*

Cooperative Collection Development: Significant Trends and Issues, edited by Donald B. Simpson (Vol. 23, No. 4, 1998). *Shows how the art of cooperation requires librarians' ability to comprehend and support "big picture" goals and the skills to incorporate "common good" objectives into local activities so that there is constructive and affirmative benefit to your own programs and services.*

Government Information Collections in the Networked Environment: New Issues and Models, edited by Joan F. Cheverie (Vol. 23, No. 3, 1998). *Explores the challenging issues related to effective access to government information.*

Going Digital: Strategies for Access, Preservation, and Conversion of Collections to a Digital Format, edited by Donald L. DeWitt (Vol. 22, No. 3/4, 1998). *"This excellent book presents a comprehensive study of crucial issues confronting librarians and archivists today. . . . From the first article to the last, it is a compelling read!" (Carol A. Mathius, MLIS, CA, Archivist, Head of Special Collections, Nicholls State University, Thibodaux, Louisiana)*

Collection Development: Access in the Virtual Library, edited by Maureen Pastine (Vol. 22, No. 1/2, 1997). *"Documents unequivocably that collaboration–between library and customer, library and vendor, and among libraries–is essential for success in today's academic library." (Kathryn Hammell Carpenter, MS, University Librarian, Valparaiso University, Indiana)*

Collection Development: Past and Future, edited by Maureen Pastine (Vol. 21, No. 2/3, 1996). *"An important navigational tool for steering through the turbulent waters of the evolving collection development environment. I highly recommend it." (Blake Landar, PhD, Philosophy, Classics, and Religion Bibliographer, University of Florida)*

Electronic Resources: Implications for Collection Management, edited by Genevieve S. Owens (Vol. 21, No. 1, 1996). *"Discusses the strengths and weaknesses of electronic resources, as well as the implications these resources have on collection management. Also provides guidance on incorporating electronic resources into library collections." (Reference and Research Book News)*

Practical Issues in Collection Development and Collection Access, edited by Katina Strauch, Sally W. Somers, Susan Zappen, and Anne Jennings (Vol. 19, No. 3/4, 1995). *With surveys, studies, and first-hand accounts of "how we did it," this book shows how fellow professionals view the evolving world of information selection, maintenance, access, and delivery.*

Access Services in Libraries: New Solutions for Collection Management, edited by Gregg Sapp (Vol. 17, No. 1/2, 1993). *"Develops a theoretical foundation for the growing phenomenon of access services in public and academic libraries–an approach to the increasingly complex problem of making materials available to patrons." (Reference and Research Book News)*

Euro-Librarianship: Shared Resources, Shared Responsibilities, edited by Assunta Pisani (Vol. 15, No. 1/2/3/4, 1992). *"A rich compendium of information about European studies, especially in relation to librarianship. . . . A worthwhile volume that will be helpful to Western European Studies librarians for many years to come." (Western European Specialists Section Newsletter)*

International Conference on Research Library Cooperation, The Research Libraries Group, Inc. (Vol. 9, No. 2/3, 1998). *"A useful . . . look at selected cooperative schemes in Britain, Europe and the United States and propose guidelines for the future." (Library Association Record)*

Reading and the Art of Librarianship: Selected Essays of John B. Nicholson, Jr., edited by Paul Z. DuBois and Dean H. Keller (Vol. 8, No. 3/4, 1986). *"A selection from over 300 completely delightful essays, representing the late author's wide and varied interests. There is much food for thought in these pages, a lively collection that is personal, intimate . . . a passionate look at the world of books." (Academic Library Book Review)*

Collection Management for School Library Media Centers, edited by Brenda H. White (Vol. 7, No. 3/4, 1986). *"A wealth of information concerning managing a school library media center collection. . . . Readable, interesting, and practical." (The Book Report: The Journal for Junior and Senior High School Librarians)*

The State of Western European Studies: Implication for Collection Development, edited by Anthony M. Angiletta, Martha L. Brogan, Charles S. Fineman, and Clara M. Lovett (Vol. 6, No. 1/2, 1984). *"An exceptionally well-edited volume . . . lively and engrossing. . . . An informative and thought-provoking overview of the current state of Western European studies and its possible future directions." (Special Libraries Association)*

∞ ALL HAWORTH INFORMATION PRESS BOOKS AND JOURNALS ARE PRINTED ON CERTIFIED ACID-FREE PAPER

Managing the Mystery Collection: From Creation to Consumption

Judith Overmier
Rhonda Harris Taylor
Editors

Managing the Mystery Collection: From Creation to Consumption has been co-published simultaneously as *Collection Management*, Volume 29, Numbers 3/4 2004.

The Haworth Information Press®
An Imprint of The Haworth Press, Inc.

New York • London • Victoria (AU)
www.HaworthPress.com

Published by

The Haworth Information Press®, 10 Alice Street, Binghamton, NY 13904-1580 USA

The Haworth Information Press® is an imprint of The Haworth Press, Inc., 10 Alice Street, Binghamton, NY 13904-1580 USA.

Managing the Mystery Collection: From Creation to Consumption has been co-published simultaneously as *Collection Management*™, Volume 29, Numbers 3/4 2004.

Cover design by Marylouise E. Doyle.

Library of Congress Cataloging-in-Publication Data

Managing the mystery collection : from creation to consumption / Judith Overmier, Rhonda Harris Taylor, editors.

p. cm.

"Co-published simultaneously as Collection management, volume 29, numbers 3/4."

Includes bibliographical references and index.

ISBN-13: 978-0-7890-3153-2 (hc. : alk. paper)

ISBN-10: 0-7890-3153-1 (hc. : alk. paper)

ISBN-13: 978-0-7890-3154-9 (pbk. : alk. paper)

ISBN-10: 0-7890-3154-X (pbk. : alk. paper)

1. Libraries–Special collections–Detective and mystery stories. 2. Detective and mystery stories–Bibliography–Methodology. 3. Fiction in libraries. 4. Reading interests. I. Overmier, Judith A., 1939- II. Taylor, Rhonda Lynette Harris, 1951- III. Collection management.

Z688.D46M36 2006

025.2780883'872–dc22

2005020982

Indexing, Abstracting & Website/Internet Coverage

This section provides you with a list of major indexing & abstracting services and other tools for bibliographic access. That is to say, each service began covering this periodical during the year noted in the right column. Most Websites which are listed below have indicated that they will either post, disseminate, compile, archive, cite or alert their own Website users with research-based content from this work. (This list is as current as the copyright date of this publication.)

Abstracting, Website/Indexing Coverage . . . . Year When Coverage Began

- *AATA Online: Abstracts of International Conservation Literature (formerly Art & Archeology Technical Abstracts) <http://aata.getty.edu>* **2004**
- *Combined Health Information Database (CHID)* **1995**
- *Computer and Information Systems Abstracts <http://www.csa.com>* **2004**
- *EBSCOhost Electronic Journals Service (EJS) <http://ejournals.ebsco.com>* **2001**
- *FRANCIS. INIST/CNRS <http://www.inist.fr>* **1983**
- *Getty Conservation Institute (GCI) Project Bibliographies <http://www.getty.edu>* **2004**
- *Google <http://www.google.com>* **2004**
- *Google Scholar <http://scholar.google.com>* **2004**
- *Haworth Document Delivery Center <http://www.HaworthPress.com/journals/dds.asp>* **1976**
- *IBZ International Bibliography of Periodical Literature <http://www.saur.de>* **1995**
- *Index Guide to College Journals (core list compiled by integrating 48 indexes frequently used to support undergraduate programs in small to medium sized libraries)* **1999**
- *Index to Periodical Articles Related to Law <http://www.law.utexas.edu>* **1989**

(continued)

- *Information Reports & Bibliographies* **1992**
- *Information Science & Technology Abstracts: indexes journal articles from more than 450 publications as well as books, research reports, and conference proceedings; EBSCO Publishing <http://www.epnet.com>* **1978**
- *Informed Librarian, The <http://www.informedlibrarian.com>* . . . **1993**
- *Internationale Bibliographie der geistes- und sozialwissenschaftlichen Zeitschriftenliteratur . . . See IBZ <http://www.saur.de>* **1995**
- *Journal of Academic Librarianship: Guide to Professional Literature, The* **1995**
- *Konyvtari Figyelo (Library Review)* **1995**
- *"LABORDOC" Library–Periodicals Section "Abstracts Section" <http://www.ilo.org>* **2001**
- *Library & Information Science Abstracts (LISA) <http://www.csa.com>* **1989**
- *Library and Information Science Annual (LISCA) <http://www.lu.com>* **1997**
- *Library Literature & Information Science <http://www.hwwilson.com>* **1984**
- *Links@Ovid (via CrossRef targeted DOI links) <http://www.ovid.com>* **2005**
- *Magazines for Libraries (Katz) . . . . (see 2003 edition)* **2003**
- *OCLC ArticleFirst <http://www.oclc.org/services/databases/>* **2001**
- *OCLC ContentsFirst <http://www.oclc.org/services/databases/>* . . **2001**
- *Ovid Linksolver (OpenURL link resolver via CrossRef targeted DOI links) <http://www.linksolver.com>* **2005**
- *PASCAL, c/o Institut de l'Information Scientifique et Technique. Cross-disciplinary electronic database covering the fields of science, technology & medicine. Also available on CD-ROM, and can generate customized retrospective searches <http://www.inist.fr>* **1983**
- *Referativnyi Zhurnal (Abstracts Journal of the All-Russian Institute of Scientific and Technical Information–in Russian) <http://www.viniti.ru>* **1986**
- *SwetsWise <http://www.swets.com>* **2002**
- *zetoc <http://zetoc.mimas.ac.uk/>* **2004**

Book reviews are selectively excerpted by the Guide to Professional Literature of the *Journal of Academic Librarianship.*

(continued)

Special Bibliographic Notes related to special journal issues (separates) and indexing/abstracting:

- indexing/abstracting services in this list will also cover material in any "separate" that is co-published simultaneously with Haworth's special thematic journal issue or DocuSerial. Indexing/abstracting usually covers material at the article/chapter level.
- monographic co-editions are intended for either non-subscribers or libraries which intend to purchase a second copy for their circulating collections.
- monographic co-editions are reported to all jobbers/wholesalers/approval plans. The source journal is listed as the "series" to assist the prevention of duplicate purchasing in the same manner utilized for books-in-series.
- to facilitate user/access services all indexing/abstracting services are encouraged to utilize the co-indexing entry note indicated at the bottom of the first page of each article/chapter/contribution.
- this is intended to assist a library user of any reference tool (whether print, electronic, online, or CD-ROM) to locate the monographic version if the library has purchased this version but not a subscription to the source journal.
- individual articles/chapters in any Haworth publication are also available through the Haworth Document Delivery Service (HDDS).

Managing the Mystery Collection: From Creation to Consumption

CONTENTS

ABOUT THE EDITORS

Judith Overmier, PhD, is Professor Emeritus, University of Oklahoma. Dr. Overmier is the author of articles on medical rare book librarianship, collecting rare science books, provenance, and the acquisition of out-of-print materials and of the reference books: *History of Biology: A Selected, Annotated Bibliography* (1989) and *Books and Manuscripts of the Bakken* (1992). She is editor of *Out-of-Print and Special Collections: Acquisition and Purchasing Options* (2002), cover story editor for the journal *Libraries & Culture* since 1989, and co-editor of *Psychology: IUPsyS Global Resource* (annually 2000 through 2004). Dr. Overmier is an avid reader and collector of mysteries and is currently writing her first mystery, *No Fishing Allowed.* She is a member of the Popular Culture Association, Sisters in Crime, and Romance Writers of America.

Rhonda Harris Taylor, PhD, is Associate Professor, School of Library and Information Studies, University of Oklahoma, where she teaches courses in the organization of information, multicultural librarianship, and library administration. Dr. Taylor has been the author and co-author of articles on library resources for and about Native Americans and also on popular culture topics. She is a life-long reader of mysteries who also has an avid interest in pop-up books, and she is a member of the Popular Culture Association.

Introduction

This volume represents the journey from the creation of the mystery story to its ultimate consumption by an avid reader. But, of particular interest to acquisitions and collection management librarians is the fact that this road oft-traveled is a circular route that also encompasses library collections. As will be seen in the various essays that constitute this issue, authors, readers, critics, scholars, and librarians interact at various junctions in a dynamic process that brings together these players and the world of information resources, and each encounter is fodder for the next act, whether creation or consumption.

To begin the cycle, mystery writer and librarian Barbara Fister provides a uniquely informed glimpse into the creative process of imagining and bringing to paper the mystery story. Her essay on "Bodies of Evidence: How Mystery Writers Imagine Their Worlds Through Research" offers explication of how mystery writers utilize library collections to create their stories and underscores the important roles of collection building and of retention of a variety of resources.

Kathy Harig brings multiple voices to her role of "mystery insider"–librarian, Sisters in Crime Liaison, mystery bookstore owner, AND daughter of a Sherlockian–to her essay, "Libraries and Sisters in Crime." She shares insights about the organization, Sisters in Crime, which promotes mysteries authored by women, and its special relationship with libraries and librarians.

Larisa Somsel, of Somsel Books, offers the acquisitions and collection development librarian an authoritative and detailed introduction to

---

[Haworth co-indexing entry note]: "Introduction." Overmier, Judith, and Rhonda Harris Taylor. Co-published simultaneously in *Collection Management* (The Haworth Information Press, an imprint of The Haworth Press, Inc.) Vol. 29, No. 3/4, 2004, pp. 1-3; and: *Managing the Mystery Collection: From Creation to Consumption* (ed: Judith Overmier, and Rhonda Harris Taylor) The Haworth Information Press, an imprint of The Haworth Press, Inc., 2004, pp. 1-3. Single or multiple copies of this article are available for a fee from The Haworth Document Delivery Service [1-800-HAWORTH, 9:00 a.m. - 5:00 p.m. (EST). E-mail address: docdelivery@haworthpress.com].

Available online at http://www.haworthpress.com/web/COL

doi:10.1300/J105v29n03_01

buying and selling books online in her revealing essay, "Buying Books Online Is No Mystery."

Public librarian Jean Bielke-Rodenbiker covers "Review Sources for Mystery Fiction," highlighting important print and Web resources for the selector.

In her essay, "'I Need a Good Mystery': Selecting for the Juvenile Reader," former school library media specialist Nancy Larson Bluemel provides an overview of the reading interests of the younger mystery reader, simultaneously providing guidance for the acquisition of mysteries for this group of patrons.

Often overlooked in library collections, but of increasing popularity, are so-called "ethnic mysteries." Library educator Connie Van Fleet, who shares responsibility for the 2003 guide, *African American Readers Advisory*, supplies the collection development librarian with a pathfinder to "African American Mysteries," while Rhonda Harris Taylor has penned an introduction to mysteries with Native American detectives.

Both Victoria Gill and Timothy Johnson provide invitations to explore two very special collections that delight followers of THE GREAT DETECTIVE and his creator (Sherlock Holmes and author Conan Doyle). These two collections, one in Canada and one in the United States, are housed in a public library and an academic library respectively, and each has an intriguing history and unique mission. Librarians will be fascinated by the sagas of the complex interactions that led to the creation of these special collections, as recounted in Gill's "The Arthur Conan Doyle Collection at the Toronto Public Library" and Johnson's "The Adventure of the Unopened Box: Building the Sherlock Holmes Collections at the University of Minnesota Libraries."

Reference Librarian Marlyn Robinson and Rhonda Hankins profile "Mysteries in a Law Library: The Law in Popular Culture Collection at the University of Texas School of Law," using an interview format that is both readable and informative.

Tracy Allen's coverage of the "Mystery and the Romance Reader" explicates the appeal of fusions of the mystery and romance genres. To assist in collection development, she gives extensive listings of subgenre titles and details of popular series.

In "Murder, Mystery, and Mayhem: The Development of a Mystery Book Discussion Group," library board member Elizabeth Arneth lends an insider's look at an often missing perspective, that of the book discussion group member. Her article demonstrates the synergy that can be generated when mystery fans and the public library collaborate, and she offers insight into both reference resources and preferred novels that will be consumed by avid mystery readers.

Academic librarian Mary P. Freier's "A Brief History of Scholarly Study of Detective Fiction, with Particular Attention to the Detective & Mystery Fiction Area of the Popular Culture Association" introduces collection development librarians to an organization and an area of study that networks creators, fans, and scholars of popular culture, specifically in the context of detective and mystery fiction.

Finally, Judith Overmier and Rhonda Harris Taylor conclude this collection with an essay on "Tracking Miriam Grace Monfredo Through Herstory, Librarianship, and Sleuthing." They interweave themes of creation, collections, and consumption of mysteries throughout coverage of mystery writer/librarian Monfredo's historical mystery series about a female librarian detective.

Judith Overmier
Rhonda Harris Taylor

Bodies of Evidence: How Mystery Writers Imagine Their Worlds Through Research

Barbara Fister

SUMMARY. Mysteries employ a combination of imagination, experience, and research for authenticity. This article explores how writers in the genre conduct their research, the role research has played in their books, what effect the research underpinning their work has on readers–and what it might mean for libraries. *[Article copies available for a fee from The Haworth Document Delivery Service: 1-800-HAWORTH. E-mail address: <docdelivery@haworthpress.com> Website: <http://www.HaworthPress.com>*

KEYWORDS. Mystery and detective stories, genre fiction, creativity and research, libraries and popular culture

---

Barbara Fister is Librarian, Gustavus Adolphus College, St. Peter, MN 56082 (E-mail: fister@gac.edu). She is also the author of *On Edge* Dell, 2002.

"I've found that the whole world is a library," Martin Cruz Smith.[1]

[Haworth co-indexing entry note]: "Bodies of Evidence: How Mystery Writers Imagine Their Worlds Through Research." Fister, Barbara. Co-published simultaneously in *Collection Management* (The Haworth Information Press, an imprint of The Haworth Press, Inc.) Vol. 29, No. 3/4, 2004, pp. 5-19; and: *Managing the Mystery Collection: From Creation to Consumption* (ed: Judith Overmier, and Rhonda Harris Taylor) The Haworth Information Press, an imprint of The Haworth Press, Inc., 2004, pp. 5-19. Single or multiple copies of this article are available for a fee from The Haworth Document Delivery Service [1-800-HAWORTH, 9:00 a.m. - 5:00 p.m. (EST). E-mail address: docdelivery@haworthpress.com].

Available online at http://www.haworthpress.com/web/COL

doi:10.1300/J105v29n03_02

In Danuta Reah's intelligent psychological thriller, *Listen to the Shadows*, a linguistic researcher finds comfort in a large university library, where she is trying to confirm a hunch that there is a link between language difficulties and violent behavior in young offenders: "She worked in the quiet of the stacks, the endless rows of shelves, the pools of light in the darkness restoring her equilibrium. As she read, she felt the excitement of seeing solid backing for her intuition" (97). For her, the library is a peaceful and familiar place where she can make sense of a disordered world. Yet that same setting is threatening, seen from the perspective of an imaginative child whom she later brings with her to the library. "It was like the story about the monster in the maze . . . More shelves, more secret shelves. Lucy had run around them, laughing, wanting to make a noise, and then she didn't know where she was. Everywhere she looked, there were just shelves. In front of her, rows and rows, and in the distance it got dark . . ." (153-54).

Mystery writers are veteran explorers of Lucy's "secret shelves" where they seek confirmation for their intuitions–and where, at the same time, like young Lucy, they sense the presence of roaming monsters just beyond the next set of stacks.

What role does research play in the creative work of constructing a mystery? And why does it matter so much to readers that crime fiction carries the ring of authenticity? As a mystery writer, I have found my training as a librarian helpful for getting background, finding facts, and generating ideas for my fiction–but I also have discovered that libraries sometimes don't have the answers I need. As a librarian, I've found it interesting to observe my own writing habits to discover the kinds of questions that are generated when writing fiction and to ponder what role our collections and services play in creative work. And as a reader, I am fascinated by the various sleights of hand writers use to suspend my disbelief and create an authoritative and authentic alternate reality. To explore these issues further, I conducted interviews with several writers about their experiences with research and polled readers about their attitudes. Canadian writer Michelle Spring summed up the dual role of research in a nutshell: It provides credibility for the reader and inspiration for the writer.

CREDIBILITY

"Novelists need to know how things work–how bodies are handled, how missing persons are traced," according to Spring. "Research supplies the facts, the background data, that enables a writer to create a fictional world. Readers have a right not to be shaken out of their involvement with the novel by something that is blatantly inaccurate."

As an example, in preparation for *In the Midnight Hour*, the complex story of the missing child who may, or may not, have turned up as an adult years later, she spent time with a forensic artist to learn how images of missing people are constructed. Spring walked the beach where the child in the story disappeared, and for another thread in the novel, she studied papers from the Scott Polar Institute about Sir John Franklin's 1845 polar expeditions. *Nights in White Satin,* which deals with historical and contemporary events and social attitudes surrounding sex work, was informed by interviews with women working in the sex industry and first-hand observations in a part of London known for prostitution–reproduced with unsettling vividness in the novel. But the research itself doesn't take the foreground. "Research should help to give readers the feel that they are really there . . . but it should do so without distracting from the all-important story."

James W. Hall, poet, essayist, and author of eleven adrenaline-spiked thrillers, is known for the expressiveness of his language, the complexity of his characters, and the inventiveness of his plots. In his creative writing courses at Florida International University, where Dennis Lehane and Barbara Parker have been among his students, he teaches a twist on the old rule: write what you *want* to know. Each of his novels started with a spark of curiosity: an old photograph of Miami, the high incidence of multiple sclerosis in the Florida Keys, new developments in pain research. He spends a month or more at the beginning of his work on a novel, starting with field work–trekking as far from his South Florida home as Borneo for his novel *Gone Wild* to collect data and to "observe characters." His goal is to become something of an expert in whatever field he is exploring.

"Novels that tell a rousing good yarn while also containing a high dose of factual information about some esoteric subject matter have always been my favorite type of book" (Cabo 179). Hall describes the thrill of the chase during the first month of a new project as "quasi-journalistic exploration. I interview people. I take lots of notes and shoot stacks of photographs. It's a time for total immersion that must provide me with enough authenticity for the next eleven months of writing," admitting a bit sheepishly, "for some inconceivable reason I have chosen ten research projects in succession that required me to go to places I would never have chosen to visit otherwise" (180). The reader may well sympathize–after all, his world is a nice place to visit, but we wouldn't want to die there.

Another rule he takes delight in turning inside-out is one of Elmore Leonard's famous maxims for writers: leave out the part that readers skip. Because of his meticulous research and the way he employs it to shape characters and drive his plots, Hall succeeds in making readers pause to examine the intriguing treasures he's turned up as he sifts his research material, even when the action beckons them on. They become parts readers *don't* skip.

Danutah Reah finds, when researching her novels, she's "looking for the fictional world," using a combination of fieldwork to experience places that she is writing about, and libraries to ground her observations. "I owe it to my readers to be accurate," she says. No matter how small the grain of truth, "it needs to be right. If it isn't, then the book isn't right–the whole fictional world collapses." But it isn't just readers who depend on her to be accurate; the subjects of her books would be betrayed if she didn't do the legwork. "At the moment, I am writing about historical events around my own father's past, events that aren't widely known in the west, and it's fundamental that I get it as right as I can, for the people whose story I am telling, and for people who may be coming across this for the first time. The book is fiction, the characters exist only in the pages, but the world they inhabit has an external reality that I have to be faithful to."

Historical mysteries pose another challenge. It isn't possible for Mary Reed and Eric Mayer to visit sixth-century Byzantium to interview the locals or stroll the marketplace and note down the sights, sounds, and smells for their series of mysteries about John the Eunuch, Emperor Justinian's Lord Chamberlain. Luckily, they have a passion for research that gives their readers an experience in time travel. "You have to drag us away from researching with grappling hooks," Reed says. "It's the thrill of the hunt, really, the chasing down of the elusive fact!" For their fifth novel in the series, *Five for Silver*, Mayer spent a day digging through digests of Justinianic law to clarify a fine legal point. "Whether in the sixth century or today," Reed points out, "the bare statements of law you see leave a lot of unanswered questions." But while the writer with a question on contemporary law can speak to someone who interprets it routinely (say, a police officer who makes frequent judgments about how to apply search and seizure laws in specific instances), historical fiction requires sifting the minutia of the historical record, insight based on a deep knowledge base, and a well-informed imagination that can fill in the blanks–or write around them without inventing facts that the author cannot confirm.

Writer Taffy Cannon suggests research should be like an iceberg: "The 10% that you use is supported by the 90% you don't." The reader may not see most of it, but what is below the surface has made a difference in infusing the work with a sense of reality. Michelle Spring sums it up by saying, "when it comes to research, less is more. The research should almost disappear into the background."

INSPIRATION

"Most of the research I do never appears in my books," Spring says without apology. "It is speculative . . . the spur to invention. Research stirs you up. It gets your imagination going." Before committing to the story told in *Nights in White Satin*, Spring spent weeks tracking down the life story of Daisy Hopkins, a nineteenth-century teenager who may have been a part-time prostitute in Cambridge. Though all that work didn't end up in the book–the historical figure gets no more than a passing reference in the novel–that pursuit provided ideas and the emotional thrust for a twentieth-century mystery. "Without Daisy, the book might never have been written."

James Hall's *Hard Aground* started with a visual cue. He came across a nineteenth-century photo of a meandering stream shaded by mossy oaks that looked nothing like the modern-day version of the Miami River. Intrigued, he spoke with the city archaeologist, who invited him to an archaeological dig along the banks of the old river. The stories he told Hall about the city's past became the inspiration for a story that evokes in double exposure both modern day Miami and the city of the past on which it rests–as well as the passions and greed that drove development in both eras.

For Mary Reed and Eric Mayer, research often is the springboard for the story. Though there's an argument to be made for outlining a plot first, then filling in the blanks, they tend to take their cues from their research because it "anchors the story more firmly in the historical period." Events in *Four for a Boy* were inspired by a brief passage in Procopios' *Secret History* that reports a man with the nickname "the Gourd" was killed in broad daylight in the church of St. Sophia. A few lines evoked an entire, complex novel. Reed adds parenthetically that she worries historical documents might upstage the fiction that uses them for inspiration: "We almost hesitate to mention *The Secret History* since anyone who reads it is bound to conclude either that truth is stranger than fiction can ever be, or that Procopios had a lot better imagination than we do!" Readers, however, are likely to find Reed and Mayer's mysteries provide easier access to the past than the centuries-old documents that give them their flavor.

At other times, Reed and Mayer's knowledge of Byzantium provides texture to a scene that doesn't particularly depend on historical facts. After Mayer read an article that mentioned sunken gardens in Constantinople, for example, Reed and Mayer decided to use one for the setting of a conversation that could have taken place elsewhere. Intended simply to add a little color, it ended up influencing the nature of the scene. "Thinking about what a sunken garden might be like in moonlight on a cold night, we started adding other things and the scene emerged more mystical than political." Indeed, Clyde Linsley, author of *Death of a Mill Girl,* set in New Hampshire in the 1830s, says the research for his novels "is often less involved with facts than with feelings, attitudes, world views and the like." It is folded into the characters and settings and infuses the action not with historical specifics, but with an integrated sense of reality.

READERS RESPOND

Mystery aficionados are often quick to spot a fake. Victoria Kemp warns, "I know enough about history to be dangerous." Barbara Fritchman Thompson, an independent research professional, points out that writers who take liberties with the facts stand to lose their market. "Authors who make a lot of mistakes are ones we rarely read more than once." In fact, her firm, Research Solutions, provides help to writers who want to get their stories straight before they go before a jury of their peers.

Writers and publishers are known to complain about the complaints they inevitably get if a book contains a factual error about guns. Michael Bane, who has given firearms seminars for writers, is pained that those readers are considered "picky." He points out that, given the number of gun owners in the United States, a writer who takes liberties with hardware is bound to be apprehended on a weapons offense sooner or later. And for the reader, that moment of disillusionment can be wholesale. "Mystery fiction requires that the reader place a level of trust in the author. When the reader finds something–a fact, an emotion, whatever–that is false or doesn't ring true, that trust vanishes in an instant. The question becomes, 'If the author doesn't know *that*, what *else* doesn't he or she know?'"

Joy Matkowski didn't get far with a novel by a best-selling author because in the first chapter a character mentions his weekly earnings as a bouncer and day laborer and a few details about his lifestyle; she did the math and concluded he couldn't possibly afford to eat the meals he describes, nor could he pay his rent. Of course most readers might let a detail like that slip by them as easily as, apparently, the author did–but Matkowski is one of the invisible toilers who catch many a faulty fact, an impossible chronology, a misspelled name, or some error in continuity before it's too late. As a copy editor she has a finely-tuned radar for anything that isn't right.

Shirley McKibbon is willing to let an occasional mistake go, but finds that getting the details right is crucial when the plot hinges on them. In one case, "I just couldn't get involved in the story because I didn't believe it . . . If the writer doesn't care enough about his or her story to get essential facts right, why should I read it?" Bob Kellogg agrees, and adds that it's best to use those essential facts to advance the story. "The ideal background becomes part of the foreground. Tony Hillerman is an excellent example of that. We learn convincing details of the Navajo life and location almost without effort, since they're frequently elements that drive the plot."

"Research is important," according to Shirley Wetzel. "Knowing how to use it is even more important." She cites Steven Saylor and Patricia Wynn as writers who get the balance right. "I love historical mysteries. I love to learn from them, and to be entertained by them. The best writers are able to do both painlessly and seamlessly, so that I end up knowing new facts without having to study them or sit through a lecture." Yvonne Klein agrees that it's frustrating when historical fiction "halts for little history lessons." When it works, the sense of being in a different period is so complete it doesn't seem to be the past at all, but the present moment. "Research has produced a complete fictional universe."

To a certain extent, the reader's expectations (and level of tolerance for detours from reality) will be shaped by the subgenre they are reading. The procedural, like the historical mystery, derives much of its flavor from the gritty details of police work. Ed McBain immersed himself in the working world of the New York Police Department for his 87th Precinct series, even to the point of reproducing actual forms in his novels. His dialogue often reads like a transcript from a recorded interrogation, complete with repetition, gaps, and equivocation. "The importance of research to me as a reader depends on the expectations the writer has raised by the type of story he or she has chosen to tell," according to writer Jim Doherty, who has spoken about researching the procedural at a writers' conference. "If it's a police procedural, for example, a sub-genre that is *defined* by its technical accuracy, then I *expect* a high degree of technical accuracy, which means I expect the writer to have done his or her homework." Of course, Doherty is fortunate to have a position that gives him a chance to do his homework while on the job–he's a police officer as well as a writer.

When asked what readers get out of the research mystery writers do, Danutah Reah points to the importance of tying the story to the reader's own life experiences. "I think most writers do obey the 'write what you know' rule in one sense. We may not know what it is like to be a killer, or to be a victim, but we've all experienced fear and threat. I think the trick is to tap into the reader's awareness and give them enough to trigger their own experiences, then they will create the world of the book in the way it works for them . . . it's important to leave readers space for their own imaginations to work."

READING THE WORLD

Research, handled well, can go beyond lessons or plot devices. It can take an unfamiliar subject and make the reader feel like an expert. A famous example is Dorothy L. Sayer's *Nine Tailors*. The mystery, centered around bell-ringing in a rural English church, is satisfying enough, but readers are often far more fascinated by the mathematical splendor of traditional British change-ringing described meticulously in the book. "I love reading mysteries," author L.C. Hayden says, "but the ones I enjoy the most are the ones that teach me something."

Fiction blends imagination and reality to arrive at a kind of truth. Crime fiction typically deals with social issues at an almost metaphysical level–what is the nature of good and evil? How do social institutions work for or against the common good? Can an individual respond ethically and effectively to a world full of injustice? These questions are not academic, but are engaged by characters struggling with crisis in a world that looks very much like our own. George Pelecanos sets his novels in a Washington, DC, that few visitors ever see, unless they miss a turn and get lost, yet his portrayal of urban neglect, racism, poverty, and the dignity of people living their lives with honor under difficult circumstances speaks more eloquently to a much wider audience than the most deeply researched sociological study. Barbara Neely shows us a part of Boston that isn't on the tour, but we get to know it and its residents and their perspectives more clearly by hearing her character Blanche White talk to us than any ethnographer could achieve through recording observations in the field. There is a curious alchemy at work that takes a writer's passions, personal experiences, and their research and transforms it into an authentic experience, even though that authenticity is conveyed through a work of imagination.

The Buckingham neighborhood in Dennis Lehane's *Mystic River* is so real the reader can draw a map of it, yet they won't be able to take the T there. Its truth is based on Lehane's upbringing in Dorchester, the descriptive touches he uses like fine brush strokes, on the genuineness of his characters and their motivations, and his vivid, evocative prose. Ed McBain's ur-procedurals focus on cops who never seem to age in a city that doesn't exist, but are nevertheless authentic in every detail. And consider this passage from Scott Turow's *Reversible Errors*, describing an urban subterranean roadway meant for access to loading docks:

> Sulfur lights glowed down here twenty-four hours a day, and over the years, the homeless had made this their chief refuge. The wilted cartons and soiled, spring-shot mattresses where they slept were piled into the recesses between the concrete buttresses supporting River Drive. Rain dribbled down between the seams in the street overhead, while grimy men in ragged clothes loitered between the roadside pillars . . . (272-3)

This novel has as one of its subject headings, "Kindle County (Imaginary place)–Fiction" yet many readers have been there. Anyone who ever ventured onto Chicago's Lower Wacker Drive before its recent reconstruction recognizes it immediately. In the same way, anyone who reads the newspaper will recognize the issue that ignites the story–are the errors that might be made when a man is sentenced to death reversible? Turow, a practicing attorney, served on the Commission on Capital Punishment formed by Illinois Governor George Ryan, and that experience provided a spark of inspiration for his novel. The commission concluded "no system, given human nature and frailties, could ever be devised or constructed that would work perfectly and guarantee absolutely that no innocent person is ever again sentenced to death" (207); Governor Ryan decided that he must commute the sentences of those on Illinois' death row as his final act in office. Turow's novel is less conclusive, but as dramatic and will give many readers a clearer understanding of the frailties of the system in all its complexity.

UNSETTLING QUESTIONS

There are probably no texts read more closely than reviews are by the writers of the books under review. A reviewer at *Publisher's Weekly* called my mystery, *On Edge*, "an unsettling debut." While I would have been satisfied with other adjectives–"brilliant" or "riveting" would have been fine–I concluded after much study that the adjective used was the *mot juste* after all.

On Edge was inspired by an idle thought I had when driving through a small town that I recalled had been the site of an inconclusive investigation into bizarre accusations of child molestation in the mid-1980s. Though in retrospect, the accusations appear to have been almost entirely groundless, the small community was torn apart by distrust, suspicion, and fear, exacerbated by the way the investigation was handled and by the international media attention it generated. I wondered just how that shared trauma had affected the community–and found myself wondering "how would they respond if they thought it was happening again?" The story that resulted is dark and violent and, yes, unsettling–if it were not, I would have failed.

For me, the book started with a question, as do most research projects. I used the medium of crime fiction to explore how we respond to crime, what role our fascination with criminal behavior plays in assuaging and sustaining our anxieties, whether our need for meaning makes us see patterns where there are none, whether our desire for justice makes us create monsters out of flawed and damaged human beings. Though I could have studied these issues in an academic mode, I chose instead to use fiction.

Perhaps ironically, for a librarian, I did almost no research about the criminal case that inspired the book, or the hundreds of others like it, until after I completed a draft of the novel. I wanted my imagination to lay the emotional boundaries first–and while I wanted a sense of authenticity, I worried about being seduced into exploiting real-life details from what must have been a horrible experience for those involved. Though it's not uncommon for crime stories to be "ripped from the headlines," this book is largely about what happens to people *behind* the headlines, those whose lives are distorted by a criminal investigation gone out of control, whose traumas are taken up by the media in a way that reflects and feeds public anxiety but distorts the truth. Though I was striving for a kind of truth in the novel, I didn't want it to mimic media accounts that had, for the most part, got it wrong.

As I wrote, I discovered factual questions that needed answering–for example, whether Chicago police officers typically load their weapons with hollow point or fully jacketed bullets. I would set the book aside to read about issues that surfaced, such as how detectives might inadvertently coax a false confession out of a suspect or about the reliability of child witnesses–but I didn't read about actual ritual abuse cases until I had finished the first round. The research I did after the fact–pouring over news accounts of investigations and trials in the 1980s, reading secondary analyses of the issue, studying official documents–suggested ways I could tweak a scene or rethink a bit of dialogue, but its major role was, in the words of the linguist in *Listen to the Shadows*, to confirm my intuition.

As a trained linguist, Danutah Reah frequently tackles "the complexities and mysteries of language" in her fiction. Her novel, *Bleak Water*, grew out of recognizing that just as linguists peel back the underlying structure of languages, a work of art can be peeled back to reveal the structure of things it parallels in reality–and can even influence events beyond its scope. Michelle Spring, too, brings to her fiction an academic background, in her case as a professor of sociology. Many of her novels explore the same questions she might have explored with sociological methods. "The things that fascinate me as a novelist are similar to the issues that captured my attention as an academic . . . the treatment is of course not at all the same. What's similar, I hope, is a tolerance; in both my academic writing and my novels, I feel strongly that my place is not to dictate how readers should feel about an issue but to explore possibilities." This latitude is not limited to readers. "As a novelist, the social issues are less ones I'm expert about, and more ones that I'm keen to explore." The murder of a small child by two other children in Britain in 1993 and school killings in the U.S. disturbed her so much it became the basis for *Standing in the Shadows*. "I started research for the novel, looking at why children commit murder, and how we as a society react to it. In the course of researching and writing the novel, I came to a kind of understanding about those issues that made me feel more at peace."

Interestingly, readers feel the same. Catherine Sheldrick Ross, a Canadian professor of library and information science, has studied what readers get out of popular fiction and recommends that libraries should recognize its value ("Readers' Advisory Service"). Though the majority of books circulated in public libraries are popular fiction titles, librarians tend to valorize the library's function of "providing information" over "providing entertainment." Ross's interviews with readers suggest that, in fact, both of these goals are met through reading genre fiction.

She quotes a nineteenth-century public library annual report: "It is certainly not the function of the public library to foster the mind-weakening habit of novel reading among the very classes–the uneducated, busy, or idle–whom it is the duty of the public library to lift to a higher plane of thinking." Few librarians would make those judgments now–yet often libraries ignore the value of what's on their shelves by not making enough of an effort to put books in readers' hands. "There is still a key role for readers' advisors to play in public libraries," Ross says, "but for a new breed of readers' advisor who pays attention to both elements in the transaction: the reader and the book." She makes a number of practical suggestions for libraries derived from readers' experiences, concluding "it is clear that libraries contain rich resources of comfort and stimulation and renewal. But how well are we doing to connect readers with the books that will give them these satisfactions? We could be doing a lot better." One place to start is to start paying more attention to how readers actually choose books and what it is that makes them read fiction in the first place.

SCHOOLS FOR SCANDAL

While librarians spend a lot of time teaching students the rudiments of information literacy, and many public libraries are beginning to include information literacy training among their services, libraries remain baffling places to many writers in part because they are not organized with creativity in mind. As Ross points out, "in the research on information seeking behaviour, only certain people have typically counted as information seekers. To qualify an individual must experience a 'problem situation,' become aware of a gap in understanding, and then formally start the search process by querying one of our systems . . . We know, in fact that in the course of everyday living people constantly encounter and use textual information without ever posing a formal question to an information system" ("Finding Without Seeking"). Her research finds that many readers learn a great deal of information from the popular fiction they read.

Retrieving information is not always the goal of a writer, and many information systems are ill-equipped to satisfy their needs. Catalogs don't easily lead to the picture on page 245 or the obscure footnote that will suddenly make a storyline fall into place. Browsing for visual images and stray ideas can be critical. Mary Reed says it's important for patrons to be able to find material for themselves in the stacks–and often, the sources she needs might be on many libraries' weed lists. "Some of the most interesting information seems to be in older books which tend to be relegated from the shelves." When considering weeding decisions, or remote storage for low use materials, librarians need to think about what creative uses some obscure book might have for their patrons, particularly when those uses may not be transparent through a catalog search. James W. Hall mentions that he wanted information about military aerial spraying on unknowing civilian populations for *Bones of Coral* and found exactly what he needed in a congressional sub-committee report. The data that became the linchpin for the novel was buried in a footnote in an obscure depository document, probably not the original intent of the GPO in disseminating the hearing, but worth bearing in mind as the future of the depository system is under debate.

Many creative writers are not even aware of the potential of libraries. I created a Web guide, *Blood at the Source: Research Tips for Mystery Writers*, inspired as I began to write fiction by the new uses I was finding for the skills I had developed as a librarian–and perturbed by the "does anyone know–?" questions popping up on discussion lists that could be easily answered by anyone who knew how to use a library. Libraries should be comfortable and familiar places for all writers. *Blood at the Source* suggests ways to making the most of libraries–how to ask a focused reference question, what services to expect, and what widely-available research tools are especially helpful to mystery writers. PsychINFO is a trove of information on human behavior, MEDLINE might just answer that minor medical point that needs to be right, and a law review article found on LexisNexis may inspire a plot twist–yet many writers don't know these resources are available. It points out the virtues of academic libraries and special collections, options many don't realize are open to them. It also gives tips for using the Web, pointing out useful government portals, legal information sites, statistical sources, and primary materials. If nothing else, I hope *Blood at the Source* will raise writers' expectations of what libraries can do for them–and let them know we'd like nothing better than to help them with their next novel.

James W. Hall was surprised by what libraries offered at the age of ten. He recounts his discovery in an essay, "Nude Woman in the Grass." Forced to spend some time in a library, and afraid the librarian might ask what he's doing there, he pops a book off the shelf at random, opens a page, and finds himself breathless: A nude woman is lying dead in a field. Just the conjunction of the words "nude" and "woman" are enough to mesmerize him, though he imagines he could be in dreadful trouble: "By evening it would be all over town: 'Little Jimmy Hall was caught reading that nude woman book in the library.'" But the librarian, who it turns out loves mysteries, reassures him as she piles books into his arms, "This isn't school." He can read whatever he wants and nobody will grade him on what he thinks. Yet, she was wrong in one sense: that introduction to the reckless power of words made it the perfect school for an imaginative ten-year-old. "Though that creaky library no longer exists in my small Kentucky hometown, and though I have fled her narrow streets and scrubby fields forever, the largest part of what I am today and what I know about the world and about the affairs of the human heart springs from that one autumn afternoon when I plucked a book from the shelf and encountered that nude woman in the grass and I began this long journey, year after year, filling myself beyond the brim with the accumulated wealth of books" (18-19, 21).

In *Listen to the Shadows*, Danutah Reah's researcher went to a library not just to find information, but to put her personal experiences and observations into a wider context of meaning. In the same sense, readers and writers alike learn something about the messy world they live in through mysteries. Crime fiction and libraries, in fact, have a lot in common: both create a space where we can explore what makes so many of us behave so badly, while in the end establishing a sense, however equivocal, of equilibrium.

NOTES

1. Quoted by Howard French in the *New York Times* in an article about Smith's research for the novel *December 6.*

2. Interviews with writers and readers quoted in this article were conducted by e-mail in December 2002 and January 2003. Contacts with readers were made through the DorothyL and Rara-Avis discussion lists.

REFERENCES

Fister, Barbara. *Blood at the Source: Research Tips for Mystery Writers.* Oct. 2002. <http://www.barbarafister.com/BloodattheSource.html>.

Fister, Barbara. *On Edge.* New York: Dell, 2002.

French, Howard W. "After 2 Visits, Taking on Japan at War." *The New York Times.* 8 Oct. 2002, E1.

Governor's Commission on Capital Punishment. *Report of the Governor's Commission on Capital Punishment.* Springfield: State of Illinois, April 2002. 14 Jan. 2003. <http://www.idoc.state.il.us/ccp/ccp/reports/commission_report/>.

Hall, James W. *Bones of Coral.* New York: Knopf, 1993.

______. "Cabo." In *Hot Damn! Alligators in the Casino, Nude Women in the Grass, How Seashells Changed the Course of History, and Other Dispatches from Paradise.* New York: St. Martin's, 2002. 179-84.

______. *Gone Wild.* New York: Delacorte, 1995.

______. *Hard Aground.* New York: Delacorte, 1993.

______. "Nude Woman in the Grass." In *Hot Damn!* 17-21.

Lehane, Dennis. Mystic River. New York: William Morrow, 2001.

Leonard, Elmore. "Easy on the Adverbs, Exclamation Points and Especially Hooptedoodle (Writers on Writing.)" *The New York Times.* July 16, 2001 pB1.

Lindsley, Clyde. *Death of a Mill Girl.* New York: Berkley, 2002.

"On Edge" [review] *Publishers Weekly* 11 Nov. 2002: 46.

Reah, Danutah. *Listen to the Shadows.* New York: William Morrow, 2001. (Published in the UK under the title *Silent Playgrounds.*)

Reed, Mary and Eric Mayer. *Four for a Boy.* Scottsdale, AZ: Poisoned Pen, 2003.

Ross, Catherine. "Finding Without Seeking: What Readers Say about the Role of Pleasure Reading as a Source of Information." *Australasian Public Libraries and Information Services* 13.2 (June 2000): 72+ *Expanded Academic ASAP.* InfoTrac. 31 Oct. 2001.

______. "Readers' Advisory Service: New Directions." *RQ.* 30.4 (Sum. 1991): 503+. *Expanded Academic ASAP.* InfoTrac. 1 Oct. 2001.

Sayers, Dorothy L. *The Nine Tailors: Changes Rung on an Old Theme in Two Short Touches and Two Full Peals.* New York: Harcourt, Brace, 1934.

Spring, Michelle. *In the Midnight Hour.* New York: Ballantine, 2001.

______. *Nights in White Satin.* New York: Ballantine, 1999.

______. *Standing in the Shadows.* New York: Ballantine, 1998.

Turow, Scott. *Reversible Errors.* New York: Farrar Straus Giroux, 2002.

Libraries and Sisters in Crime

Kathy Harig

SUMMARY. Founded in 1986 by mystery author Sara Paretsky, Sisters in Crime (SinC) is devoted to promoting mysteries written by women. In 1991, in order to spread the word about SinC and its authors to libraries and librarians, SinC staged its first presence at the annual American Library Association. A SinC Library Liaison position was established to coordinate this effort. SinC also established Speakers' Bureaus to coordinate and encourage requests for SinC author appearances in libraries. At the same time, libraries have been important to the writing life of SinC authors and for the promotion of their books. From the beginning, SinC produced *Books in Print* of SinC authors' work to distribute to libraries, bookstores, and the general reading public, and this article discusses the relationship between libraries and bookstores in promoting and acquiring mysteries. It concludes with recommendations for stocking and developing a comprehensive mystery collection in libraries and promoting mysteries through readers' advisory work with all age groups. *[Article copies available for a fee from The Haworth Document Delivery Service: 1-800-HAWORTH. E-mail address: <docdelivery@haworthpress.com> Website: <http://www.HaworthPress.com> © 2004 by The Haworth Press, Inc. All rights reserved.]*

Kathy Harig, MS, retired in December 2001 after twenty-four years as Branch Manager, Enoch Pratt Free Library, Baltimore, MD. She is the owner of Mystery Loves Company Booksellers in Baltimore, MD, which she co-founded in 1991. She has been Library Liaison for National Sisters in Crime since 1991.

Address correspondence to: Kathy Harig, 9621 Pastora Place, Columbia, MD 21045.

[Haworth co-indexing entry note]: "Libraries and Sisters in Crime." Harig, Kathy. Co-published simultaneously in *Collection Management* (The Haworth Information Press, an imprint of The Haworth Press, Inc.) Vol. 29, No. 3/4, 2004, pp. 21-39; and: *Managing the Mystery Collection: From Creation to Consumption* (ed: Judith Overmier, and Rhonda Harris Taylor) The Haworth Information Press, an imprint of The Haworth Press, Inc., 2004, pp. 21-39. Single or multiple copies of this article are available for a fee from The Haworth Document Delivery Service [1-800-HAWORTH, 9:00 a.m. - 5:00 p.m. (EST). E-mail address: docdelivery@haworthpress.com].

Available online at http://www.haworthpress.com/web/COL

doi:10.1300/J105v29n03_03

KEYWORDS. Mysteries, fiction collections in libraries, library programming, Sisters in Crime, ALA conferences

THE FOUNDING OF SISTERS IN CRIME

> Until recently, most women in mystery fiction were either ornaments and/or spectacularly dead. Women who wrote mysteries sometimes suffered a worse fate–they were ignored by reviewers.[1]

In 1986, mystery author Sara Paretsky was thinking about spreading the word about female mystery authors. She and a number of women who read, wrote, bought, or sold mysteries had met in Baltimore in October 1986 to found a group in support of female mystery writers, Sisters in Crime (SinC), at the Bouchercon convention, named for mystery author Anthony Boucher. There was a perception that women writers were reviewed less frequently, that books on the softer side of the genre were taken less seriously than those on the graphically violent side, and that male writers received bigger contracts and advances. SinC sought to change all that. According to the by-laws, the purpose of Sisters in Crime is:

> To combat discrimination against women in the mystery field, educate publishers and the general public as to inequities in the treatment of female authors, raise awareness of their contributions to the field, and promote the professional advancement of women who write mysteries.

Sisters in Crime promotes all types of writing in the mystery/suspense genre from cozy to hardboiled, as well as true crime, non-fiction, novels, and short stories for readers of all ages.[2]

> The 1992 membership brochure tells of the first few years of Sisters in Crime: Sara Paretsky was the driving force in galvanizing and organizing the group. In May of 1987, the first steering committee was elected and consisted of Charlotte MacLeod, Dorothy Salisbury Davis, Sara Paretsky, Nancy Pickard, Susan Dunlap. Kate Mattes, and Betty Francis. The group sent a letter to the New York Times pointing out that in 1985, of the 88 mysteries reviewed, only 14–or 16%–were written by women. They also began counting reviews in other major publications hoping to collect

> enough data to chart whether or not their perception of inequality was correct.[3]

This important study was mentioned in 2002 as a top priority for the organizational goals of the association. Although I was unaware of it at the time, that meeting in 1986 in Baltimore, the very city where I worked as a librarian, would profoundly change my life.

MYSTERIOUS DOINGS AT THE LIBRARY

As the daughter of a dedicated Sherlockian, I was surrounded by mysteries. I loved them as a child and still do. A friend once told me that a good librarian is just like a detective. But it wasn't until I attended an author signing at The Butler Did It Bookstore in Baltimore in 1987 that I was really hooked. Here were "real" British women mystery authors eager to talk to me about their stories. The authors of the day were the late Sarah Caudwell and Patricia (Penny) Moyes. Both Sarah and Penny were formidable creatures with heavy British accents. I had always loved the British mysteries the best, and here I was in the company of two of England's greatest mystery writers. Gail Larson, the proprietor of The Butler Did It, was a perfect hostess, knowledgeable and feisty, and I envied her ability to surround herself with such witty, literate people. The afternoon passed pleasurably with tea, scones and clotted cream, and a visit from the Mayor's representative with a plaque proclaiming that day "Sarah Caudwell and Patricia Moyes Day" in Baltimore. I also met my future business partner Paige Rose, who managed the bookstore. When I went back to my library, the Roland Park Branch of the Enoch Pratt Free Library, I had an idea. I called Gail to thank her for her hospitality and asked if she might be able to work with me to bring authors to my library for a program. She was enthusiastic and we began our plans.

"MYSTERY LOVES COMPANY EVENINGS" AT THE LIBRARY

Gail and I planned an event in May 1987 at the Roland Park library, featuring Robert Baylus. I came up with the name "Mystery Loves Company Evenings." The concept was to use all three floors of the library on an evening when it would be normally closed to the public. The public would enter by the front door where desks and tables had been pulled back and chairs arranged. (This event was before computer cables made it prohibitive to move furniture.) The evening would begin with an author panel discussion with questions and answers from the audience. Book lists and puzzles would be distributed. Refreshments based on Virginia Rich's culinary mystery recipes would be served on the circulation desk. Then the guests would have the choice of viewing a mystery film in the basement, playing a mystery treasure hunt game using mystery books on the library shelves, or playing an interactive mystery role-playing game upstairs on the third floor. The authors would circulate and talk with the guests as the night progressed. Well, the public loved it! Here is what one enthusiastic guest said:

> Dear all of you,
>
> Lily begged me to go to your Mystery Loves Company evening and I, no mystery buff, acceded. What a treat! I haven't stopped talking about it. I may have *become* a mystery buff. It was all grand. Many Thanks–E. Thayer[4]

The event was featured in all the newspapers with pictures of the authors and me. "Mystery Loves Company Evenings" became an annual event at the library to be hosted each spring during Preakness week in May.

In May of 1990, the Malice Domestic Convention, featuring cozy mystery writers, was held in Bethesda, Maryland. Six Sisters in Crime authors agreed to carpool their way forty miles up from Bethesda to Baltimore to present an "Evening with Sisters in Crime" at the Enoch Pratt Free Library. Here's how we promoted it:

> Spend an evening with some of today's top mystery writers. Learn about their craft and get a sneak preview of their latest works . . . They are the creators of a new breed of women detectives who have the savvy and the guts of their male counterparts.[5]

We chose the Waverly Branch since it had an auditorium that seated one hundred. Attending were Sisters in Crime mystery authors Susan Dunlap, Carolyn Hart, Sharyn McCrumb, Margaret Maron, Nancy Pickard, and Dorothy Sucher. I was privileged to moderate the ensuing panel discussion for the one hundred mystery readers who attended the evening's festivities. The audience was eager to learn how they did their research, why they wrote about murder, where their ideas came from, how they developed their characters, what it was like to be a published author, and what was their advice to budding authors. Then, as now, I have noticed that most people have never met a published author, and it is quite a thrill for them when they do. The evening was a great success, with a book signing afterward managed by The Butler Did it. I had arranged an honorarium for each author, but they each gave the money back, saying, "Please buy mysteries for the library."

THE CHESAPEAKE CHAPTER OF SISTERS IN CRIME

I received a note from writer Barbara Lee in October 1990 asking me to attend a meeting to form a local Chapter of Sisters in Crime at the house of mystery author Dorothy Sucher. My time had come to get officially involved with this now dynamic group. According to "archival information" from Maureen Collins[6] twenty-eight women attended that first meeting. From the beginning, Sisters in Crime, unlike other mystery groups such as Mystery Writers of America, has welcomed everyone into their egalitarian organization. Its membership includes published and unpublished writers, librarians, agents, editors, reviewers, teachers, readers, fans, and anyone who loves mysteries by women. Officers of the Chesapeake Chapter were chosen, and Margaret Fromer was elected president, and I was chosen to be vice-president. Other officers were Maureen Collins, secretary, and Lee Mewshaw, treasurer. The rest of the officers are interesting to note since they show the focus of the organization and the period in which it was formed:

Program:	Barbara Lee
Newsletter:	Caroline Stafford
Bylaws:	Doris Long
Desert Shield:	V.G. Jordan

Programming was the key. If we could not attract a following to the membership, the group would flounder and die. Everyone was eager to help Barbara with ideas for programming; the more extreme and outrageous the better. The newsletter position was also critical since it galvanized and communicated with the membership. Bylaws were a must if we were to be affiliated with the National Sisters in Crime group. Finally, Desert Shield was our commitment to send books to servicepersons stationed overseas in the Middle East during Desert Storm.

The focus for the fledgling group would be:

- Networking
- A chapter calendar and bibliography
- A newsletter designed to be sent to editors and agents
- Preparation of membership list and mailing labels
- Assistance with publicity
- Legal advice about copyrights and trademarks
- Desktop publishing and graphics design at low cost[7]

We met for a Board meeting once a month at a board member's home. The general membership meeting was held the first Saturday of each month at Bish Thompson's, a seafood restaurant in Bethesda. The membership meetings were held at lunch-time with full five-course lunches and a speaker afterwards. Through various mailings, the attendance grew to seventy-five and more at these monthly luncheons. We had speakers from rape crisis groups, a serial profiler, a shoplifting expert, a scene-of-the-crime police expert, female and male private eyes, a forensic pathologist, a psychic who worked with the police, a former master of disguises for the CIA, and many of our own members who were published authors. We went on field trips to shooting ranges, penitentiaries, the FBI headquarters in DC and the FBI Academy in Quanitico, VA, morgues, and gun shops.[8] We talked about finding an agent, getting a publisher, and promoting the mystery after it was published. In between meetings, authors met in small critique groups to evaluate each other's work. The Chesapeake Chapter became one of the largest and most dynamic Sisters in Crime chapters in the United States.

SISTERS IN CRIME AND PARTICIPATION IN THE AMERICAN LIBRARY ASSOCIATION CONFERENCE

In the fall of 1990, I spoke to mystery writer Carolyn Hart, President of Sisters in Crime and author of the Annie and Max Darling "Death on Demand" mysteries, about my idea for Sisters in Crime participation at the American Library Association (ALA) Convention. I was astounded that more publishers did not feature fiction authors in their exhibits and in programming. I would visit a well-known publisher's booth at ALA and inquire about the publication date of a new mystery, and they would be unfamiliar with it. There would be no posters proclaiming the new Joan Hess or Anne Perry book. In 1990, few mystery authors graced the numerous panels during the conference, and fiction novels, book selection, or reader's advisory work were rarely on the agenda. As a librarian who specialized in fiction, particularly mysteries, I was out to change all that, given the Sisters in Crime board's permission. Carolyn thought it was an excellent idea and encouraged me to pursue it with a proposal to the board. My target was the Atlanta, Georgia annual ALA convention in June 1991. Sisters in Crime had just commissioned a stunning graphic map of the United States showing locations of female authors' mystery series. I arranged for a booth in the ALA exhibit area and decorated it with the maps and Sisters in Crime *Books in Print* and membership brochures. I invited authors to come to the booth and scheduled a panel discussion and breakfast to be held on Sunday, June 30, 1991. A note in the SinC newsletter encouraged authors who could not attend to send books and promotional bookmarks and covers and other giveaways promoting their books. These giveaways have become increasingly creatively inspired as authors and publicists use every trick in the book to help librarians and readers to remember and read their books. The most inspired handout for 1991 was Joan Hess's "Best Loved Recipes from Ruby Bee's Bar and Grill, Maggody, AK." As the author stated to me, "If you fret about cholesterol and calories you're plum out of luck."

Mystery author and SinC Publicity Chair Elaine Raco Chase got us valuable publicity in the June 15, 1991 issue of *Library Journal*. Our booth and breakfast in Atlanta 1991 featured Sisters in Crime authors Patricia Carlson, Susan Dunlap, Carolyn Hart, Joan Hess, Sharyn McCrumb, Margaret Maron, Patricia Houck Sprinkle, and Elizabeth Daniels Squire. Sisters in Crime now had a presence at ALA. I recounted the experience in an article I wrote for the national and Chesapeake Chapter SinC newsletters:

> Images of the SinC Booth T-111 at American Library Association/Atlanta June 28-July 2 (1991): Two SinC Presidents on their knees on the floor furiously signing SinC maps while adoring librarians and publishing fans grab them out of their hands, more librarians eagerly receiving copies of the new edition of the SinC *Books in Print*, brisk tee-shirt sales to fans with some curious, and remarkably funny, reasons for buying them. (The librarian who brought two shirts to give to her two sisters WHO WERE NUNS!)
>
> SinC at ALA/Atlanta. An idea whose time was obviously well overdue. But it was a natural alliance. Librarians are tremendous

> mystery fans. Sales of mysteries to libraries are a substantial percentage of all total sales. Librarians are great promoters of mysteries to their patrons. Bring them together for a while, give away free books and promotional materials . . . and watch the magic happen.
>
> Linda Grant edited and produced the BIPs; and Gavin Faulkner printed and shipped the BIPs and SinC brochures. And what a shipment! Nearly twenty boxes of materials greeted me in the booth on Friday in Atlanta. With a borrowed plastic display rack, a few hangers and many energetic helpers, the booth took shape, enough to win President Sue Dunlap's enthusiastic praise.
>
> Was it hard work? Yes, but we had a great cast of helpers. Was it rewarding? My yes. Good will and business contacts abounded and invitations were extended for speaking engagements and trips to future conventions.[9]

Then National SinC President Sue Dunlap was extremely pleased with the Atlanta ALA events.

> For the organization, we've gotten a lot of notice, will get a slew of new members who will bring with them enthusiasm and good ideas. Librarians are more familiar with us and will be more at ease asking authors to come to their libraries, so they and their readers will benefit.[10]

Past SinC President Carolyn Hart said: "Thank you for making possible the most effective promotional appearance ever achieved by Sisters in Crime."[11] She encouraged me to stay on as chair of library events for SinC and the next ALA in San Francisco.

> We should be able to do even better there. I definitely hope we can achieve both a panel and a breakfast. We have so many wonderful writers in CA . . . that we should be able to man a booth staffed by three authors for every hour the booth is open. This is going to be great.[12]

Many suggestions and ideas came from that first ALA appearance. I outlined them in a letter to Sue Dunlap July 12, 1991.

> I'm sending cards of several library groups who want a SinC presence at their next convention. I think there should be an effort on

> the part of SinC authors to go to regional and state library conventions, either with a booth or as a panel discussion. I'm sure you would be welcomed with open arms.
>
> Finally every chapter should have a speaker's bureau to handle these regional and state requests. You, yourself could contact the California Library Association about their next conference. They also have monthly programs around the area where authors and librarians could serve on a panel to discuss mystery issues and violence towards women in fiction, etc.[13]

This ALA convention was also the scene of what was to be for me a very important cocktail party; it was thrown for SinC members and friends by the Bantam-Doubleday-Dell Publishers. It was at this party in July 1991 that I overheard Joan Hess say to Sharyn McCrumb that Gail Larson was selling the Butler Did It bookstore in Baltimore. I sat there with my friend and Smithsonian librarian Mary Rosenfeld and discussed what fun it would be to own a mystery bookstore. In less than a month and a half, in August 1991, I became the proud co-owner of a mystery bookshop in Baltimore. Gail Larson sold her shop to Sue Feder and me. We moved the business to Fells Point, named it Mystery Loves Company, and Paige Rose became our store manager. I continued my work as Branch Manager at the Roland Park Branch of Enoch Pratt until I took early retirement after Paige's death in December 2001 to work full-time at the store. I have continued to serve as Library Liaison for Sisters in Crime since the Atlanta ALA conference. Since then SinC has had a presence at all of the Annual and Midwinter conferences of the American Library Association, a total of twenty-three conferences over twelve years.

SISTERS IN CRIME SPEAKERS BUREAU

Elaine Raco Chase, National Publicity Chair, in the September 1994 SinC *Newsletter*, stated:

> We need more speakers! . . . I get at least 4-6 requests a week from libraries and then follow-up letters that tell me how wonderful our SinC authors were and how great the response was from the guests. Over 60 people heard Lee Harris at the Friends of the Libraries of Woodbridge, NJ. Over 100 copies of her books were

> purchased, and funds raised will be used to aid the township libraries. Miriam Monfredo spoke to an audience of 85 at North Tonowanda Library and sold all her books. Now the library wants to sponsor a mystery festival![14]

Every issue of the SinC *Newsletter* lists libraries that have contacted the Speakers' Bureau looking for authors for events they would like to plan. Current National Sisters in Crime President Kate Flora explains how a Sisters in Crime Speakers' Bureau works:

> Here in New England, Sisters in Crime runs a very active Speakers' Bureau. We have about twenty-five writers involved, and we speak at about twenty libraries a year. Usually, we send panels of three writers with an assigned moderator, who speak on a pre-selected topic. We send libraries our brochure that suggests topics. We've also participated in a number of special events, chief among them our talk and lunch, called Soup and Suspense, and our talk and dessert party, especially popular for Valentine's Day and Sunday afternoons, called Death and Chocolate or Death and Dessert. These titles came to us from librarians, and were adopted by us to use in other venues. Many of these events have become repeat performances, with libraries expecting us to return on a yearly basis where they can meet new authors or hear about new books from authors who have become old friends.
>
> Along with their generous hospitality, librarians are often the source of useful statistics, such as the percent of mysteries to general fiction published, 28.1%, and the percent of mysteries to general fiction checked out at the library, 35.1%, both statistics furnished by a librarian in Manchester, New Hampshire.[15]

The listing in the SinC *Books in Print* by "Location of Authors" is a handy way to see what authors live in the general area of a library needing authors as speakers. Event organizers can contact the Speakers' Bureau through Beth Wasson, the SinC Executive Secretary in Lawrence Kansas at (785) 842-1325. Baltimore mystery author Laura Lippman tells of the warm welcome she has gotten in libraries.

> For a traveling author, it's always a bright spot on the schedule to do an event at a library. I know some short-sighted souls fret only about the places that "sell" books, but I think they've lost sight of

the fact that libraries are consumers and the purchase has already been made. So library events really are about the shared love of books, not commerce.[16]

SinC MYSTERY AUTHORS' VIEWS OF LIBRARIES AND PROGRAMMING

From the very beginning of Sisters in Crime, libraries and librarians have had a special place in the lives of authors and the promotion of their mysteries. Canadian mystery author Vicki Cameron has a very important relationship with her local library:

> Our library is very small, serving a village of less than 500 people, and the surrounding township, all rural, mostly dairy farms. Our library's budget is so small they buy first the best sellers to keep the clients happy, then some non-fiction to build up the collection. What's left goes to other books. I donate my books, and other mysteries I have read. The librarian is always happy to accept them, and more clients get hooked on mystery. I've noticed over the last couple of years that there are new mysteries on the shelves from mid-list authors which I didn't donate. So I guess we have some converts.[17]

Michigan mystery author Jeanne Dams, whose character Dorothy Martin an expatriate American in England is a favorite of librarians and library patrons, says this:

> I can't say enough good things about libraries. They taught me to love reading in the first place. They buy my books. They ask me to speak, and bring together lively, intelligent people for an audience. They all say that mysteries are among the favorites of their patrons. They're warm, friendly places with lots and lots of books–what's not to love?[18]

Sisters in Crime National Past President Eve Sandstrom, author of several mystery series under her own name and currently two chocoholic mysteries under the pseudonym Joanna Carl, has these suggestions for libraries:

> My experience with libraries and SinC is limited, because I don't belong to a local chapter. But most libraries have public meeting

> rooms, and I've always wondered why more chapters don't use them for meetings.
>
> As a writer, I love libraries and I've found them great places for promoting books. I do urge all of them to develop policies, which allow BOOKSTORES to sell books for writers during appearances at the library. This is so much more convenient and professional.
>
> But librarians are wonderful, and many of them are mystery fans.[19]

Mystery author Elaine Viets, National Sisters in Crime's Publicity Chair and author of the soon to be published Dead-End-Job mystery series, tells us,

> Libraries have played a crucial role in my work. Librarians have answered my research questions, no matter how strange. Libraries have promoted my writing and introduced my books to new readers. The St. Louis Public Library has its Signature Series, which brings in non-fiction writers from around the country, from Susan Sontag, to Mary Higgins Clark, to me. The Broward County library has the Literary Fest. This is a weekend-long event, where writers from around the country speak at local schools, sign their work, participate in panels, and attend dinners hosted at some of the finest houses in Lauderdale. The Fest authors include bestsellers as well as local writers. Finally, libraries have helped my audio career. I recorded all four of my mysteries on tape, and my audio company quit abridging books because of pressure from libraries, who wanted uncut works. Thank you, thank you.[20]

Chesapeake SinC President Donna Andrews sees the link between SinC and Chapter literary efforts:

> Sisters in Crime is a great organization for anyone who's interested in getting published–I learned a lot when I was getting started, from the experts who spoke to our chapter and from my fellow members. But now that I'm published, I also appreciate how belonging to Sisters in Crime lets me give back to the mystery world–not just by helping newer writers, but also through the organization's support for literacy projects. Of course, supporting

literacy isn't exactly altruistic for a writer, is it? If we don't help spread literacy, who the heck will read us in the future?

Seriously, librarians are an important channel for getting news about good mysteries out to readers. Ads and bookstore displays will tell anyone who pays attention to them what the publishers and the book chains are trying to hype–the bestselling books. But so many good writers who are not bestsellers (including, of course, most of our Sisters in Crime members) might never reach their readers if it weren't for other, quieter channels–like thoughtful recommendations from librarians who take the time to learn what their readers like and what new books might be interesting to those readers.[21]

SISTERS IN CRIME BOOKS IN PRINT *AND LIBRARIES*

One of the benefits and main ways that Sisters in Crime promotes women's mystery fiction is through the publication of Sisters in Crime's *Books in Print*. Originally published twice a year, but now published annually, SinC *Books in Print* is compiled from submissions by member authors. The 2003 version of SinC *Books in Print* is seventy-five pages long. It contains entries from 573 Sisters in Crime authors worldwide with separate sections on mysteries in German from our German chapter, short story anthologies and collections, non-fiction and reference books, mysteries for minors, mysteries written for children and young adults, an index of authors by location, and an index of publishers. According to Kate Flora, Sisters in Crime's current President,

> Among the projects that support and promote our members, we publish a Books in Print catalogue distributed each year to more than 10,000 wholesalers, distributors, libraries, bookstore chairs, independent bookstores, and mystery bookstores, as well as to thousands of individual readers.[22]

Canadian mystery author Vicki Cameron has been the compiler and editor for the *Sisters in Crime Books in Print* since 1999. SinC *Books in Print* is published by Gavin Faulkner of Rowan Mountain Literary Associates. SinC *Books in Print* is especially relevant for librarians since it cites ISBN numbers for accurate ordering of mysteries from publishers and vendors. Representing over 350 publishers, large and small, conglomerate and independent, of books, audio books, and e-books, it provides the librarian responsible for ordering mysteries in public, school, academic, and special libraries the perfect acquisition. SinC *Books in Print*'s value is evident in the enthusiastic librarians who grab it "hot-off-the-press" from our booth at ALA. At the reference desk, it gives readers' advisory librarians an essential reference work for citing, recommending, and interlibrary loaning mystery fiction. For those librarians who are mystery readers–and few aren't–it is a work to devour from cover to cover, since it tells not only what is currently in print, but what mysteries will be published in the near future. Many librarians have two or more copies of this wonderful reference tool, one to consult at the library and one to browse at home.

RELATIONSHIP OF BOOKSTORES AND LIBRARIES

From August of 1991 until I retired from the Pratt Library in December 2001, I wore two hats, one as a librarian and one as a bookseller. My husband had a famous quote with which he assailed me with as I was going out the door: "Are you selling them, or giving them away today?" What is the relationship between bookstores and libraries? Both support and recommend mysteries to their patrons and customers. The valuable and extensive reading experience I acquired while a Pratt librarian more than amply prepared me for the business of "hand-selling" I do everyday at Mystery Loves Company. But aren't they in competition for one another's business? In times of economic hardship, libraries should gain readers.

But bookstores and libraries can have a wonderful symbiotic relationship if they work together. Case in point is the Baltimore bookstores' cooperation with the City of Baltimore's Office of Promotion and the Arts and the Pratt Library in presenting the annual Baltimore Book Festival where we showcase the best that Maryland has to offer in literature in a three-day outdoor festival. Many states and cities now sponsor such literary events with lectures and workshops. First Lady Laura Bush has sponsored two such national book events on the Mall in Washington, DC.

Many times a library can offer an honorarium to entice famous authors to a town when they might miss coming to a bookstore. When space was a premium in our store for a big signing with Maryland Senator Barbara Mikulski, we worked with the Pratt library to use the reading garden of the former Fells Point Library for an elegant outdoor lecture and tea where Mystery Loves Company sold books. Open to the public, we had over 200 in attendance. I get calls at the store every week from Pratt and other local libraries, even once from Virginia and West Virginia, asking what I would have called a reference question about mysteries in my former life as a librarian. I certainly refer customers to the library should I not have what they want. I frequently compile bibliographies that I share with libraries, and they share their book lists with me.

But as a member of Sisters in Crime and a bookstore owner, my expertise now is knowing authors personally; that is, talking to authors daily and learning about their works in progress and when the books will be available. This is what makes a specialty store really special. I'm also very savvy about a variety of publishers: At the store we are regularly inundated with all types of information about the tiniest of specialty publishers. In this day of publish-on-demand and small boutique publishers, the only way to keep ahead of the curve is to read and absorb all that information. Librarians are now largely removed from this information due to central purchasing and must rely on their acquisitions departments to keep up with all that data. To make quality decisions about books that are published on demand, sometimes without the aid of any outside editing, you must read the book itself. There is no other way. Even then, mistakes in editing and production slip by. So every book that enters the store is checked, and at least five percent are rejected and sent back to the publishers. But several of the publish-on-demand books are best sellers in our store, so it is worth it to get to know this evolving subsection of publishing.

Once again Sisters in Crime, through its networking and newsletter, keeps us current, in this case about trends in publishing and the strange world of the mega-publishers, such as Bertelsmann and VHPS, which are no longer U.S.-owned. The implications this has for the reading public in the United States is rather frightening when you realize that an overseas editorial board is determining what is being printed by the majority of our publishers.

MYSTERY ACQUISITION AND USE IN LIBRARIES

Beverly Earls, Adult Services Coordinator of the Memphis-Shelby Public Library, says this about mysteries and libraries:

> Mysteries are our second most popular genre after romance . . . Between July 1994 and April 1995 we added 2,190 mysteries system

> wide, and they circulated 8,332 times for a turnover rate of 3.80. I think the message this sends is that the public enjoys genre fiction and when given a good choice of new titles will check the books out in droves. Memphis not only loves mystery writers, they can put them on the library's own cable TV Channel, WYPL, as well as on a FM radio reading service.[23]

In my own Roland Park Library Branch, fiction was half of our circulation. A great share of this was mystery fiction. Library patrons came in practically panicking because they did not have a new mystery to read. Interest was inter-generational. One reader started at age eleven, another would be still reading in her nineties. Most of all, they wanted recommendations from librarians and other readers as to what to read next. Most large public libraries publish book lists. They concentrate on the tried and true formula of "If you liked this type of mystery, try this author." Either in book list, extensive bibliography, or handy bookmark, the recommended mystery list assures that large stacks of mysteries will leave the library in happy hands.

At the Enoch Pratt Free Library Central Fiction Department, Helen Blumberg, the Department Head, talks about her favorite genre:

> Mysteries have always been the single most popular genre among our customers. There are several reasons for this. First, mysteries have so many subgenera that most fiction readers can practically be assured of finding one to their liking. After all, what other genre includes romance, history, the supernatural, technology, humor, contemporary urban life, multiculturalism, gay/lesbian, psychology, etc.? Second, mysteries appeal to readers who enjoy the challenge of a puzzle and of pitting their wits against those of the author. Third, since many mystery authors write series, readers form a strong attachment to the characters and follow them as their lives change from book to book.
>
> We have had great success recommending historical mysteries to young adults who have to read a historical novel. The settings and characters are authentic and the plots capture the teens' interest. If the protagonist happens to be a young adult, so much the better.
>
> Our centralized ordering system targets the top authors by using ordering plans. Our selectors track the second tier authors and en-

> able us to maintain complete runs of series. Having several knowledgeable and voracious mystery readers on our staff helps, too![24]

John Charles, librarian at the Scottsdale Public Library and author of *The Mystery Readers' Advisory: The Librarian's Clues to Murder and Mayhem*, wrote to me:

> It should not be a surprise to anyone who works in a public library that mysteries are popular with readers. In a survey done by the Romance Writers of America in 2001 mystery/detective/suspense fiction comprised 26.6% of all popular fiction sales in the United States. When *Library Journal* surveyed book expenditures in 1997 it found mystery fiction commanded the highest percentage of adult book expenditures by libraries for genre fiction selection. Even a quick glance at what is being returned on any given day in an individual library will demonstrate just how popular mysteries are.
>
> While some libraries may embrace the trend towards increasingly centralized selection and others may look towards mega bookstores such as Barnes and Noble as the blueprint for building their own cookie cutter collections, the truth is that if a library truly desires an excellent and unique mystery collection, it will involve some time and effort on the part of its staff.[25]

John offers the following six points for building a better mystery collection in public libraries:

1. Begin by assessing your own mystery collection. Before you can start ordering, you need to know what you are working with. Get out in the stacks and see what your own patrons are finding when they look for mysteries.
2. Add a few genre specific review sources to your selection mix. While the standard library review journals (*Booklist*, *Library Journal*, *Publisher's Weekly*) do cover a wide range of mystery titles, looking at such fan oriented publications as *Mystery News*, *The Drood Review of Mystery*, or *Murder Most Cozy* will expand the depth and scope of your collection.
3. Don't forget other formats. All too often when libraries do mystery selection, their focus is solely on books. But there are lots of wonderful mystery audios (on both cassette and CD) and mysteries on video and DVD that your readers would just love to see in your collection.

4. Remember the old mysteries. Usually when we select books for our library, we focus just on new titles, but if your library collection is anything like mine, you will need to replace your classic mystery titles on a regular basis.
5. Weeding is essential. Even if it isn't as much fun as ordering, your mystery collections should be weeded on a regular basis to keep the collection fresh and inviting to your readers.
6. Consider joining a mystery fan group like Sisters in Crime or try attending a mystery genre conference such as Left Coast Crime, Bouchercon, or Malice Domestic to name a few. Both provide wonderful ways to learn more about the genre and form connections with authors.[26]

SISTERS IN CRIME TODAY

Today, in 2003, Sisters in Crime has more than 3,200 members (expected to reach 3,600 by year's end), of whom 939 are published mystery writers and 472 are published in other fields. There are forty-six local chapters, including chapters in Canada, Germany, and Australia, an Internet chapter, and the Guppies, a support group for pre-published writers.[27] For a membership application, either go to the Internet Web site http://www.sistersincrime.org, call Beth Wasson, Executive Director of Sisters in Crime, at (985) 842-1325, or pick up an application at the Sisters in Crime booth at the next American Library Association convention. Ours will be the booth with the long line of eager librarians clustered around it and the happy mystery folks behind it eager to put the best of the genre into your waiting hands. As National SinC President Kate Flora says,

> Reach out to the camaraderie for which Sisters in Crime is famous, and keep reading, keep writing, keep recommending mysteries to everyone, everywhere.[28]

AUTHOR NOTE

The author is indebted to those authors and librarians who assisted her with her research and shared their experiences with libraries and Sisters in Crime. The majority of the quotes come from personal e-mail and letters to the author. The author refers the reader to the Sisters in Crime Web site http://www.sistersincrime.org and the Sisters in Crime membership brochure for further information about the organization. Other sources quoted are from national and chapter Sisters in Crime newsletters that are a benefit of Sisters in Crime membership.

REFERENCES

1. Carol Z. Edelman, "Mysterious Doings at the Roland Park Library," *The Messenger,* 23 May 1991.

2. Kate Flora, "Welcome to Sisters in Crime," Sisters in Crime, <http://www.sistersincrime.org>, [30 December 2002].

3. "An Introduction to Sisters in Crime," [Brochure], 1992, 2.

4. Emily Thayer, letter to Kathy Harig, 22 May 1988.

5. "An Evening with Sisters in Crime," [Press release], 4 March 1990.

6. Maureen Collins quoted in e-mail from Donna Andrews to Kathy Harig, 31 December 2002.

7. Collins, Ibid.

8. Various authors, *Chesapeake Chapter Sisters in Crime Newsletters* and issues of *Criminal Tendencies*, August 1991-95.

9. Kathy Harig, "Sisters in Crime at ALA/Atlanta," *Criminal Tendencies*, Volume I, August 1991, 5-6.

10. Susan Dunlap, letter to Kathy Harig, 5 July 1991.

11. Carolyn Hart, letter to Kathy Harig, 3 July 1991, 1.

12. Hart, Ibid, 2.

13. Kathy Harig, letter to Susan Dunlap, 12 July 1991, 2.

14. Elaine Raco Chase, *Sisters in Crime Newsletter*, September 1994, 15.

15. Kate Flora, e-mail to Kathy Harig, 2 January 2003.

16. Laura Lippman, e-mail to Kathy Harig, 3 January 2003.

17. Vicki Cameron, e-mail to Kathy Harig, 9 December 2002.

18. Jeanne Dams, e-mail to Kathy Harig, 10 December 2002.

19. Eve Sandstrom, e-mail to Kathy Harig, 10 December 2002.

20. Elaine Viets, e-mail to Kathy Harig, 20 December 2002.

21. Donna Andrews, e-mail to Kathy Harig, 6 January 2003.

22. Flora, "Welcome to Sisters in Crime," Ibid.

23. Beverly Earls, "Tennessee Library Supports Genres" in *Sisters in Crime Newsletter*, June 1996, 6.

24. Helen Blumberg, e-mail to Kathy Harig, 7 January 2003.

25. John Charles, e-mail to Kathy Harig, 30 December 2002.

26. Charles, Ibid.

27. Flora, "Welcome to Sisters in Crime," Ibid.

28. Flora, Ibid.

Buying Books Online Is No Mystery

Larisa Somsel

SUMMARY. This article discusses buying books online, includes popular sites where you can buy books online, and identifies important considerations for online shoppers. *[Article copies available for a fee from The Haworth Document Delivery Service: 1-800-HAWORTH. E-mail address: <docdelivery@haworthpress.com> Website: <http://www.HaworthPress.com> © 2004 by The Haworth Press, Inc. All rights reserved.]*

KEYWORDS. Out-of-print books/acquisitions, mystery and detective fiction/acquisitions, Internet/bookstores, second-hand books

Whether you are an employee of an institution completing a collection or an individual buying books for your personal use, the Internet has made it easier than ever to find out-of-print and hard to find books. But like all Internet transactions, the anonymity of ethernet means that you must do a little more research to make sure that you protect yourself when making a purchase. The phrase *caveat emptor* has never been more appropriate.

With millions of used books available online, it may not be so much of an issue of how to find the books that you are seeking, but rather a question of how to get the best deal while protecting yourself.

Larisa Somsel is an Online Bookseller at Amazon.com. Her inventory is searchable at http://www.amazon.com/shops/somselbooks (E-mail: somselbooks@aol.com).

[Haworth co-indexing entry note]: "Buying Books Online Is No Mystery." Somsel, Larisa. Co-published simultaneously in *Collection Management* (The Haworth Information Press, an imprint of The Haworth Press, Inc.) Vol. 29, No. 3/4, 2004, pp. 41-52; and: *Managing the Mystery Collection: From Creation to Consumption* (ed: Judith Overmier, and Rhonda Harris Taylor) The Haworth Information Press, an imprint of The Haworth Press, Inc., 2004, pp. 41-52. Single or multiple copies of this article are available for a fee from The Haworth Document Delivery Service [1-800-HAWORTH, 9:00 a.m. - 5:00 p.m. (EST). E-mail address: docdelivery@haworthpress.com].

Available online at http://www.haworthpress.com/web/COL

doi:10.1300/J105v29n03_04

FROM WHOM ARE YOU BUYING?

If you are already shopping at a local independent or mystery book store and are a frequent customer, you may want to consider those venues first when looking for an out-of-print or hard to find book. Many mystery bookstores have online sources or reciprocal relationships with other vendors and can help you find what you need. An added benefit of this approach is that you are still supporting your local bookstore. If your local retailer cannot assist you, then the Internet makes every bookstore local.

There are a variety of types of vendors online. Some are traditional brick and mortar stores with online presences, like Mystery Ink in New York (http://www.mysterink.com). Others, like Greenwich Village's Partners & Crime (http://www.crimepays.com), have a catalog online but prefer phone orders, although the inventory can be found on Abebooks.com. Some are online-only stores, like Grave Matters (http://www.gravematters.com/). Some are very professional businesses; some are run from the owners' homes. Unfortunately, it often does not matter what type of seller or business that a vendor is. Like all businesses, some online booksellers have higher levels of customer service than others. I sell used books from my home, but strive to maintain a high level of customer service, and I have a five star feedback on Amazon. Just keep in mind that these are not always traditional bookstore dealers with whom you are negotiating. Thus, there are a number of guidelines that can help assure successful transactions.

First, be sure to research a seller before buying. Take the time to check the return policy, shipping and handling information, and shipping costs. On some sites, such as Alibris, eBay, and Amazon.com, you can check a seller's feedback rating. Feedback is left by previous customers and rates the quality of service that they received. This scoring is one good way to evaluate a seller to determine if she is legitimate and conscientious. Such assessments from customers include indicators of whether vendors are accurately rating their books and providing timely service. Steer clear of sellers with a history of negative feedback. Another way to evaluate a seller is to e-mail or phone her directly to learn more about the book that you wish to purchase. Person-to-person customer service reflects the quality of the establishment and the professionalism of the management. Also be sure to request photos or scans for high priced items and learn the return policy of the seller with whom you are working, just in case that option is needed. In return, after you have completed a sale, remember to leave positive feedback for a vendor if you were satisfied with the transaction and negative feedback if totally unsatisfied. Amazon recommends that before you leave negative feedback, you try to work out a resolution in cases where you are not satisfied. Remember that some non-traditional sellers operate out of their homes or have odd hours and may not respond immediately to your requests. It is reasonable to give sellers at least twenty-four hours to communicate with customers. Sites such as Amazon and Alibris have their own return and refund policies that may override individual sellers and provide greater protection for the buyer. On some sites, returns must be within seven days of receipt, and on other sites the limit is within thirty days.

BOOK BUYING SITES

The following selected list of book buying sites provides contact information and highlights notable aspects of each business:

Advanced Book Exchange
http://www.abebooks.com

Forty million books offered by 10,000 booksellers (some of their inventory, but not all, is cross-listed on Amazon, Barnes and Noble, and eBay/Half.com). Neat feature: want list.

Alibris
http://www.alibris.com

Twelve to fifteen million out-of-print, out-of-stock-indefinitely, and rare books and four million in-print books. Partnerships with Books in Print, YBP Library Services (supplier to academic libraries), and Blackwell's Book Services. Formerly Interloc.

Amazon.com
http://www.amazon.com

"The Godfather" of online book and merchandise sites. It has an incredible number of books, both new and used, and it has partnerships with Abebooks.com and Alibris.com.

Barnes and Noble
http://www.bn.com

This brick and mortar goliath has more than twenty million listings from its nationwide network of out-of-print, rare, and used book dealers.

eBay and Half.com
http://www.ebay.com, http://half.ebay.com

eBay is an auction site with everything from books to butter churns. Half.com is eBay's fixed price (non-auction) venue. Both sites' drawback is fewer professional sellers, which means that prices can be lower, but service isn't always guaranteed.

Library Book Sales
http://www.librarybooksales.org

The Library Book Sales project was developed by the California State Library System to enable libraries and Friends of Libraries around the world to sell their better books online. The full-featured project is free (small commission on sold books) and encourages libraries to learn and then earn more money than they could get from local library sales. LibraryBookSales.org matches you with rare, collectible, and quality books that have been donated to public libraries. The money that you spend goes directly to the library that sells you the book. The listing site has over 200 partner libraries and more than 50,000 books.

BOOK SEARCH ENGINES

The following search engines are useful for global searching:

AddALL
http://www.addall.com

AddALL is a free service that searches for the best deal in books available online. It has separate search engines for new books, used books, movies, and music. It was built by book buyers for book buyers. AddALL is an independent and impartial Web site, not owned by any bookstore.

The search result is therefore totally objective. The used book search engine accesses fourteen different book selling sites, including: Abebooks.com, Alibris, Antiqbook, Biblioroom, Bibliology, Bibliophile, Bibliopoly, Biblion, Chapitre, Elephantbooks, ILAB (International League of Antiquarian Booksellers), Powells, Maremagnum, and Half.com.

Bookfinder
http://www.bookfinder.com

BookFinder.com is a one-stop search site that lets users view the collections of over 40,000 sellers of new, used, rare, and out-of-print books. The forty million titles available comprise the largest book catalog available anywhere, either online or offline. The search engine accesses over thirty-four different sites.

MYSTERY BOOKSELLERS ONLINE

There are so many mystery booksellers online that I could not include them all in this listing. Instead, see the compilation below for directories of mystery bookstores and sellers:

- Cluelass.com
  http://www.cluelass.com
- Independent Mystery Booksellers Association
  http://www.mysterybooksellers.com/
- Sisters in Crime
  http://www.sistersincrime.org
- Mystery Readers International
  http://www.mysteryreaders.org/
- Thrilling Detective
  http://www.thrillingdetective.com/

WHAT ARE YOU BUYING?

For most collectors and libraries, condition will be the number one determining factor when purchasing an out-of-print book, so make sure you understand what you are buying. When buying used books online it is important to read each seller's description of the book carefully.

Terms used vary between sites and sellers and can lead to confusion when the hardback book that you thought you ordered arrives as a paperback edition. Traditional brick and mortar book dealers have long described book condition by using terms that were originally defined by the periodical, *AB Bookman's Weekly*. Following is a summary of these terms:

- *As New.* To be used only when the book is in the same immaculate condition in which it was published. There can be no defects, no missing pages, no library stamps, etc., and the dust jacket (if it was issued with one) must be perfect, without any tears. (The term *As New* is preferred over the alternative term *Mint* to describe a copy that is perfect in every respect, including jacket.)
- *Fine.* Approaches the condition of *As New*, but without being crisp. For the use of the term *Fine* there must also be no defects, etc., and if the jacket has a small tear, or other defect, or looks worn, this fact should be noted.
- *Very Good.* Can describe a used book that does show some small signs of wear, but has no tears on either binding or paper. Any defects must be noted.
- *Good.* Describes the average used and worn book that has all pages or leaves present. Any defects must be noted.
- *Fair.* Indicates a worn book that has complete text pages (including those with maps or plates) but may lack endpapers, half-title, etc., (which must be noted). Binding, jacket (if any), etc., may also be worn. All defects must be noted.
- *Poor.* Describes a book that is sufficiently worn that its only merit is as a *Reading Copy* because it does have the complete text, which must be legible. Any missing maps or plates should still be noted. This copy may be soiled, scuffed, stained or spotted and may have loose joints, hinges, pages, etc.
- *Ex-library.* Copies deaccessioned from libraries must always be designated as such *no matter what the condition of the book.*
- *Book Club.* Such editions must always be noted as such *no matter what the condition of the book.*
- *Binding Copy.* Describes a book in which the pages or leaves are perfect but the binding is very bad, loose, off, or nonexistent.
- *Dustjacket.* In all cases, the lack of a dustjacket should be noted if the book was issued with one.[1]

The Independent Online Booksellers Association, Antiquarian Booksellers' Association of America, and the International Book Collector's Association endorse these standard terms. However, the arrival of a slew of new sellers and new selling venues means that these terms are sometimes used more loosely and are subject to interpretation. To add to the confusion, Amazon.com has its own set of terms that it asks its sellers to use:

- *New.* Just like it sounds: a brand-new, unused, unread copy in perfect condition.
- *Like New.* An apparently unread copy in perfect condition. Dust cover is intact; pages are clean and are not marred by notes or folds of any kind. Suitable for presenting as a gift.
- *Very Good.* A copy that has been read, but remains in excellent condition. Pages are intact and are not marred by notes or highlighting. The spine remains undamaged.
- *Good.* A copy that has been read, but remains in clean condition. All pages are intact, and the cover is intact (including dust cover, if applicable). The spine may show signs of wear. Pages can include limited notes and highlighting, and the copy can include "From the library of" labels.
- *Acceptable.* A readable copy. All pages are intact, and the cover is intact (the dust cover may be missing). Pages can include considerable notes–in pen or highlighter–but the notes cannot obscure the text.[2]

If you have any questions about the condition of a book beforehand, you should e-mail or telephone the seller. If you see a book listed on Amazon in "Good" condition with no further details, e-mail for clarification. Online sellers are often limited in the number of words that they can use for a description, and they often abbreviate to compensate. For more detailed book condition terms check out these Web sites:

- Independent Online Booksellers Association
  http://www.ioba.org/terms.html
- A Book Collector's Glossary by Carl Noe
  http://www.trussel.com/books/glossary.htm
- rec.collecting.books FAQ
  http://www.massmedia.com/~mikeb/rcb/
- Bibliomania's links to eight terminology sites
  http://bibliomania.net/Terminology.html

- Abebooks glossary
  http://dogbert.abebooks.com/docs/HelpCentral/Glossary/index.shtml

While condition is often important, you may decide that condition is less important when a book is extremely scarce or if you are buying it for personal reading or for research. One of my clients did a conference session on mystery books set in Norway. As you may guess, this is not a popular genre that is easy to track down or even to find in print. There are thirty-five English-language mysteries set in Norway. Initially we were able to find all but ten titles, and it was the search for the remaining ten that led us to thoroughly test the limits of online book buying. Out of the ten remaining books and authors, we were able to acquire five copies within a year. One of these books we purchased twice because the first copy was in "reading copy" condition with stained boards, missing title pages, and ex-library markings. Four months later, we were able to purchase a better copy whose only flaws were a faded spine and spine slant. The rest of these books are still being sought.

WAITING FOR BOOKS TO COME TO MARKET

For books that are not immediately available, you many want to try Abebooks' "Want List," a service that keeps you informed when a specific book comes on the market. This was an excellent tool for acquiring our Norwegian mystery book collection. To use this service at Abebooks.com, you enter and save a list of books that you are seeking and as booksellers add inventory to the online database, you will receive an e-mail notifying you of the new content. Your want list can include author, title, publisher, and/or keywords. On my want list I have a book titled *Sorting of the Samsells*, a genealogy book about my husband's side of the family, a mystery book titled *Lewker in Norway*, a listing of the keywords "Hocking Valley" (another genealogy interest), and the author Emma Stahler Smith (my great-great-grandmother). As with all search strategies, the more specific you are, the better the results that you receive. For instance, the keywords "Wood County" could result in books on Wood County, Texas, rather than Wood County, Ohio. Abebooks.com is a terrific service with no obligation to purchase. It also means that you have to be on the ball when books become available. A reading copy of *Lewker in Norway* by G. Carr became available for the first time in a year and was snatched up quickly by another lucky buyer.

When shopping on Amazon you can pre-order a book that is not currently available as a used copy, operating on the premise that their sellers add inventory every day and one will soon become available. You can define the condition that you require (New, Like New, Very Good, etc.) and the price at which you are willing to purchase. As soon as a book that matches your condition and price becomes available, your credit card is automatically charged and your order processed to the independent seller. The downside to this strategy is you do not have a chance to approve the order, as it processes automatically. You can, of course, cancel with the seller immediately if necessary. Remember that for both of these services, dealers can check the pre-order/want list and that fact may result in an increased price.

PRICING AND HOW TO PAY

Credit cards are the most commonly accepted form of payment on the Internet. If you are concerned about credit card fraud, check to make sure the payment site is secure (as indicated by https, rather than http before the Web site address) and carefully read each site's privacy and security disclosures. Alibris, Amazon, Half.com, and Barnes and Noble accept credit cards and process them internally, sharing only your order information and mailing address with sellers. Some sites share your e-mail address with sellers, too. On Abebooks, sellers can choose to use Abebooks' payment service or accept payment directly. Librarybooksales and eBay do not handle any payments; arrangements are made between library and buyer. In these cases, most vendors will accept checks, money orders, or online payment through sites such as PayPal.com. Most sellers will accept a purchase order from an institution such as a library, but may not from an individual. For high priced items, use an escrow service, in which a reliable third-party handles deposits.

You can use sites such as AddALL to compare the price for a book from a number of dealers. Just make sure you are looking at comparable items when evaluating prices. For serious collectors and high-priced books, be sure to thoroughly research prices in a price guide and to read some of the basic resources on book collecting, such as John Carter's *ABC for Book Collectors* and Allan and Patricia Ahearn's *Book Collecting 2000*. Prices on the Internet may have extreme fluctuation as seller inventory and buyer demand shift.

When paying, make sure your credit card and billing and shipping addresses are correct. Many a book has gone astray because a buyer forgot to update a preferred mailing address. Many sellers are wary of online buying with their credit cards. While these fears may be overblown, there are some steps that you can take to protect yourself. Talk to your credit card company representatives for their recommendations and remember that most card companies have some kind of fraud protection (whether online or off).

SHIPPING AND RETURNS

Most dealers ship books via Media Mail rate, which has replaced the Book Rate class. This rate is slower than regular First Class mail. If you need a book quickly or live in Alaska or Hawaii, you should pay extra and upgrade your shipping class to Priority Mail. In some cases, such as used books bought through Barnes and Noble, the book is first sent to the company headquarters, and then sent on to you after its condition is confirmed by Barnes and Noble. If you want insurance or delivery tracking, make arrangements with the seller as these services are often extra and may include extra fees. Sites such as Amazon, Abebooks, and Barnes and Noble will charge customers a set shipping and handling fee and only pass a portion of that onto the seller, keeping the "handling" to cover their expenses such as Web site maintenance and credit card processing. At Amazon, the buyer is charged $3.49 for standard shipping and handling, but the seller only receives $2.26, which is enough to cover Media Mail rates but not First Class or Priority for hardbacks. Amazon's Expedited shipping costs the buyer $5.49 and pays the seller $5.05, more than enough for Priority. Keep in mind that your shipping and handling covers both the parent company's percentage and the postage and packaging expenses of the seller.

Before returning a book, it is best to notify your seller. Barnes and Noble and Abebooks require that you contact them directly within a specific time frame before returning. In some case you will receive a credit for shipping. If you are returning a book because the condition of the book did not meet your expectations, you can usually expect a full refund. If you are returning a book because you did not like the novel or you are finished reading it (believe me, this scenario happens!), then you can probably expect no refund. Remember that these are bookstores, not libraries. In cases where a buyer and seller cannot come to an agreement on a refund, most parent sites have their own refund policies. Amazon calls theirs an "A to Z Guarantee."

DIFFERENT BOOKS, DIFFERENT NEEDS, DIFFERENT PRICES

A quick scan of some mystery books on the Internet illustrates the wide variety of book editions, conditions, and prices available for the general reader and the collector. None of these books were listed in the two print price guides that I checked.

P.D. James, *Cover Her Face.* 1962. The London First Edition published by Faber and Faber in a hardcover with a pictorial dust jacket starts at $7,500. An ex-library edition, signed, ranges from $4,100-3,500. The American First Edition signed sells between $1,565-800, unsigned $700-350. A brand new paperback edition is $10.80. A used paperback edition is $1-2.

Ellery Queen, *The Roman Hat Mystery.* 1929. NY: Stockes, 1929. $1,950-1,250. $500 with no dust jacket. A brand new hardcover edition is $40. A used paperback edition in very good condition ranges from $5-15. A 1979 First Golden Anniversary Edition, signed (one of 250), sells for between $100-250.

Agatha Christie, *The Mysterious Affair at Styles.* 1921. First British Edition. $11,000. This is the first novel introducing Hercule Poirot. A vintage Penguin paperback (Penguin # 6; 1935) retails for approximately $30. A brand new paperback edition is $5.99. A used paperback edition in very good condition lists as low as $1.

DIFFERENT VENDORS, DIFFERENT EXPERIENCES

A recent discussion on an online book sellers forum illustrates the variety of experiences that you can have buying books online. A few months ago there were two sales of a rare Val Kilmer poetry book. The differences between these two sales, how they were conducted, and the results are a good example of the online buying experience. Both of these sales were on eBay auctions, a good venue for capturing the attention and bidding action of Val Kilmer collectors. The book was a limited edition poetry book entitled *My Edens After Burns* (New Mexico: Blue Feather Press, 1987). The book had a very limited print run (approximately 2,000) and was written for family and friends as a gift, and then recalled because Val Kilmer feared the poems would be misconstrued and taken out of context.

A seller who also sells on Amazon.com sold the first auction. She had only sold on eBay a few times and while she had some feedback posted, it did not include a large number of responses, thereby indicating that she was somewhat new on eBay. The seller included a good description and six scans of the item cover, autograph, contents, and the one small flaw. The auction lasted ten days, and the mint condition book sold for $4,200 to a serious collector who had contacted the seller directly for more information.

Two weeks later a different seller listed the same book on eBay. The seller was brand-new to the service, with no customer feedback posted, and she included no pictures of the book. The auction lasted only five days and included a number of bidders who were listed as new to eBay (a practice commonly believed to be employed by sellers bidding on their own items to raise prices). The rare and expensive book listed standard mail shipping, with no special insurance or overnight fees included. The auction ended at $800 and did not meet the initial reserve price. The seller later re-listed the auction with one photo and closed at $4,300, but the item remained unsold because the auction had a reserve price of $5,000. It is unknown if this book was ever sold or offered for auction again by this seller.

The hunt for out-of-print books is no longer a mystery. Buying books online can solve your book acquisition problems. As a buyer you must pay attention to condition descriptions, price, customer service, and payment security, just as you would in a bookstore or when ordering from a catalog. For more in-depth information on buying books online, read *Buying Books Online: Finding Bargains and Saving Money with Booksense Stores, Amazon Marketplace, and Other Online Sites* by Stephen Windwalker.[3]

Happy hunting! With so many mystery books available online your hunt may never end, and your mailbox will never grow cold.

REFERENCES

1. International Book Collector's Association, <http://www.rarebooks.org/bookcondition.htm>, 1999.

2. Amazon.com, Inc., <http://www.amazon.com/exec/obidos/tg/browse/-/1161242>, 1996-2003.

3. Windwalker, Stephen. *Buying Books Online: Finding Bargains and Saving Money with Booksense Stores, Amazon Marketplace, and Other Online Sites*. MA: Harvard Perspectives Press, 2002.

Review Sources for Mystery Fiction

Jean Bielke-Rodenbiker

SUMMARY. Mysteries are an increasingly popular genre with library patrons. The following article discusses sources that librarians can use to find reviews and other information about mystery fiction. Professional journals and fan publications are discussed; online sources attached to these venues are also included. Since subscriptions to print sources may be limited, selected Web sources are covered. Finally, selected sources for further research are briefly discussed. *[Article copies available for a fee from The Haworth Document Delivery Service: 1-800-HAWORTH. E-mail address: <docdelivery@haworthpress.com> Website: <http://www.HaworthPress.com> © 2004 by The Haworth Press, Inc. All rights reserved.]*

KEYWORDS. Mystery fiction–reviews, review sources, mystery reviews, mysteries–reviews

Mystery fiction has become increasingly popular over the last twenty years. It can be very difficult to keep up with all the new authors, new titles, and new entries in series. The following discussion will highlight

---

Jean Bielke-Rodenbiker, MLIS, is Adult Services Librarian, Southdale Area Library, Edina, MN.

Address correspondence to: Jean Bielke-Rodenbiker, 5028 Nicollet Avenue, Minneapolis, MN 55419.

The author is grateful to Constance Hill, Minneapolis Public Library, for her support during the writing of this article.

[Haworth co-indexing entry note]: "Review Sources for Mystery Fiction." Bielke-Rodenbiker, Jean. Co-published simultaneously in *Collection Management* (The Haworth Information Press, an imprint of The Haworth Press, Inc.) Vol. 29, No. 3/4, 2004, pp. 53-71; and: *Managing the Mystery Collection: From Creation to Consumption* (ed: Judith Overmier, and Rhonda Harris Taylor) The Haworth Information Press, an imprint of The Haworth Press, Inc., 2004, pp. 53-71. Single or multiple copies of this article are available for a fee from The Haworth Document Delivery Service [1-800-HAWORTH, 9:00 a.m. - 5:00 p.m. (EST). E-mail address: docdelivery@haworthpress.com].

Available online at http://www.haworthpress.com/web/COL

doi:10.1300/J105v29n03_05

some of the resources available to librarians to help them with this task. The professional publications that have mystery reviews will be discussed, as will some of the genre and fan magazines. Finally, there will be brief reviews of some of the Internet sources available. Many of these resources will have links to other information of value in collection development.

For brevity's sake, this article will offer a sampling of the review sources available. Keep in mind that local sources will often prove a valuable resource as well; many local newspapers, for example, offer book reviews at least on an irregular basis, if not a weekly basis. Many specialty bookstores with a Web presence will also have reviews, and these can be a valuable resource.

PRINT SOURCES: PROFESSIONAL JOURNALS

Booklist

Appearing twice monthly, *Booklist* has been produced by the American Library Association publishing committee since 1920. *Booklist* is one of the periodicals aimed at librarians, and the reviews are generally written by subject specialists. The aim is to identify and review new titles in specific subject areas; the aim is not to predict what will be financially successful, but to point out necessary and/or exciting additions to a particular field or genre. Some of the issues focus on a particular genre or subject. Generally one will not find negative reviews here, and a review can be seen as a recommendation for purchase. Reviews are generally short and to the point, giving the overall essence of the book. Those titles deemed to be outstanding are marked with a star. Reviews are attributed, with the reviewer's name at the end of the review. Approximately 40,000 adult books are reviewed yearly, and *Booklist* features articles, author interviews, bibliographies, and more.

There is also a corresponding Web site for *Booklist*: http://www.ala.org/booklist. Here you will find an index to the publication, with access to the reviews. After clicking on "Main Entry Index" for the volume you see, clicking on the title of the novel or article will take you to it. When this author checked, the index with links was approximately six weeks behind. Also, under the heading "Cumulative Indexes to Booklist Magazine" one finds PDF formatted, printable pages indexing entire volumes, i.e., one year of the publication. This is an index only, with volume ninety-eight totaling sixty-four pages. Further down the page, there is main entry indexing to *Booklist*, as well as access by letter of the alphabet. Use of these tools can save time if one is not sure when a review may have appeared.

Kirkus Reviews

Generally aimed at librarians and others with a presumed scholarly interest, *Kirkus Reviews* has been in print since 1932. Fiction and non-fiction for adult and juvenile audiences are covered, with separate indexes at the ends of the juvenile and adult sections. While reviews are not individually attributed, contributors are listed at the bottom of the first page with the information about editors, etc. Each review includes the necessary purchasing information.

Mystery fiction is reviewed separately from regular fiction, although here, as with any of these sources, it is a good idea to check regular fiction reviews for those titles that are not strictly mystery, but will be in demand by mystery readers. Generally reviews tend to be approximately 200-250 words, with the "in brief" reviews being shorter; however, some are as short as ten sentences, with others as long as half a page. The last paragraph generally gives the overall opinion of the work; the main review gives a synopsis of the plot. Books deemed to be of special merit are marked with a black star by the title and are listed on the "Of Special Note" page at the beginning of the issue. Reviews range from glowing to denigrating; in fact, *Kirkus* will sometimes pan a title other review sources have praised. Sections of this publication are also available for free online: http://www.kirkusreviews.com.

Library Journal

Aimed at librarians, and not solely a review source, *Library Journal* is generally considered to be the least critical of the major review journals. Contributing librarians pen evaluative reviews in areas of their expertise, writing with a librarian audience in mind. The "Mystery Reviews" are generally found after the fiction reviews and are not separately found in the table of contents at the beginning of each issue.

These reviews are attributed; mystery reviews are quite often written by one person, although when this is not the case, the reviewer's name and affiliation appear after the review. There may also be additional mystery reviews by other reviewers under the category "Additional Mystery." Length of reviews can range from fewer than one hundred words to over 300. Since this is a publication geared to libraries and librarians, reviewers will often specify whether a title is or is not worth purchasing for a library. Consequently, there may be a less than glowing review that indicates the title should still be purchased for the library due to anticipated demand or purchased for a library where there has been demand for that author. Or, it may state that it is a marginal purchase. Reviewers may also recommend a title or author to purchase instead of, or in addition to, the reviewed title.

Publishers Weekly

An international news magazine of the publishing industry, *Publishers Weekly* (PW) identifies materials that are marketable on a national basis or those that will be promoted heavily in mass media. Articles concerning industry trends, interviews with authors, and reviews are valuable for collection development as well. PW also informs about size of print runs, publicity and promotion, etc. Articles about the publishing industry may also be of interest.

Reviews are timely; galleys must be sent approximately three months in advance to be included, and no reviews are done after publication. An issue will often focus on a particular topic: Christian publishing, women's fiction, audio-books, etc. Reviews are found in the PW "Forecasts" section, and many reviews conclude with a forecast or comment about potential demand factors. Information for purchase is included at the beginning of each review, and publication month is at the end. Mystery reviews are generally found after fiction. Reviews are not attributed, but editors are listed at the beginning of the magazine on the "How to Reach Us" page, and contributing editors are listed as well. "Hot" titles have stars, with the title printed in red. Reviews average 250 words and give a plot synopsis. Generally, since this publication is tied to the publishing industry, even less-than-glowing reviews will find some positive aspect about a work.

PRINT SOURCES: GENRE/FAN PUBLICATIONS

Below is a sampling of some of the genre publications available. These magazines are geared toward mystery readers/aficionados, and writers themselves, therefore, the coverage will be more specific to mysteries/thrillers/suspense and the like, and more of these titles will be reviewed. Patrons quite often ask for some of these periodicals as well, so it may be worthwhile to circulate them if possible.

Deadly Pleasures

This Anthony Award winning publication is edited and published by George Easter. Published four times yearly, *Deadly Pleasures* is composed primarily of book reviews and news of forthcoming releases. There are regular columns as well, such as "Reviewed to Death," in which the same book is reviewed by different people. This is a useful technique–one is able to compare reviewers side by side, and it gives an in-depth review of a particular work. The same work could have rave reviews and pans within one or two pages.

Generally, there will be one author featured per issue, with reviews and interviews. *Deadly Pleasures* also publishes a list of the best mystery and crime novels each year in several different categories. Each features a capsule synopsis, as well as a notation alerting the reader to other sources that gave a glowing review. "Quarterly Question" poses a question to readers, who respond with their answers. From a librarian's perspective, this can be interesting insight into what the public may be reading, or what "mystery buffs" are seeking. "Sneak Previews" alerts the reader to forthcoming titles. "Recent Recommended Paperbacks" breaks titles into the categories "soft to medium boiled" and "medium boiled to hard boiled," "hard boiled" being the nitty-gritty hard-as-nails mysteries.

Deadly Pleasures has regular reviewers as well, each with their own style and rating methods. The periodical contains a good number of reviews, and there are often reviews for titles not reviewed elsewhere. While most reviews are of works emanating from United States authors, there are sections covering reviews from the United Kingdom, including new titles that are coming out in England. Some of the reviewers have regular columns, and these reviews are listed in the table of contents under the reviewers' names rather than the column title. This is a good periodical title to use as a review resource.

The Web presence for this publication is http://www.deadlypleasures.com. There is a sampling of the magazine's contents here, but the Web site is not full content. A new review is posted weekly, with a monthly interview with a mystery author. The forthcoming books section, "Recent Crime Novels," is duplicated in its entirety, as is the information on crime fiction conventions. The "Mystery Links" section has a collection of links pertinent to the interests of mystery readers and librarians alike:

other mystery magazines, publishers, crime fiction conventions, and other general mystery links.

Drood Review of Mystery

Jim Huang's *The Drood Review of Mystery* has been in publication for twenty years and is an excellent source for mystery reviews. *Drood* is a two-time winner of the American Mystery Award for best fan publication and a 2001 Anthony Award nominee. The periodical reviews titles from large publishers, but also covers books from lesser known sources, which fills a niche some of the other publications may not. It has been called the best source for serious fans of mystery and suspense literature, especially since the passing of *Armchair Detective*. The self-proclaimed mission is "to give our readers fair and reliable reviews of current mysteries, along with comprehensive guides to new titles and thoughtful commentary on the genre."

Drood Review comes out six times a year, and each issue contains reviews and essays on a topic of interest to mystery fans. Most issues are between twenty to twenty-five pages in length. There is a mixture of longer reviews that are a page or more in length and shorter capsule reviews. Usually there are about twenty-five reviews in each issue, and approximately 1,400 yearly. Its reviews are perhaps more analytical than those of some of the other mystery publications. Each review is attributed; generally the longer reviews have the authors' names, while the capsule reviews have the initials of the reviewers. These can be translated by looking at the editorial information, which may not be on the first page, but is somewhere near the beginning of each issue.

The *Drood Review* also publishes a guide to books that are scheduled to be published in the coming months. This guide lists author, title, and a short synopsis, closing with publisher, expected date, and expected price. Format is also included: first edition, paperback, etc. The *Drood Review* is a good source to use for reviews and information about forthcoming publications.

Mystery News

This thirty-six page tabloid format review periodical has been in publication since the early 1980s. It was acquired by L. Kaczmarek and C. Aldrich as Black Raven Press in 1997. The press was formed to publish this periodical, with the door being open for other publishing ventures in the future. *Mystery News* won the Anthony Award as best fan publication of 2000. Available at bookstores, by subscription, and at some libraries, it comes out in the even numbered months of the year, for a total of six issues yearly.

Each issue lists the names of the reviewers, but there is no information about them. The reviewers generally discuss more than one title, and the reviews are grouped by reviewer. There is an index by title reviewed found on the inside first page, and this is quite helpful. This organization allows the reader to look for a review by title if desired, but also allows those interested in a particular reviewer to find their reviews easily. Each issue contains over fifty reviews, along with some features such as mystery news, convention information, etc. Each review ends with a "quill" rating: a five quill rating is considered a must-read. Since the reviewers are fairly constant, one can get a taste for what they tend to review and if their reviews are useful for one's purposes. As with patrons, each reviewer seems to have different taste and this is reflected in the reviews. Each review is generally a mix of synopsis of the plot and what the reviewer liked (or did not like) about the novel. Comments about the plot, writing style and overall opinion about the novel are often featured in the reviews as well. The unbiased reviews vary from a half quill to five; there are unfavorable reviews here as well as favorable. The February/March issue features a list of the reviewer's favorites for the previous year–the February/March 2002 issue features favorites of 2001.

Previews of forthcoming books are near the end of the magazine on pages thirty to thirty-four. They are divided into "hardcover" previews and paperback. An interesting feature here is the division into categories: Each of the previews is under an appropriate category, including amateur sleuth, legal thriller, British mysteries, etc. Each preview provides a short synopsis, along with publishing information.

The accompanying Web site for *Mystery News*, http://www.blackravenpress.com, is also useful. This extensive Web site features "what's new," which seems to be updated quite frequently. In this section one finds information on author chats, awards, new reviews added to the page, convention information, and more. There are also links to publishers, mystery conventions, award nominees and winners, and other links of interest.

The Web site also features many reviews that are not found in the magazine itself. New reviews are added on a timely basis, and the newest reviews are marked with "new!" in red letters, making it simple to just look at the newest reviews. Clicking on the link takes one directly to the review. When last checked there were over sixty reviews on the

Web page. Combined with the magazine, this is quite a good source for reviews.

Mystery Readers Journal

Billed as "The Journal of Mystery Readers International," this journal is the publication of that organization. Mystery Readers International is open to anyone interested in or involved in mystery fiction. One receives the journal upon joining the organization. It is a quarterly journal, with each issue focusing on a specific theme. Past issues have focused on "Culinary Crime," "Pacific Northwest Mysteries," and "Oxbridge." Upcoming features include "Music and Mystery," "Religious Mysteries," and "Spring Gardening Mysteries."

Issues feature short articles by mystery authors and others that pertain to the theme of the issue. Other features include information about members, mystery group information, and a column by the founder of the group, Janet Rudolph. A disclaimer at the beginning of each issue states that unattributed material is written by her.

What reviews were seen within the issues reviewed were included within the articles. Therefore, most reviews or discussion was limited to books that fit the particular theme of an issue. While the issues were interesting reading, there are better sources for libraries to use for reviews.

The publication's Web site does have some features of interest to librarians. At http://www.mysteryreaders.org one can find listings of mystery groups by state. While this information is in the magazine, it is probably more cost-effective to use the Web site for this information. While probably not all-inclusive, the compilation is a good starting point.

There is also a good list of mystery periodicals on this Web site. A short annotation and contact information is included under each title. E-mail and Web addresses are also included as applicable.

The Mystery Review

This quarterly publication originates in Canada and mainly covers English, Canadian, and American mystery fiction. Features include interviews with authors and other mystery personalities, information about new releases, book reviews, and thematic articles. Recent interviewees have included Joan Hess and P. D. James. When there is no interview, there may be a profile of an author and their mysteries, such as an overview of the Anna Pigeon mysteries by Nevada Barr. Recent article topics have included "They Call it the Murder Home," "Martha Grimes' Children" (about children in the Richard Jury novels), and "Horror in the Mysteries of Agatha Christie." The column, "A Global Mysterious View," discusses mysteries set in other countries; Cuba, German language, and Finland were recent topics. The occasional "Between the Lines" column discusses various mystery themes, generally in the form of a bibliographic essay.

The reviews are generally quite substantial and are occasionally written by other mystery authors or literary professionals. Each review is attributed, with a short sentence about the reviewer and possibly their qualifications/interests at the end. A short paragraph about the author of the reviewed book follows the review. There are usually twenty to twenty-two pages of reviews, and each review tends to be about a page in length. Each review has a "dagger" rating–four daggers are an excellent rating, and the rating scales down in half dagger increments. Since each review is done by a different reviewer, each has its own particular flavor or style. Some give a detailed synopsis and biographical information about each author, while some discuss their own reactions to the novels in depth, and others summarize in only a sentence or two. These reviewers will finish a book whether they enjoy it or not: It isn't unheard of for a book to receive only half a dagger. Many titles receive three to four daggers, but reviewers are very clear about why they give only one or two daggers. Many of the reviewers do reviews for each issue, so a reader can get an idea of where individual reviewer tastes may lie and how it compares with her/his own. This publication may have fewer reviews than some of the other sources, but the reviews are in-depth, which may better suit some professional needs.

Mystery Scene

This established publication celebrated its eighteenth anniversary with its latest issue, number seventy-seven. It also changed hands in June of 2002. Longtime owners Ed Gorman and Martin H. Greenburg turned over control to Kate Stine, a consultant and editor in the mystery field. Gorman will remain involved as a contributing editor and columnist for *Mystery Scene*. It is not really known what types of changes, if any, will be in store for this magazine.

Mystery Scene is known not only for its reviews, but for its interviews with authors and industry professionals, publishing and bookselling industry news, writing tips, commentary, and more. It offers an inside look at the craft of writing, and a taste of the industry itself. "The Writing Life" section features authors discussing their latest books: the inspiration, their thoughts about protagonists, plot twists, why they do it. "The Publishing Biz" discusses the business end; there may be an interview with a publisher, or a discussion about bookstores partnering with libraries.

Reviews are not a main feature of this publication. Generally there are about twelve pages of reviews per issue; in a publication averaging eighty to ninety-plus pages, this is not a large percentage. The authors discussing their latest books provide an alert about what is being published, but of course these notices could not be considered reviews. The main interest here is the discussion of the craft and business of writing, with some reviewing provided. Therefore, depending on the need, there may be better publications for reviews.

WEB SITES

Web sites can be a real help in finding reviews of mystery fiction, especially when periodical budgets are tight. There are numerous mystery-oriented Web sites available now, many with reviews. Reviewers can vary from professionals in the publishing fields to those who write reviews as a hobby. These Web sites can be invaluable sources for librarians, and particularly for those individuals who are not as familiar with the genre as they would like. Web sites can also be useful for finding reviews written by readers and to get an idea about what mystery readers like. A sampling of sites available will be discussed here. Bookstores with a Web presence may be an additional source for reviews. Web sites that accompany or are sponsored by a publication are discussed with that publication.

Books'nbytes
http://www.booksnbytes.com

This Web site calls itself "Your Home for Mystery, Science Fiction, and Fantasy Authors!" and one will find reviews of these here. The mystery reviews are found by clicking on the button titled "Mystery Reviews." Under the "Mystery" button, topics such as author/book information, awards, conventions, interviews can be found. There is a category for true crime reviews, as well.

Under the "Mystery Reviews" category, the reviews are accessed three ways. There is a category for reviews posted within fifteen days;

these are the newest reviews, and some of the books are not yet published. Reviews can also be accessed by title or author. The review page states that most reviewers are not paid, and therefore they generally do not read books they do not expect to like. There is a fifty-page rule as well: If the reviewer cannot get through the first fifty pages of a novel, she does not read it and does not review it. Therefore, most reviews tend to be positive, if not glowing. Reviews are credited, and there is information available about the reviewers. Many of the reviewers are members of the online newsgroup, rec.alt.mystery. This group discusses crime fiction and true crime literature. On the dates this site was reviewed, many of the mystery reviews were written by one person, and looking at the archives this was true there as well.

This is a good site to access for reviews, especially for forthcoming books, if one takes the reviews with a grain of salt. If one likes the reviews of the main reviewer, this site is perfectly fine, but if not, there are other sites out there on the Internet. Books'nbytes can also be used as a source for "non-professional" reviews, that is, for reviews written by readers and not professionals in the field.

Cozies, Capers and Crimes
http://www.coziescapersandcrimes.com

Booked as a "newsletter for booklovers," this Web site consists of reviews, news on the mystery front, convention information, interviews, tidbits of interest, and in the latest edition (October/November), gift ideas. The editor (and sole owner) is the former manager of the Mystery Bookstore in Dallas, Texas. Reviews are attributed, and some of the reviews are written by published authors in the mystery field. Reader input is also encouraged. Publisher and date of publication is listed at the beginning of each review, and there will often be a link to the author's Web page or author interview at the end of the review. General coverage includes novels published within the last six months.

Reviews vary in length from a few paragraphs to a page; some have extensive plot synopses while others discuss only enough to get an idea of the story. Most of the reviews include at least a cursory discussion of writing and plot and why or why not the reviewer enjoyed the novel. Length of reviews is anywhere from two to six or more paragraphs, the average being four to five paragraphs. The reviews tend to be positive, but comments about editing, or negative comments may be included. There were a good number of reviews in the current issue; the print preview showed fifty-six pages. However, the reviews don't seem to be in any particular order, and there is no indexing or sorting mechanism in place. Scrolling is the only way to navigate the reviews. Two archived issues were available; scrolling to the bottom of the newsletter brings up the link.

While there is not a definite update timeframe listed, it is possible to sign up to receive an e-mail notification when the new issue is mounted on the Web site. The newsletter is distributed via e-mail and then added to the Web site.

I Love a Mystery Newsletter *http://iloveamysterynewsletter.com*

This Web site has reviews for hardcover, paperback, and trade paperback mysteries. There is also news and commentary available on the site. The newsletter is published online in the months of March, May, June, September, and November. It is on "hiatus" December through February, although there may be occasional updates during that time. For more information about the site, click on the "about us" button on the bottom of the page.

Reviews can be seen by author (author index), title (table of contents), or by reviewer, simply by clicking the appropriate button. Reviewers have their own Web pages, where information about them might be found along with their reviews. For the most part, reviewers are from the United States, Canada, and the United Kingdom. Novels from large and small publishers are reviewed, but e-books are not. New authors are reviewed here as well, along with well-established authors.

There is an extensive number of reviews to be found here. Clicking on the "Table of Contents" brings one to a list of titles reviewed; the latest ones added are denoted by "New" highlighted in yellow. October/November reviews were at the top; scrolling down brought up the August/September reviews. Some titles are listed more than once, which means that more than one reviewer has written a review on the book. Clicking on the title brings up the review, where one finds publishing information as well: publisher, date, and for smaller presses, ISBNs, to facilitate ordering. The page will be the reviewer's page: The reviews are not in alphabetical order, but are placed on the reviewer's pages, and access to individual titles is provided by clicking on the title. As mentioned, by clicking on the reviewer's name one sees the titles that individual has reviewed. The site was on hiatus when checked.

The reviews vary in length somewhat, but none are overly long. Many of the reviews are positive, but if a reviewer has reservations about a title, she says so. Generally the reviews contain a plot synopsis and the reviewer's reaction to/opinion about the novel.

At the time the site was reviewed, the last two "issues" were all that were posted, and it was not evident that earlier issues were available on the Web site. The editor states that work on a solution is underway. Access is through the Mystery Vault Web site; however, one goes to the parent directory and must follow that to the archives. It would be a good idea to check this site monthly to keep up-to-date.

January Magazine
http://www.januarymagazine.com

Launched in 1997, *January Magazine* covers many different types of books, fiction and non-fiction. It is one of the first online literary magazines. Its focus is not only on reviews, but on authors themselves.

Mystery reviews are available by clicking on the link "crime fiction." While the reviews in this section were not updated frequently, and are not great in number, the "Rap Sheet" column is a good resource. This column can be seen through the Web site, but is also available by signing up for a free subscription.

Updated monthly, the reviews and commentary in the "Rap Sheet" are provided by J. Kingston Pierce, the crime fiction editor for *January Magazine*. "Pierce's Picks" are fairly short reviews of forthcoming novels found to be of particular interest and provide a short synopsis rather than a review of each title. Inclusion in this section denotes a positive recommendation, covering novels that Pierce believes are worth noting.

The "New and Noteworthy" column, also written by Pierce, consists of longer, essay-type reviews of particular novels. These reviews are generally quite long and may include mention of, or comparison to, other novels in the genre. "Other Voices" has reviews written by other *January* contributors, and these reviews are attributed. They are quite lengthy as well. The reviews within "Rap Sheet" are of a more literary bent than some of the other review sources (print or online). There are plot synopses along with discussions about the writing style, the conventions used, etc. This site is a good resource for literary-style mystery reviews.

The Mystery Reader
http://www.themysteryreader.com

Companion to the *Romance Reader* site, this Web site is edited by D. N. Anderson. The introduction to the site states that it has hundreds of reviews. Including the archives, this claim may well be accurate.

This Web site is easy to navigate; different subgenres are listed along the left side of the page, with the date of the last update underneath. Clicking on the subgenre gives access to the latest reviews, listed by title with publisher information, date reviewed, and reviewer's initials. The newest reviews are available by clicking on "New Reviews" at the top center of the page. At the bottom of each subgenre page is a rating key, which is a helpful reminder. A very useful and unique feature is a "violence" rating: non-violent, standard violence but not too graphic, and graphic violence. Since many patrons do not like a lot of violence in mysteries (preferring implied over specific), this is a very useful feature. This rating is also helpful when looking for mysteries to recommend to teen readers. When on one of the subgenre pages, the other genres and an archive link are along the left side to aid in navigation between the pages.

Mysteries are rated by stars: A five is outstanding, while a one means "don't bother." These reviews are not all positive; reviewers are not afraid to discuss problems they had with novels right along with what they liked about particular titles. Plot synopses are included, as well as opinions about the plot, writing, and whether the book is recommended, and in some cases, for whom. A novel could be recommended even if there are caveats. This occasionally was the case with the three-star reviews; there may have been some problems with plot, writing, etc., but not enough to totally discredit the work. The reviews vary in length from approximately fifty lines to over one hundred.

Reviews are attributed, both by initials at the subgenre level and the name of reviewer at the end of the review. Information about each reviewer is available by clicking on the contributor's button on the first page, then on the individual author's name. Each reviewer has written some introductory information about her/himself; some state the types of mysteries they prefer. There is more information about the reviewers here than most Web sites give.

This site is one of the most often linked to by other sites: It's been around awhile and is a credible resource for mystery reviews. A newsletter is available by subscription: An e-mail will be sent with updates no more frequently than once a week.

New Mystery Reader Magazine
http://www.newmysteryreader.com

This is a fairly new Web site that contains short stories, articles, and reviews. It has reviews and summaries of new books and a section for reader recommendations. There is also a section with author interviews. The editor states that the intent is to focus on calling attention to new and exciting mystery authors while including old favorites.

Since the site is new, there are not yet an exhaustive number of reviews, but under the new hardcover category there were about thirty-five reviews, so the archive should grow quickly at this rate. Many of the reviews are written by the editor of the Web site, and there will be more reviewers added. Clicking on links for "New Hard Cover," or "New Paperbacks" takes one to a page with title, author, a small snapshot of the book, and a "thunderbolt" rating. Newer books are at the beginning, with older releases on subsequent pages. Reviews are from October through December, with some January additions. There is no explanation for the ratings, but five thunderbolts seem to be the highest rating. Clicking on the title leads to the review. There is also a link for hardcover archives. There is not a review date listed for when reviews were written, but this addition has been suggested and may be implemented in the future.

Generally the reviews by the editor are fairly concise. There is a brief synopsis, enough to give a feel for the book's content without giving anything away. The end of the review discusses appeal factors: what the reviewer liked about the book and why. The other reviewers tend to write longer reviews: There are more synopses, but not much more discussion of the plots. The thunderbolt rating does not carry over to the review page, but this may change.

Again, this is a new Web site, so there are some small changes that could be made. But overall this should be a valuable resource for reviews, especially in light of their stated mission to highlight new authors since this is a sorely needed area of coverage.

Reviewing the Evidence
http://www.reviewingtheevidence.com

This Web site was begun to help fill a perceived lack of availability of book review Web sites. It was evidently begun some time ago, as there are nearly 1,300 reviews in the archives of the Web site.

The most recent reviews are on the front page of the Web site. There were twenty at the time the page was accessed. Clicking on the title takes one to the review, where the title, author, publishing information, and number of pages are at the beginning, along with a snapshot of the cover. Other reviews are accessed by clicking on the "REVIEWS" button on the left side. The last twenty reviews are listed on the beginning of the review page. These are different reviews than on the first page.

The reviews are of a variety, ranging from items not yet published to books ten years old or more. A review that is newly posted may not be of a new release. The reviews on this Web site are searchable: One can click to sort by author or title. Once this is done, reviews can be re-sorted by review date or publication date. While somewhat convoluted, this is a good way to find reviews for new material on this site, especially since the newest reviews are not always of the newest books. There is no labeling by letter of the alphabet, so one must guess upon what page a certain letter may be. Doing a title search can eliminate this problem. Some titles are reviewed more than once: This fact is noted on the review itself, along with links to the other reviews of that title. This duplication can also be seen if the list is sorted by title, of course. It did not appear to be possible to sort reviews by author. It is preferable to have search/sort capabilities, especially with the great number of reviews to be found on this site.

Reviews are attributed; there is information about some of the regular reviewers under the reviewers' category. Guest reviews are attributed and there may or may not be short informational paragraphs about them at the end of the review. There seem to be quite a few reviewers. There is no rating or ranking system; one must read the review to find the reviewer's opinion. As with most sources, each reviewer has a different style. The reviews vary considerably in length and writing style: Some reviews include a detailed plot synopsis and discussion of various elements, some essentially describe the plot with little discussion, and some are some combination of both styles. This is a useful source for finding reviews.

SOURCES NOT REVIEWED

These sources were not included in the previous discussion but may be worth exploring.

Mystery Ink
http://www.mysteryinkonline.com

Along with reviews, this Web page has a "reference and recommendation" section with such features as an "If You Like" chart to determine other authors a reader might like, a guide to mystery series, and other guides that are useful to acquisitions librarians.

Over My Dead Body
http://www.overmydeadbody.com

This is the Web presence for the magazine of the same name. An exhaustive number of reviews can be found here, and the newest reviews are updated irregularly. This Web site is good for archived reviews, and when updated, is a good source for new reviews.

BOOKSTORES

Some bookstores produce review sources, with reviews contributed by staff, readers, or both. Below is a selection of bookstores with reviews; look at *Mysterious Strands* (link below under the category "Mystery Links") for others to investigate. Publishers often put out a newsletter or some type of alert for new books as well; check their Web sites for information. Of course, publishers will not mount a negative review, but use these notifications as prepublication alerts.

- Creatures 'n Crooks Bookshoppe
  http://www.cncbooks.com/index2.html
- The Mysterious Bookshop
  http://www.mysteriousbookshop.com
- Murder, Ink
  http://www.murderink.com
- The Poisoned Pen
  http://www.poisonedpen.com

FORTHCOMING BOOKS

Both of these Web sites have an excellent section listing forthcoming books.

Cluelass
http://www.cluelass.com

Click on Bloodstained Bookshelf–updated monthly.

Stop You're Killing Me
http://www.stopyourekillingme.com

New releases are divided into hardcover and paperback. There is also a useful author/character index which lists author series, other works, and publication dates.

GENERAL MYSTERY SOURCES

Mysterious Strands
http://home.att.net/~csilberblatt/mystery.htm

Exhaustive collection of links concerning mysteries, including links to author Web pages, and bookstores. See also: "Deadly Directory" via http://www.cluelass.com. Click on "Deadly Directory Online."

Booklist
P.O. Box 607
Mt Morris, IL 61054-7564
888-350-0949
blst@kable.com

Kirkus Reviews
770 Broadway
New York, NY 10003
http://www.kirkusreviews.com

Library Journal
360 Park Avenue S.
New York, NY 10010
800-588-1030
ljinfo@reedbusiness.com

Publishers Weekly
360 Park Avenue S.
New York, NY 10010
800-278-2991
http://publishersweekly.com

Deadly Pleasures
George Easter–DP
P.O. Box 969
Bountiful, UT 84011
george@deadlypleasures.com

Drood Review of Mystery
484 East Carmel Drive #378
Carmel, IN 46032
http://www.droodreview.com

Mystery Readers Journal
c/o MRI (Mystery Readers International)
P.O. Box 8116
Berkeley, CA 94707
510-845-3600
whodunit@murderonthemenu.com

The Mystery Review
P.O. Box 488
Wellesley Island, NY 13640
613-475-4440
mystrev@reach.net

Mystery News
PMB 152
105 Townline Road
Vernon Hills, IL 60061
caldrich@blackravenpress.com
lkaczmarek@blackravenpress.com

Mystery Scene
331 W. 57th Street Suite 148
New York, NY 10019
http://www.mysteryscene.org

"I Need a Good Mystery": Selecting for the Juvenile Reader

Nancy Larson Bluemel

SUMMARY. Mystery series have been a favorite choice of juvenile readers ages ten to fourteen since the publication of Nancy Drew and the Hardy Boys over seventy years ago. Because of this popularity, the genre is an effective teaching tool across the curriculum when appropriate titles of good quality are selected. *[Article copies available for a fee from The Haworth Document Delivery Service: 1-800-HAWORTH. E-mail address: <docdelivery@haworthpress.com> Website: <http://www.HaworthPress.com> © 2004 by The Haworth Press, Inc. All rights reserved.]*

KEYWORDS. Mystery fiction, mystery–juvenile, mystery–selection, mystery–study and teaching

Note: Choosing a word to define the age of the readers with whom this article is concerned has been a challenge. The most commonly used term is young adult, generally including readers from grades six through

---

Nancy Larson Bluemel, MLIS, PhD, is a retired School Library Media Specialist, an adjunct instructor for library education, and a vendor representative.

Address correspondence to: Nancy Larson Bluemel, 725 Hillcrest, Denton, TX 76201.

[Haworth co-indexing entry note]: "'I Need a Good Mystery': Selecting for the Juvenile Reader." Bluemel, Nancy Larson. Co-published simultaneously in *Collection Management* (The Haworth Information Press, an imprint of The Haworth Press, Inc.) Vol. 29, No. 3/4, 2004, pp. 73-82; and: *Managing the Mystery Collection: From Creation to Consumption* (ed: Judith Overmier, and Rhonda Harris Taylor) The Haworth Information Press, an imprint of The Haworth Press, Inc., 2004, pp. 73-82. Single or multiple copies of this article are available for a fee from The Haworth Document Delivery Service [1-800-HAWORTH, 9:00 a.m. - 5:00 p.m. (EST). E-mail address: docdelivery@haworthpress.com].

Available online at http://www.haworthpress.com/web/COL

doi:10.1300/J105v29n03_06

twelve. High school students tend to read mysteries published for the adult market. Children's literature brings to mind books written for children from babyhood through elementary school. Neither level will be addressed here. This article will focus on books that appeal primarily to students from grades six through eight. However, this is a difficult age bracket for which to select because of the wide range of reading abilities and personal preferences. Many sixth graders still need or enjoy books at the fourth/fifth grade level while many eighth graders are already demanding the same popular authors enjoyed by their parents. The typical middle school library collection contains books in a fourth to tenth grade range.

Some school districts have junior high schools with grades seven through nine instead of middle schools. Others have intermediate schools containing grades five and six. In an effort to cover all of these variations, the terms juvenile reader and juvenile mystery will be used here. While sometimes considered archaic designations, they will hopefully, in this case, help to clearly designate the group being addressed as roughly between the ages of ten to fourteen.

INTRODUCTION

Mysteries. What is it about them that has, for decades, kept readers anxiously awaiting the next publication of their favorite author? And when the wait becomes too long, to begin the search for a carbon copy sleuth? "If you like Sherlock Holmes you'll love . . . " Perhaps it is because they allow us to escape the realities of our commonplace daily existence by plunging us into an unknown world of intrigue and suspense. Or, maybe it is the challenge that drives us as we strive to deduce from the clues the name of the perpetrator of the crime before the author dramatically reveals it in the final chapter. Whatever the reason may be, mysteries have been a habit-forming genre for generations of adults, teenagers, and even children.

A BRIEF HISTORY

Young adult readers have historically been readers of mystery and detective stories written for the adult market, e.g., Arthur Conan Doyle, Agatha Christie, Ellery Queen, Dashiell Hammett, and Erle Stanley Gardner. That fact remains true today as older teens are fans of Sue

Grafton, Mary Higgins Clark, Tony Hillerman, John Grisham, and other best selling authors. Younger readers, those in their preteen and early teenage years, had few other options until Edward Stratemeyer created the Hardy Boys series in 1926, followed by Carolyn Keene's Nancy Drew series in 1930. Prior to their publication, characters in other series such as the Bobbsey Twins occasionally solved a mystery, but Nancy Drew and the Hardy Boys actively pursued tracking down criminals (Mason, 1975). Readers eagerly followed their adventures. Though the plots were formulaic and often viewed negatively by critics of children's literature, both series flourished.

Clearly a market for juvenile mysteries existed, including those with female sleuths. The Stratemeyer Syndicate added the Dana Girls series. Grosset & Dunlap published the popular Cherry Ames books, stories of a nurse who turned to solving mysteries. Trixie Beldon was the country girl heroine of the series published by Whitman Company. Movie stars such as Ginger Rogers and Jane Withers solved mysteries on the side in other Whitman editions (Mason, 1975). These young women and celebrity detectives were but a few of the popular amateur detectives of the 1930s, '40s, and '50s.

CHARACTER SERIES

Enthusiasm for mystery series has not declined since the heyday of Nancy, Frank, and Joe. Fans today continue to read revised, updated, and new editions of those adventures of early juvenile detectives. However, beside them on bookstore and library shelves are new protagonists. There is a certain comfort to be found in series with continuing characters, as if meeting old friends in familiar surroundings. There is a natural curiosity about what will happen to them next.

Today's juvenile readers, who as children grew up with Donald Sobol's Encyclopedia Brown and E. W. Hildick's McGurk mysteries, can look forward to meeting teenager Orville Jacques, the hero of a series by T. M. Murphy. The stories combine mystery with life lessons in a Cape Code setting. As with the first book *The Secrets of Belltown*, the five other titles all begin with *The Secrets of . . .* (http://www.belltownmysteries.com).

Readers with an interest in foreign locations can follow the adventures of a thirteen-year-old boy, Finnegan Zwake, who solves mysteries around the world. This series by Michael Dahl currently includes five titles (http://www.finneganzwake.com).

K. C. Flanagan, Girl Detective, also takes readers to exotic places. The six books in the series all have tropical settings, the first being *Panic in Puerto Vallarta*. Some readers may associate with the family circumstances of "14 3/4-year-old" K. C. and her eighteen-year-old brother Rudy. They have divorced parents with "Significant Others," who collectively provide the teens with their opportunity to travel extensively. The authors of this favorably reviewed series are Susan Murray and Robert Davies (http://www.amazon.com).

Canadian author Mary Woodbury introduced her seventh grade sleuth, Polly, to readers in 1994. The first title in the series, *The Invisible Polly McDoodle,* was the recipient of the Canadian Children's Book Centre "Our Choice" Award (http://www.writersunion.ca/w/woodbury.htm).

MYSTERY/GHOST/HORROR SERIES

Mysteries are not always strictly "whodunits" with the detective solving a traditional crime. The blending of mystery with the supernatural or horror story is extremely popular with today's readers. A ghost and a music box that plays by itself in Betty Ren Wright's book *Haunted Summer* (1996), and dolls who leave clues to a murder in *The Dollhouse Murders* (1983), make her a favorite choice in bridging the age gap between children and juvenile readers of this genre.

R. L. Stine's name has become synonymous with the mystery/horror genre. Younger readers of his *Goosebumps* books move eagerly, as middle-schoolers, on to the eerie and goulish *Fear Street* series. Similarly, younger fans of the Christopher Pike series, *Spooksville,* have many titles to anticipate as they mature. *Final Friends* and *Remember Me* are two popular trilogies, along with a lengthy list of individual titles, written by the prolific Pike.

AWARD WINNING MYSTERIES

Many authors who write for the juvenile market bring to it a quality which rivals and often surpasses that of books written for adults. Their books are favorably reviewed in the nation's most respected journals, and many of them have been recipients of prestigious awards given for children's and young adult literature. The American Library Association and its divisions annually bestow several awards. Many highly acclaimed authors have been selected for their mystery novels. Some of those awards and well-known winners are:

ALA Best Books for Young Adults

Lois Duncan. *Don't Look Behind You*, 1990
Philip Pullman. *The Shadow in the North*, 1988 and *The Tiger in the Well*, 1991

ALA Recommended Books for the Reluctant Young Adult Reader

Jay Bennett. *Sing Me a Death Song*, 1991 and *Coverup*, 1992
Joan Lowry Nixon. *Secret Silent Screams*, 1989; *Whispers from the Dead*, 1990; and *High Trail to Danger*, 1992

Newbery Award

Ellen Raskin. *The Westing Game*, 1979
Zilpha Keatley Snyder. *The Headless Cupid*, 1972 (Honor Book)

The Edgar

The only award given strictly for juvenile mysteries is the Mystery Writers of America's Edgar Allan Poe Award. It is named in honor of the man credited by many as the father of the detective story. Poe introduced C. Auguste Dupin in *The Murders in the Rue Morgue* in 1841. That tale and his following detective stories contained nearly every element still used by mystery writers today (Gilbert). The Edgar was first awarded in 1946. Over the years various categories have been added or deleted. Phyllis A. Whitney was the winner of the first Best Juvenile Award in 1961 for *The Mystery of the Haunted Pool* (http://mysterynet.com/edgars/previous/juvenile.shtml). In 1989, the Best Young Adult Novel category was added. That award went to Sonia Levitin for *Incident at Loring Groves* (http://mysterynet.com/edgars/previous/youngadult.shtml). The impact of Nancy Drew on mystery fiction for juveniles was again acknowledged when the Mystery Writers of America honored Mildred Wirt Benson in 2001. As Carolyn Keene, she authored twenty-three of the first thirty books in the series (http://www.mysterywriters.org/awards/Mildren_Wirt_Benson.html). Another record holder is Joan Lowry Nixon, who is the only four-time Edgar award winner in the category of juvenile and young adult mysteries.

AN INTERDISCIPLINARY GENRE

Teachers frequently develop units across content areas in order that students might see the linkage between subjects. Teaming, a process in which teachers of different subjects taught at a specific grade level meet on a regular basis to plan cooperatively, is common practice in schools across the country. Mysteries are a natural for use in the school curriculum. In those mysteries which are well-written, characters have depth and the story line is multileveled. They are highly crafted novels with the added appeal of intrigue and suspense. Mysteries are one of the most popular choices in free voluntary reading. By capitalizing upon that popularity and selecting those titles which blend genre (that is, mysteries whose plots or settings contain historical fiction, science, art, culture, etc.) teachers can add another dimension to their teaching strategies.

As a former school librarian, I have seen mysteries used successfully on many occasions. In my former school, there was an emphasis on cultural studies. A major component of the curriculum was the study of the history, geography, and culture of the nations of the world. In addition to conducting research on their individually selected country, each student was required to read a novel set in that country and compare their impressions from it to the factual findings of their research. Mysteries set in other countries, whether historic or current, were always popular choices. For example, the first of Philip Pullman's three books about Sally, a sixteen-year-old orphan in Victorian England, was often selected by students studying that country. *Ruby in the Smoke* gave students the opportunity to compare the accuracy of descriptions of life in that era with historical facts they gleaned from reference sources.

Similar types of assignments can be used to enhance critical thinking skills in any subject area. For example, Henry Winterfeld's reprinted classic, *Detectives in Togas*, adds life to the study of ancient civilizations. Kathleen Karr appeals to the morbid curiosity of young scientists in her book *Skullduggery* and its sequel, *Bone Dry*. These novels tell the story of Matthew Morrissey, apprenticed to a phrenologist who travels the world in search of the buried skulls of famous people. The books combine mystery with the history of nineteenth century science. Rodney Johnson's Rinnah Two Feathers mysteries reflect his Sioux heritage, and their favorable reviews make them an appropriate complement to multicultural studies. E. L. Konigsburg's Newbery Medal winning classic, *From the Mixed-Up Files of Mrs. Basil E. Frankweiler*, is the perfect art tie-in as siblings hide out in the Metropolitan Museum of Art and solve the mystery of the creator of a beautiful statue.

A relatively recent spin-off of the popular American Girl books, the American Girl History Mysteries, appeals to avid fans of the original stories. Each of the volumes in the series features a girl solving a mystery at an important time in America's past. Book 3, *The Night Flyers* by Elizabeth McDavid Jones, was the winner of the 2000 Edgar Award. It is set in the time period of World War I. Disappearing homing pigeons and enemy spies portray an era in U.S. history with which many twenty-first century students are unfamiliar.

SELECTION

Juvenile readers love mysteries! One of the tools I used as a librarian to help me build a collection that contained books that excited students was a "genremeter." Constructed with the aid of the industrial tech teacher, it was a series of plastic tubes set in a wooden base. Each tube had a label: mystery, fantasy/sci-fi, historical fiction, realistic, etc. As students returned books that they had read, they dropped marbles in the appropriate tubes. Each year it was a neck-to-neck race between mystery and fantasy/sci-fi!

Selecting new mysteries for the collection, however, was a more difficult task than adding fantasy/sci-fi for two reasons. In many selection tools, mysteries are included in the category of realistic fiction. Ferreting them out involves reading each annotation and is very time consuming. Secondly, there are many bibliographies and indexes devoted entirely to fantasy and/or science fiction. Despite the popularity of mysteries, such bibliographies/indexes are rare indeed. How can a school librarian keep the mystery fans happy and the collection current?

STUDENTS

Ask the readers! Those students who follow character series or the mystery/ghost/horror series such as those described above know what is new and forthcoming. They are also a good source for acquiring new books. Because of budget constraints librarians are often reluctant to spend money on publications geared to the mass market, and many students are happy to donate (especially paperbacks) after they have read the latest installment.

AWARDS AND BEST BOOKS LISTS

Almost every state has a reader's choice award. Because students, not adults, select the winners, they tend to be very popular with readers of like age across the country. Mysteries frequent the lists so watch for annual announcements in journals and on state library association Web sites.

In addition to the American Library Association awards and the Edgars, "best" lists are helpful sources in locating mysteries published within the last year. Many journals, such as *School Library Journal* and *Booklist*, publish lists of their top juvenile picks annually. Booksellers, publishers, newspapers, educational associations, special interest organizations, and public libraries are also among those entities that compile their recommendations, and again, mysteries for juvenile readers are often included.

SELECTION TOOLS AND REVIEW SOURCES

Any of the journals commonly subscribed to by schools for access to reviews are good sources for locating newly published mysteries. Bibliographies and indexes of books for children and young adults which are published on a one time or irregular basis can be helpful in selecting recommended "classic" titles that are still in print or for adding newer works that may have been missed at the time of publication. The *Middle and Junior High School Library Catalog*, published by the H. W. Wilson Company, indexes mysteries under the heading "Mystery fiction." The titles included are all recommended, making this an excellent source for insuring quality additions to the collection.

THE WWW

Web sites are invaluable in locating current awards, "best" lists, author biographies, and other information pertinent to mysteries. Of particular interest are the following sites:

http://www.mysterywriters.org

The Web site of Mystery Writers of America publishes the Edgar Award winners and nominees in all categories.

http://www.amazon.com

Provides editorial reviews, reader reviews, synopsis of plot, author background, book cover photo, and sample pages of books.

http://www.mysterynet.com

An online mystery network with links to many mystery awards, including lists of all previous years of Edgar winners. Also features links to mystery books, TV programs, movies, and lesson plans utilizing mysteries for teachers.

http://www.overbooked.org/

A portal specializing in literary and genre information. Has links to awards, reviews, reading lists, authors, and Kids Love a Mystery, which is a literacy outreach of Mystery Writers of America.

http://www.ala.org

The American Library Association homepage offers a link to Libraries and You, which links to all of the awards given by ALA and its divisions.

KNOW YOUR AUTHORS

One of the best ways to select mysteries is to keep abreast of authors of juvenile literature whose work is recognized by their peers and their audience as being of high literary quality. Just a few writers whose books include mystery and detective novels, in addition to authors previously noted, are Caroline Cooney, Avi, T. Ernesto Bethancourt, Willo Davis Roberts, Mary Downing Hahn, Todd Strasser, M. E. Kerr, Eve Bunting, Lynn Hall, Theodore Taylor, Will Hobbs, and Phyllis Reynolds Naylor. These are names which appear frequently on recommended lists.

There are many other authors whose total body of work includes fewer mysteries, but who are nonetheless, worthy of inclusion in any collection. Virginia Hamilton is a gifted writer best known for her depiction of the Black experience. Her historical fiction mystery *The*

House of Dies Drear was the 1969 Best Juvenile Edgar Award winner. Being able to identify authors such as Hamilton and include them with the creative writers more commonly associated with mystery will add depth to the selection of tales of crime available for those younger readers whose mantra is "I need a good mystery!"

REFERENCES

Print

Carter, Betty. *Best Books for Young Adults*. 2nd ed. Young Adult Services Library Association, 2000.

Donelson, Kenneth L. *Literature for Today's Young Adults*. 3rd ed. HarperCollins, 1989.

Gilbert, Elliot L. *The World of Mystery Fiction*. Bowling Green, OH: Bowling Green State University Popular Press, 1983.

Mason, Bobbie Ann. *The Girl Sleuth*. Old Westbury, NY: The Feminist Press, 1975.

Price, Anne and Juliette Yaakov, editors. *Middle and Junior High School Library Catalog*. New York: H. W. Wilson, 2000.

Spencer, Pam. *What Do Young Adults Read Next? A Reader's Guide to Fiction for Young Adults*. Detroit, MI: Gale Research, 1994.

Volz, Bridget Dealy. *Junior Genreflecting: A Guide to Good Reads and Series Fiction for Children*. Englewood, CO: Libraries Unlimited, 2000.

Web Sites

http://www.mysterynet.com
http://www.ala.org
http://www.amazon.com
http://www.belltownmystries.com
http://www.finneganzwake.com
http://www.mysterywriters.org
http://www.overbooked.org/
http://www.writersunion.ca/w/woodbury.htm

African-American Mysteries

Connie Van Fleet

SUMMARY. African Americans who have spent formative years in the United States have a viewpoint grounded in a specific culture. This paper defines "African American mystery" as crime or detective fiction written by African Americans. African American mystery novels have grown in number and diversity over time. As the audience has grown, publishers and reviewers have given more attention to the genre. While the stories are not necessarily about race, they are richly imbued with African American culture and themes. An overview of review sources, an annotated bibliography of four essential background sources, a classified list of African American mystery novels, and a list of award-winning African American mysteries are included. *[Article copies available for a fee from The Haworth Document Delivery Service: 1-800-HAWORTH. E-mail address: <docdelivery@haworthpress.com> Website: <http://www.HaworthPress.com> © 2004 by The Haworth Press, Inc. All rights reserved.]*

KEYWORDS. African American, authors, awards, bibliographies, black, crime, detective, genre, mysteries

---

Connie Van Fleet, PhD, is Professor, School of Library and Information Studies, University of Oklahoma, 401 West Brooks, Room 120, Norman, OK 73019-6032.

[Haworth co-indexing entry note]: "African-American Mysteries." Van Fleet, Connie. Co-published simultaneously in *Collection Management* (The Haworth Information Press, an imprint of The Haworth Press, Inc.) Vol. 29, No. 3/4, 2004, pp. 83-99; and: *Managing the Mystery Collection: From Creation to Consumption* (ed: Judith Overmier, and Rhonda Harris Taylor) The Haworth Information Press, an imprint of The Haworth Press, Inc., 2004, pp. 83-99. Single or multiple copies of this article are available for a fee from The Haworth Document Delivery Service [1-800-HAWORTH, 9:00 a.m. - 5:00 p.m. (EST). E-mail address: docdelivery@haworthpress.com].

Available online at http://www.haworthpress.com/web/COL

doi:10.1300/J105v29n03_07

WHY AFRICAN AMERICAN AUTHORS?

This article defines "African American mystery" as crime or detective fiction written by blacks who have spent formative years in the United States. While authors from among the African Diaspora have an important voice, they have not experienced the same societal forces and cultural norms that are unique to African Americans. Some white authors have attempted to include honest and sympathetic portrayals of African American detectives, and a few have succeeded, but it is often difficult for those who have not experienced first-hand what it means to be black to strike the right note or to gain credibility. For African American authors, a worldview is inherent, not learned. Hughes Allison, the first black author to appear in *Ellery Queen's Mystery Magazine*, argues for the importance of authentic first-hand experience in shaping not only characters, but mood and form of the mystery:

> Could tough, hard-boiled Sam Spade or suave, gentlemanly Ellery Queen enter that dark, costly museum room [of Negro culture] and single out the culprits? While it's possible they could, it's improbable they really would. For neither . . . is equipped to think with his skin. Moreover, merely apprehending the room's culprits is not the most important factor involved. (Woods in McDonald and McDonald 1999, 70)

The value of an underlying perspective shaped by the black experience persists as modern African American mystery writers with individual worldviews shape the genre and attract new audiences. Black authors have taken divergent approaches to the issue of race. While some black authors echo their white counterparts with one-sided characters whose blackness is nothing more than a description of complexion, others will provide it as identifiable "blackground" (Soitos 1997), and still others use black culture to add an important dimension of the character's personality and outlook.

These last writers bring the complexity and awareness of the social novel to the genre. While the stories are not about race, they are richly imbued with African American culture and themes. Being black does not drive the story, but it is impossible to imagine the story from a different point of view, with different characters, in other neighborhoods. Typical are modern crime writers Walter Mosley and Paula Wood. "Because race is almost never the main event in their stories, these [modern crime] writers don't look at racial issues as problems to resolve. They look at them as clues about how society works, or doesn't work" (Jones 2002).

African American authors appeal to different audiences by providing a means for outsiders to understand the culture through an engaging story and by affirming personal and cultural identity for other African Americans. They invite the reader to "explore cultural differences–in perception, in way of life, in visions of the world–and act as links between cultures, interpreting each to each, mainstream to minority and minority to mainstream" (Macdonald and Macdonald 1999, 60).

PRODUCTION AND PUBLISHING TRENDS

Emergence

The entry of African American authors into the mystery genre is a fairly recent phenomenon, although scattered examples date back over one hundred years (Woods 1995). Most scholars of African American detective fiction date the true beginning of the genre to 1932, when Rudolph Fisher published the first detective novel with all black characters, *The Conjure Man Dies*. In 1948, *Ellery Queen Magazine* published its first short story by an African American author (Woods 1995; Soitos 1997). Nine years later, Chester Himes received the Grand Prix for Best Detective Novel of The Year 1957 for *A Rage in Harlem*, originally published as *For the Love of Imabelle*, a crime caper featuring Grave Digger Jones and Coffin Ed Johnson, two black, hard-boiled Harlem policemen. "Black experience novels" written in the gritty ghetto realism style by criminals and drug addicts were the primary mode of expression in the 1960s and 1970s (Dietzel 1997). It was not until the 1980s that there was significant production of the style of detective stories that are most popular today and only a decade ago that the genre exploded with the variety of authors, characters, and themes that characterize the field African American mystery today.

Publishing

African American mystery stories, as is typical of the genre, first appeared as serials and later gained some national attention as short stories published in mystery magazines. Some early authors were published by major houses in their crime and detective imprints (Vintage Crime, Random House) or in paperback (Dell, Avon). The greatest single provider of popular African American fiction throughout the 1970s into the early '90s was Holloway Publishing House, which still remains a good source for genre literature by black authors. Holloway House Publishers sold more than five million copies of Robert Beck (writing as Donald Goines) books and established the profitability of the African American genre market (Dietzel 1997).

Currently, African American mysteries are much more readily available than in previous years. A number of the vintage black urban experience novels have been re-issued by various university presses or by Norton under the "Old School Books" imprint. The most popular writers are published under various imprints of such major houses as Doubleday, Alfred A. Knopf, Norton, Penguin, Simon and Schuster, Viking, and Random House. Some have specific lines, such as the Random House Group's Strivers Row imprint, featuring African American authors.

Smaller specialty presses may specialize in new authors or may focus on aspects other than ethnicity. For instance, the protagonists in Nikki Baker's Virginia Kelly series and Penny Mickelbury's Gianna Malone series are lesbians and those series are published by Naiad Press, while Mickelbury's Carole Ann Gibson series is published by Simon and Schuster.

Reviews

From the Harlem Renaissance through the Black Arts movement, genre literature has largely been ignored by audiences and critics and has been criticized for its perceived shallowness and transience by African American authors, scholars, and literati, who felt it did not represent the best efforts of the black community. Although some African American authors and scholars are still critical of light, popular fiction written by other African Americans, most have adopted a much more accepting attitude.

As demand and popularity has grown, mainstream sources have paid increasing attention. *Publishers Weekly* and *Booklist* now review African American mystery and crime fiction regularly, often with special features in the February issues. Online bookstores amazon.com and Barnes&Noble.com provide searchable databases of their lists, publisher descriptions of novels, excerpts of reviews from other sources, and original reviews by readers.

Review sources dedicated solely to black writers are beginning to appear. *QBR The Black Book Review*, edited by Max Rodriguez, is an outstanding source dedicated exclusively to reviewing books about the Africana experience. It includes reviews of fiction, nonfiction, poetry, children's books by writers from the Diaspora, as well as essays. Sample issues and subscription information are available on the Web (http://www.qbr.com/), but its primary medium is print on paper.

Available exclusively on the Web, the African American Literature Book Club–AALBC.com. (http://aalbc.com) is an ambitious commercial site, whose goal is "to increase everyone's knowledge of the diversity of African American literature, facilitate the exchange of opinions, satisfy your online book buying needs, and serve as a resource and vehicle of expression for aspiring and professional writers." Founded by Troy Johnson, AALBC provides a regular newsletter with full length articles and book reviews. Reviews, written by regular reviewers, are straightforward and often offer very divergent opinions.

In addition, the growing family of African American general interest magazines includes book reviews as regular features. *Essence* includes a monthly list of fiction and nonfiction, hardcover and paperback bestsellers based on reports of retail sales by African American bookstores.

THEMES IN AFRICAN AMERICAN MYSTERIES

Telling a good story with engaging characters and an interesting puzzle is basic to good mystery writing, and African American mystery writers ground their work in these traditional forms. The styles and approaches among these authors are widely varied, however. There is a rich mixture of character, style, and theme.

Character

As is the case with much current mainstream mystery, character is a key appeal factor. The race of the protagonist is an obvious attribute and is often significant in the selection of a mystery. African American authors give black readers characters they recognize or with whom they can identify. Their philosophies, approach to life, language, and communities are familiar. Other readers are given a glimpse into a world that may be unfamiliar and thus is intriguing or instructive.

It would be a mistake, however, to assume that that the protagonists of African American mysteries share a single view of their ethnic identity, view of society, or ways of coping. Characters may range from the slyly manipulative Blanche White (Barbara Neely), a domestic worker who relaxes in her employer's bubble bath, to pragmatic but cynical Easy Rawlins, who functions as an uneasy buffer between the black community and white justice system, to calmly efficient Marti McAlister (Eleanor Taylor Bland), widowed homicide detective, who worries about her children losing their black cultural identity.

The roster of African American detectives is diverse and readers of all ethnicities may find themselves identifying with some of the protagonists. Some of the characters are just scraping by, while others are solidly middle class and some very wealthy. While professionals are increasingly represented, working class characters abound. Characters may be from the South or North, from small towns or big cities. Readers may feel kinship with other mothers who are attempting to find a balance between home and work or with Vietnam veterans who are marginalized in society. They may enjoy the homey feel of community or the comfort of gossiping with a best friend. They may identify with the ever-present challenges in romantic relationships, whether straight or lesbian.

Color and Color Bias

Skin color is an issue approached in several ways. Readers who are not African American are sometimes amazed by the variation in description of skin color and often surprised at the depth of color consciousness within the black community.

"Passing," pretending to be white, is a part of the social context of a number of stories. Some authors take a very pragmatic approach and will rather matter-of-factly mention that a relative of a minor character is passing in order to secure better employment and quality of life. For some, passing has had tragic consequences that drive the characters (*One Must Wait*, Carole Mickelbury). Still others keep a protagonist's passing a mysterious secret and use its revelation as a plot device (*Harlem Redux*, Persia Walker).

While some protagonists, such as Woods' Charlotte Justice, do not actually pass for white, they recognize that their relatively pale skin color in some ways gives them an advantage in the workplace. Gary Hardwick, on the other hand, turns the tables and explores the meaning of color from the opposite point of view in his Justice series, which features a white cop who grew up in the ghetto and is more "black" than his African American partner.

More frequent are references to the extent to which color bias plays a role within the black community. Stories of the "paper bag" test (in which one is considered acceptable only if one's skin is lighter than the bag) and the pigmentocracy populated by the "light-bright" (in which upper class, lighter skin blacks consider themselves superior to other African Americans) are used to raise awareness, express black pride, and in some cases, as plot devices (*Blanche Among the Talented Tenth*, Barbara Neeley). Some authors attempt to explore the deeper motives and implications of this systematic bias, while others have no patience with people who deny their black heritage and try to "act white."

Professional and romantic relationships are sometimes inter-racial and usually bring out the best in both partners. A number of detective teams are "salt and pepper": Marti MacAlister and Vik Jessenovik (Bland); Danny Cavanaugh and Marshall Jackson (Hardwick); Starletta Duvall and Dominic Parisi (Smith-Levin). Inter-racial romances are common: Larry Cole and Kate Ford (Holton); Ivan Monk and Jill Kodama (Phillips); Gianna Malone and Mimi Patterson (Mickelbury); and Virginia Kelly and a series of white lesbian lovers (Baker). While most of the inter-racial romances are in themselves positive, their impetus may be negative. After long talks about the problems with black men and white women, Starletta and roommate Vee both enter into romantic relationships with white men.

Class Conflict

Conflict between classes, both among and within races, is a fact of life and a common theme in African American mysteries, providing a dynamic tension among characters. Wealth and prestige often serve as a mask for unethical behavior and a barrier to discovering the truth. This theme permeates Barbara Neeley's Blanche series, in which the wealthy upper classes, both black and white, are populated by people who are corrupted by greed and power. Chassie West (*Sunrise*) and Gary Phillips (*Violent Spring*) use the lure of economic development as the impetus for both class and racial conflict for her story.

Family and Friends

The important role of family and community in African American mysteries is perhaps the greatest innovation that black authors bring to the genre (Décuré 1999, 163-168). While the relationships are sometimes demanding and often irritating, they offer the protagonist love, loyalty, and support. Mothers and children are present to a much greater degree than in mainstream mysteries. Strong, independent, and capable heroines frequently confer with their mothers, with one series built around the interaction of mother and daughter (Mama series, Nora DeLoach).

The frequent presence and central role of children in black mysteries are rare in other detective novels. Crimes against children often drive the stories in the Marti MacAlister series, for instance. But the children are not simply faceless victims; they are individuals to be cherished. The series contrasts the life of forgotten children with that of Mari's own beloved son and daughter. Hard-boiled Easy Rawlins adopts two children over the course of his series; Blanch White rears her sister's two children; and private investigator Tamara Hayle is a single mother whose son is central to her life and story. Even the humorous Loudermilk series from Haywood, in which retirees Dottie and "Big Joe" take off in an Airstream to avoid their adult children, demonstrates the strength of family ties when the couple is reluctantly drawn into case after case to protect their errant progeny.

Setting

At one time, the setting of African American mysteries was limited to large urban areas, particularly New York and Chicago and Washington, DC. New Orleans is a popular locale as well. Mosley helped move the setting to the west coast, with his descriptions of Los Angeles and its evolution from 1960 onward. Greer's CJ Floyd series moves to the interior with stories set in Denver; John Ridley's crime novels are set in Las Vegas.

Settings are now rural as well as urban, often rich in the author's exploration of small town characters and life, and may range from New England (Virginia Kelly series, Baker) to Otis, South Carolina (Mama series, DeLoach). Vacations go terribly wrong for Wesley's Tamara Hayle (Jamaica), Bailey's Lizzie Stuart (Cornwall, England), and Carter's Nanette Hayes (Paris) when settings take on an international flavor.

Most intriguing is the strong sense of community, of belonging to a neighborhood. Gunner (Haywood) is at home in Mickey Moore's Trueblood Barbershop, where he has an office in the back, and the Acey-Deuce Bar, which he frequents and shares with the other regulars. The Abyssinia Barber Shop and Shine Parlor serves as Ivan Monk's (Phillips) base of operations and the interaction with other customers (who may or may not be getting haircuts) provides a light touch and a feeling of authenticity. Tamara Hayle's first and best source of information is Jan's Beauty Biscuit, which also serves as an important source of support and comfort. Community comes alive as we recognize the assortment of regulars and the easy camaraderie of places where we are recognized and accepted.

Style

Style ranges from the pleasant cozy of the Mama series to the very dark noir style of Wright's *Justice Denied.* Many of the amateur detective novels are lighthearted and optimistic. Wrongdoing is clearly an aberration and once the isolated case is solved, everyone returns to a benign everyday world. "Cozy," in its traditional sense, may be too mild a word for the joy of living evident in these novels. Life is not just to be enjoyed, it is to be relished. Descriptions of good friendships, food, and stylish clothing are vivid, and an appreciation of the opposite sex is earthy and expected. Humor is often interjected through clever dialogue; problems are met head on with a wry acceptance.

Even in the less buoyant mysteries, humor within the closed community–the inspired put down, the mocking description of the outsider–pervades. These mysteries are darker, stronger. There is no bright, optimistic world to which the characters will return. But in the case of authors like Mosley, Woods, or Bland, good people and good communities are worth protecting and there is, at least, hope and security if individuals act with courage and personal integrity.

The very darkest side of the African American mystery is revealed in the crime novel, which takes place in a world of cynicism and despair where death and violence are commonplace. Its characters live lives of desperation and hopelessness, beaten by the system and their own poor judgment. The dialogue is brutal, coarse, and derogatory, the language borrowed from the streets. Sex replaces love and gang loyalty substitutes for friendship. In these noir stories, the descriptive passages are grim, but often compelling.

Universality

African American mysteries succeed on many levels because the themes they address and the characters who inhabit them speak to many audiences while preserving the unique aspects of black culture. Loyalty and betrayal, community and family, overcoming hardship with dignity, and the difficulty and necessity of individual affirmation and integrity are themes that speak to us all. As with many mysteries, they allow us to address serious issues, often unconsciously and painlessly, while providing escape and entertainment.

CATEGORIES OF AFRICAN AMERICAN MYSTERY AND CRIME FICTION

Generally, there are three main types of stories that are loosely characterized as mysteries: detective stories, crime novels, and psychological suspense. Most black detective stories are murder mysteries. Most mystery readers select by author and then by the detective, so popular series are usually developed around the character. In the author list provided at the end of this article, titles are categorized first by the professional status of the detective (amateur, police, or private detective), then by gender of the detective, another factor important to many readers.

Crime novels are characterized by violence, brutality, graphic descriptions, and adult language. The two main categories, old school or black experience novels and contemporary crime fiction, are identifiable not only by the time period in which they were first published, but in approach. Old School novels are typically written in the ghetto realism style, which frequently depicts a protagonist with only limited choices trapped in a recurring nightmare of hopelessness and violence and whose destiny is to a large degree preordained by circumstances beyond his control. Protagonists in contemporary crime novels are no more sympathetic. In fact, while society and environment may play a role, the characters in contemporary crime novels are more often seen as having more choice and therefore greater responsibility for their own situation.

Finally, psychological suspense has not been a popular subgenre with African American authors. Although this subgenre may include many facets, the most common among black mysteries deal with an ordinary person pushed to the limit.

A classified list of prominent authors and characters is provided at the end of this article to assist selectors unfamiliar with African American mystery and crime fiction. In addition, the next two sections discuss resources to supplement the review sources described earlier.

FOUR ESSENTIAL BACKGROUND SOURCES

Andres, William L., Frances Smith Foster, and Trudier Harris, editors. *The Oxford Companion to African American Literature*. New York: Oxford University Press, 1997.

This comprehensive work is comprised of well-researched and clearly written essays by notable scholars. It includes numerous entries relevant to African American mysteries, with topics ranging from the very broad ("crime and detective fiction") to the very specific ("Easy Rawlins"). This reference work is entertaining as well as informative, and librarians may want to browse as well as look for specific information.

Bailey, Frankie Y. *Out of the Woodpile: Black Characters in Crime and Detective Fiction.* Westport, CT: Greenwood Press, 1991.

Bailey's analysis of the popular image of African Americans in crime and detective fiction is limited to neither books nor African American authors. It includes an exploration of depictions in all popular media. In this way, it offers a broader contextual basis for scrutinizing the depiction of African American characters. The directory of "black characters in crime and detective fiction, film, and television" is very useful, and the symposium and survey of authors makes for interesting reading. This title is scholarly, but accessible to the intelligent reader.

Woods, Paula L. *Spooks, Spies, and Private Eyes: Black Mystery, Crime, and Suspense Fiction of the 20th Century*. New York: Doubleday, 1995.

Every collection should have this critical anthology; everyone interested in black mystery fiction should read it. Woods shares the personal impact of finding out about earlier authors, traces the evolution of African American mystery and crime fiction, and provides carefully selected representative work from the most influential authors.

Landrum, Larry. *American Mystery and Detective Novels: A Reference Guide.* Westport, CT: Greenwood Press, 1999.

Landrum's work is not devoted exclusively to African American crime and detective fiction, although significant portions of the "related formulas" and "authors" chapters address this body of work.

The strength of this volume is in placing the work of African American mystery writers into context, both intellectually and chronologically.

BIBLIOGRAPHIES

Selectors will find that identifying African American authors and titles is difficult, but familiarity with authors and characters is key in developing African American mystery collections. NoveList (http://www.novelist.com), originally conceived by Duncan Smith and offered by EBSCO, is the best of subscription online resources for genre fiction. The comprehensive database features title, author, subject, and keyword searches; annotations written by librarians; clearly written essays and useful lists.

Each year, the Black Caucus of the American Library Association (BCALA) recognizes excellence through the Black Caucus Literature Awards (available online at http://www.bcala.org/awards). Categories include adult fiction and nonfiction by African American authors, first novelist, Outstanding Contribution to Publishing. The Web site is not restricted to mysteries, although the genre is well represented among award recipients and descriptions will help to identify relevant titles.

A search of the Web lists hundreds of sites dedicated to African American mysteries and black literature. Many of these are pages developed by public libraries and typically feature lists of African American mysteries that may or may not include catalog links. Others are bookstore homepages. Some links are to African American mystery writers' personal Web pages, which vary in usefulness. Among these, Gayle Tiller's Web site (http://www.galetiller.com) is notable for its list of e-books published by black writers.

Although becoming dated (the bibliography of "new releases" was last updated June 6, 2001), the African American Mystery Page (http://www.aamystery.com/) still stands out for its extensive book list, links to information about African American authors, and links to other pages about black literature and concerns. It also contains a short list of reference sources.

CONCLUSION

African American mysteries are growing in number and popularity and more are being solicited, published, and marketed as the audience has increased and proven profitable. African American authors bring to the genre a worldview grounded in their cultural experience. Their characters and styles are diverse and they bring fresh perspectives to the mystery genre. But while African American authors explore new trends and part of their appeal is in their point of view, their stories are attracting ever-wider audiences as they address universal themes. Ultimately, they succeed in the same way that all mysteries succeed, because they tell stories of good and evil, of adventure and personal triumph, or present interesting puzzles that entertain and amuse.

AFRICAN AMERICAN MYSTERY AND CRIME WRITERS

Detective Novels

Amateur Detectives–Female

Baker, Nikki. Virginia Kelly Series.
Carter, Charlotte. Nanette Series.
Edwards, Grace. Mali Anderson Series.
Garland, Ardella. Georgia Barnett Series.
Grimes, Terris McMahan. Theresa Galloway Series.
Mickelbury, Penny. Carole Ann Gibson Series.
Neely, Barbara. Blanche White Series.
West, Chassie. *Loss of Innocence*.

Amateur Detectives–Male

Arnold, N. Xavier. *The Genocide Files*.
Carter, Stephen L. *The Emperor of Ocean Park*.
Gibson, John. *Dummy*.
Greer, Robert O. CJ Floyd Series.
Walker, Persia. *Harlem Redux*.

Amateur Detectives–Teams

Bates, Karen Grigsby. *Plain Brown Wrapper*.
DeLoach, Nora. Mama Series.
Haywood, Gar Anthony. Loudermilk Series.

Police Detectives–Female

Darden, Christopher and Dick Lochte. Nikki Hill Series.
Mickelbury, Penny. Gianna Maglione and Mimi Patterson Series.
Olden, Mark. *The Ghost.*
Woods, Paula L. Charlotte Justice Series.

Police Detectives–Male

Holton, Hugh. Larry Cole Series.
Olden, Marc. Manny Decker Series.

Police Detectives–Teams

Bland, Eleanor Taylor. Marti MacAlister (and Vik Jessenovik) Series.
Hardwick, Gary. The Justice Series.
Smith-Levin, Judith. Starletta Duvall (and Dominic Parisi) Series.

Private Eyes–Female

Coner, Kenyetta. *The Mockingbirds: A Maxine Michaels Mystery.*
Wesley, Valerie Wilson. Tamara Hayle Series.
West, Chassie. Leigh Ann Warren Series.

Private Eyes–Male

Haywood, Gar Anthony. Aaron Gunner Series.
Meadows, Lee E. Lincoln Keller Series.
Mosley, Walter. Easy Rawlins Series.
Phillips, Gary. Ivan Monk Series.

Crime Novels

Crime Novels–Old School

Cooper, Clarence Jr. *The Scene.*
Goines, Donald. *Daddy Cool.*
Himes, Chester. Grave Digger Jones and Coffin Ed Johnson Series.
Pharr, Robert Dean. *Giveadamn Brown.*
Simmons, Herbert. *Corner Boy.*

Crime Novels–Contemporary

Hardwick, Gary. The Detroit Series.
Phillips, Gary. Martha Chainey Series; *The Perpetrators.*
Ridley, John. *Stray Dogs*; *Love Is a Racket*; *Everybody Smokes in Hell*; *The Drift.*
Tramble, Nichelle D. *The Dying Ground: A Hip-Hop Noir Novel.*

Psychological Suspense Stories

Gause-Jackson, Arlene. *Howling Against the Wind.*
Joe, Yolanda. *Falling Leaves of Ivy.*
Wright, William. *Justice Denied: A Novel of Ultimate Revenge.*

Award-Winning African American Mysteries

Bates, Karen Grigsby. *Plain Brown Wrapper.* New York: Avon Books (an imprint of HarperCollins), 2001. ISBN 0380808900 (paper). 321 p. BCALA Literary Award Honor Book, 2002.
Bland, Eleanor Taylor. *See No Evil.* New York: St. Martin's Press, 1998. ISBN 0312169108. 274 p. Marti MacAlister (and Vik Jessenovik) Series. BCALA Literary Award Fiction Honor Book, 1999.
Carter, Stephen L. *The Emperor of Ocean Park.* New York: Alfred A. Knopf (A Borzoi Book), 2002. ISBN 0-375-41363-4. 657 p. BCALA Literary Award First Novelist Award, 2003; A Book-of-the-Month Club Main Selection.
Edwards, Grace. *A Toast Before Dying.* (The Mali Anderson Series) New York: Bantam Books: 1999. ISBN 0-55357-953-3 (paper, reprint edition). 293 p. BCALA Literary Award Fiction Honor Book, 1999.
Haywood, Gar Anthony. *Fear of the Dark.* (The Aaron Gunner Series) New York: St. Martin's Press, 1988. ISBN 0-312-01796-0. 185 p. Shamus Award Best First Private-Eye Novel, 1987.
Himes, Chester. *A Rage in Harlem.* (The Grave Digger Jones and Coffin Ed Johnson Series) First Vintage Books Edition 1989. New York: Vintage Crime (A Division of Random House), 1957, 1985. ISBN 0679720405 (Originally published as *For the Love of Imabelle.*) 159 p. Grand Prix for Best Detective Novel of the Year 1957.

Mosley, Walter. *Devil in a Blue Dress*. (The Easy Rawlins Series) New York: W. W. Norton, 1990. ISBN 0-39302-854-2. 219 p. Edgar Award Nominee Best First Novel, 1991; John Creasey Award 1991; Shamus, Best First Novel, 1991.

Mosley, Walter. *Black Betty*. (The Easy Rawlins Series) New York: W. W. Norton, 1994. ISBN 0-39303-644-8. 255 p. Publisher's Weekly Best Books of 1994.

Neely, Barbara. *Blanche on the Lam*. (The Blanche White Series) New York: St. Martin's, 1992. ISBN 0-312-06908-1. 180 p. Agatha Award Best First Novel, 1993; Anthony Award Best First Novel, 1993; Macavity Award Best First Mystery Novel, 1993.

Olden, Mark. *The Ghost*. New York: Simon & Schuster, 1999 (1998). ISBN: 0-684-83467-7. 313 p. BCALA Literary Award Fiction Honor Book, 2000.

Simmons, Herbert. *Corner Boy*. New York: Old School Books, W.W. Norton & Co, 1996. (1957). ISBN 0-393-31465-0. 250 p. Houghton Mifflin Literary Fellowship, 1957.

West, Chassie. *Killing Kin*. (The Leigh Ann Warren Series) New York: Avon, 2000. ISBN 0-06-104389-3 (paper). 329 p. Anthony Nominee Best Paperback Original, 2000; Edgar Nominee Best Original Paperback, 2000.

Woods, Paula L. *Inner City Blues*. (The Charlotte Justice Series) New York: W. W. Norton, 1999. ISBN 0-393-04680-X. 316 p. BCALA Literary Award First Novelist, 2000.

REFERENCES

Dècurè, Nicole. 1999. In search of our sisters' mean streets: The politics of sex, race and class in black women's crime fiction. In *Diversity and Detective Fiction*, ed. Kathleen Gregory Klein, 158-185. Bowling Green, Ohio: Bowling Green State University Press.

Dietzel, Susanne B. 1997. Pulp fiction. In *The Oxford Companion to African American Literature*, ed. William L. Andres, William L., Frances Smith Foster, and Trudier Harris, 610-612. New York: Oxford University Press.

Jones, Malcolm. 2002. It's black, white–and noir: Crime writers are taking a hard-boiled look at race. *Newsweek*. http://stacks.msnbc.com/news/767591.usp. 5 pages.

Macdonald, Gina and Andrew Macdonald. 1999. Ethnic detectives in popular fiction; new directions for an American genre. In *Diversity and Detective Fiction*, ed.

Kathleen Gregory Klein, 60-113. Bowling Green, Ohio: Bowling Green State University Press.

Soitos, Stephen F. 1997. Detective and crime fiction. In *The Oxford Companion to African American Literature*, ed. William L. Andrews, Frances Smith Foster, and Trudier Harris, 82-84. New York: Oxford University Press.

Wood, Paula L. 1995. *Spooks, Spies, and Private Eyes: Black Mystery, Crime, and Suspense Fiction of the 20th Century*. New York: Doubleday, 1995.

The Native American Detective

Rhonda Harris Taylor

SUMMARY. While the Native American detective is a recent phenomenon in popularity, portrayals of Native Americans that have been present in the earliest examples of American literature and in well-known American mystery stories have usually been stereotypical. Listings of authors who have penned mysteries with Native American detectives are available to acquisitions librarians in print and Web resources. *[Article copies available for a fee from The Haworth Document Delivery Service: 1-800-HAWORTH. E-mail address: <docdelivery@haworthpress.com> Website: <http://www.HaworthPress.com> © 2004 by The Haworth Press, Inc. All rights reserved.]*

KEYWORDS. Native Americans, American Indian, detectives, mystery, stereotypes

THE CONTEXT

It is not an exaggeration to say that portrayals of Native people have been present in the earliest examples of literature generated within the

Rhonda Harris Taylor, PhD, is Associate Professor, School of Library and Information Studies, University of Oklahoma, 401 West Brooks, Room 120, Norman, OK 73019-6032.

[Haworth co-indexing entry note]: "The Native American Detective." Taylor, Rhonda Harris. Co-published simultaneously in *Collection Management* (The Haworth Information Press, an imprint of The Haworth Press, Inc.) Vol. 29, No. 3/4, 2004, pp. 101-105; and: *Managing the Mystery Collection: From Creation to Consumption* (ed: Judith Overmier, and Rhonda Harris Taylor) The Haworth Information Press, an imprint of The Haworth Press, Inc., 2004, pp. 101-105. Single or multiple copies of this article are available for a fee from The Haworth Document Delivery Service [1-800-HAWORTH, 9:00 a.m. - 5:00 p.m. (EST). E-mail address: docdelivery@haworthpress.com].

Available online at http://www.haworthpress.com/web/COL

doi:10.1300/J105v29n03_08

United States. But the pattern of that portrayal of Native Americans in American literature has been of stereotypes that have been repeatedly identified in a substantial body of criticism, including works by Shames and Stedman. Similarly, the juxtaposition of the mystery story plot with Native American characters has a long history but evidences a too-familiar pattern of stereotypes substituting for characterization. Those stock portrayals equate ancestry with the worst of human attributes. One relatively early example is that most well-known and popular classic in American literature, Mark Twain's 1876 novel, *The Adventures of Tom Sawyer*. On a nocturnal visit to the local graveyard, those quintessential American heroes, Tom Sawyer and Huck Finn, witness a murder committed by Injun Joe. Later, while searching for buried treasure in a haunted house, the two boys stumble across a plot by Injun Joe, the "bloody-minded outcast" (248), to seek a murderous revenge upon the Widow Douglas. As "The Young Detectives" (203), the two boys attempt to follow the villain to his hideout. When "'that murderin' half-breed'" (78) ultimately dies trapped in a cave, it is emphasized that he "was believed to have killed five citizens of the village" (249).

Over a century after Mark Twain's novel appeared, Rex Stout, the creator of Nero Wolfe, whom McBride has crowned the "greatest" detective of the twentieth century (xi), would place "Henrietta, a halfbreed bootlegger" (27) within the pages of *Death of a Dude* (1969). She is a "leather-skinned woman with stringy black hair," and her responses to queries are, of course, "grunted" (28). After Stout's death, Robert Goldsborough would continue the adventures of Nero Wolfe, and in his 1990 mystery, *Fade to Black*, the murderer would be revealed as the son of a man who claims Cherokee heritage.

The creation of the first character who was both Native American and a detective has been attributed to Manly Wade Wellman. In 1946, he introduced David Return, ironically a character whose Native American heritage was of a fictitious tribe (Macdonald and Macdonald 101). Return appeared in two short stories in *Ellery Queen's Mystery Magazine* in April of 1946 and in February of 1947 (Contento). However, the Native American detective with a widespread popular following is a relatively recent phenomenon, and its initiation can arguably be credited to Tony Hillerman, whose first mystery with a Navajo detective, Lieutenant Joe Leaphorn, was published in 1970 as *The Blessing Way*. Hillerman's influence on this subset of the genre may have come full-circle when his *Skinwalkers* (featuring Leaphorn and Navajo Tribal Police Sergeant Jim Chee) became the first American "Mystery" television series production, airing in November of 2002 as a project by film director Chris Eyre, who is Native American (PBS; Harlaub).

Thematically, the mystery that features a Native American detective carries with it considerations of: what role, if any, is played by the heritage of Native American writers who pen for the genre as compared to the perspectives and experiences of non-Indian writers, including the possibility that Native writers may "remain true to literary conventions found in Native American literature" and thus create their "own kind of detective fiction simultaneously within and outside the genre" (Stewart 167); what is the role of the hybridity of post-colonial detectives, who "are themselves blendings of western police methods and indigenous cultural knowledge, and their abilities are greater because of this hybridity" (Christian 13); the question of "does the mystery structure empower its [Native American] characters or merely squeeze them into a popular fictional pattern" (Coale 35); and the question of "does the ethnicity simply provide interesting local color or is it essential to the nature of the detective or to the social milieu in which s/he works?" (Macdonald and Macdonald 79). Finally, there is the dilemma of what constitutes "Native American" as a designation of heritage and culture. If the Latino detective is a meld of the Indigenous and other ancestries/traditions, is s/he also Native American (considering, for instance, Rudolfo Anaya's Sonny Baca character, introduced in 1995 in *Zia Summer*)?

THE RESOURCES

Acquisitions librarians should be conscious that in this arena of the mystery story that revolves around Indian protagonists, defining what constitutes a "mystery" can be challenging. Is James Welch's 1990 novel, *The Indian Lawyer*, a mystery, or simply a novel with a law/crime theme? Oftentimes, those Native American writers whose works might be considered to be mystery stories will be covered more extensively in critiques of Native American literature than in discussions of the mystery genre.

Acquisitions librarians will find it fairly easy to locate listings of authors who have created characters of Native American detectives. They are compiled in a number of resources, both print and Web, emanating from a variety of sources (for full citations, see the References section at the end of this essay): Macdonald and Macdonald's "Ethnic Detectives in Popular Fiction" (100-101); "Indians" in Mackler's *Murder . . . by*

Category (184-187); Dancing Badger Consultants' "'American Indian Mysteries': A Crossover Genre Not Quite There" (http://www.dancingbadger.com/indmyst.htm); Jacob's "Ethnic Detectives" category in "Booktalking Blitz: Recent Trends in Mysteries" (http://www.genrefluent.com/blitz5.htm); Kiser's "Native American Mysteries," (http://www.santafelibrary.org/namystery.html); the Manchester (Connecticut) Public Library's list at http://library.ci.manchester.ct.us/ra/readlists/nativeamericanmysteries.html; and "Native American Mysteries" on *Reader's Advice* at http://www.readersadvice.com/readadv/000302.html. Consulting several of these compilations should lead to generation of a fairly comprehensive list of the works in this area. Also informative for acquisitions purposes will be the Web sites of/about individual authors, easily found by using any good search engine. Finally, it should be noted that there are a few film productions that feature Native American detectives, including two productions that were frequently panned by reviewers: *The Dark Wind* (1991), adapted from Hillerman's novel of the same name, and *Thunderheart* (1992).

REFERENCES

Anaya, Rudolfo. *Zia Summer*. New York: Warner Books, 1995.

Christian, Ed. "Introducing the Post-Colonial Detective: Putting Marginality to Work." *The Post-Colonial Detective*. Ed. Ed Christian. NY: Palgrave-St. Martin's, 2001. 1-16.

Coale, Samuel. *The Mystery of Mysteries: Cultural Differences and Designs*. Bowling Green, OH: Bowling Green State U P, 2000.

Contento, William G. "Mystery Short Fiction, 1990-2002." 2002. <http://users.ev1.net/~homeville/msf/index.htm>.

Dancing Badger Consultants. "'American Indian Mysteries': A Crossover Genre Not Quite There." *At Wanderer's Well: A Magazine of Literature and Opinions*. 7 July 2003. <http://www.dancingbadger.com/indmyst.htm>.

The Dark Wind. Dir. Errol Morris, 1991.

Goldsborough, Robert. *Fade to Black*. New York: Bantam, 1990.

Hartlaub, Peter. "Eyre Turns His Camera on American Indians; But Race Isn't the Focus of Director's 'Mystery.'" *The San Francisco Chronicle* 24 Nov. 2002. 22 Jan. 2003. <http://web.lexis-nexis.com/>.

Hillerman, Tony. *The Blessing Way*. New York: Harper & Row, 1970.

Jacob, Merle. "Booktalking Blitz: Recent Trends in Mysteries." Chicago Public Library. March 2002. <http://www.genrefluent.com/blitz5.htm>.

Kiser, Marcia. "Native American Mysteries." 23 July 1998. Santa Fe Public Library. <http://www.santafelibrary.org/namystery.html>.

Macdonald, Gina and Andrew Macdonald. "Ethnic Detectives in Popular Fiction: New Directions for an American Genre." *Diversity and Detective Fiction.* Kathleen Gregory Klein. Bowling Green, OH: Bowling Green State U Press, 1999. 60-113.

Mackler, Tasha. *Murder . . . by Category: A Subject Guide to Mystery Fiction.* Metuchen, NJ: Scarecrow, 1991.

Manchester Public Library. "If You Like Tony Hillerman's Native American Mysteries, Try. . . ." "Manchester Public Library: The Reader's Connection." Nov. 2001.

McBride, O. E. *Stout Fellow: A Guide Through Nero Wolfe's World.* New York: iUniverse, 2003.

"Native American Mysteries." *Reader's Advice.* 1 July 2003. <http://www.readersadvice.com/readadv/000302.html>.

PBS. "Redford's Wildwood Enterprises and PBS Bring 'Skinwalkers' to the Small Screen." *PBS News.* 21 Feb. 2002. <http://www.pbs.org/insidepbs/news/skinwalkers.html>.

Shames, Priscilla. *The Long Hope: A Study of American Indian Stereotypes in American Popular Fiction, 1890-1950.* Ann Arbor, MI: University Microfilms, 1969.

Stedman, Raymond William. *Shadows of the Indian: Stereotypes in American Culture.* Norman: U of Okla. P, 1982.

Stewart, Michelle Pagni. "'A Rose by Any Other Name': A Native American Detective Novel by Louis Owens." *Multicultural Detective Fiction: Murder from the "Other" Side.* Ed. Adrienne Johnson Gosselin. New York: Garland Publishing, 1999. 167-183.

Stout, Rex. *Death of a Dude.* New York: Bantam-Viking, 1969.

Thunderheart. Dir. Michael Apted. Columbia, 1992.

Twain, Mark. *The Adventures of Tom Sawyer.* Garden City, NY: Junior Deluxe Editions-Harper & Row, n.d.

Welch, James. *The Indian Lawyer.* New York: Norton, 1990.

The Arthur Conan Doyle Collection at the Toronto Public Library

Victoria Gill

SUMMARY. The Arthur Conan Doyle Collection, one of the Toronto Public Library's special collections, dates from 1971. The areas of collection were clearly laid down in the first two major purchases: original material by Conan Doyle and others using his characters in any format, and secondary material to support these works.

Many significant purchases in the collection's early days gave it a sound foundation, upon which it has been possible to continue to build in later times of budgetary restraints.

The collection has strong ties to the world of Sherlockian enthusiasts; donations and information from them have been important over the years and continue to be so. The recent formation of a Friends group for the collection is of great significance, not merely in fundraising, but in showing support and in raising public awareness of the collection. *[Article copies available for a fee from The Haworth Document Delivery Service: 1-800-HAWORTH. E-mail address: <docdelivery@haworthpress.com> Website: <http://www.HaworthPress.com> © 2004 by The Haworth Press, Inc. All rights reserved.]*

Victoria Gill, MA, MLS, has been Curator of the Arthur Conan Doyle Collection since 1991.

Address correspondence to: Victoria Gill, Special Collections Department, Toronto Reference Library, 789 Yonge Street, Toronto, ON M4W 2G8, Canada (E-mail: vgill@tpl.toronto.on.ca).

[Haworth co-indexing entry note]: "The Arthur Conan Doyle Collection at the Toronto Public Library." Gill, Victoria. Co-published simultaneously in *Collection Management* (The Haworth Information Press, an imprint of The Haworth Press, Inc.) Vol. 29, No. 3/4, 2004, pp. 107-119; and: *Managing the Mystery Collection: From Creation to Consumption* (ed: Judith Overmier, and Rhonda Harris Taylor) The Haworth Information Press, an imprint of The Haworth Press, Inc., 2004, pp. 107-119. Single or multiple copies of this article are available for a fee from The Haworth Document Delivery Service [1-800-HAWORTH, 9:00 a.m. - 5:00 p.m. (EST). E-mail address: docdelivery@haworthpress.com].

Available online at http://www.haworthpress.com/web/COL

doi:10.1300/J105v29n03_09

KEYWORDS. Conan Doyle, Sherlock Holmes, special collections, Toronto Public Library

It has never seemed strange to me that Toronto Public Library should have its unique collection devoted to Conan Doyle and his works, including that most well-known of detectives, Sherlock Holmes. Among the main users of public libraries are those adults who consult travel guides, search for gardening tips, and seek investment advice from time to time, but there are also those individuals whose regular habit is to visit the library every couple of weeks in search of recreational reading, which often means mysteries. So a collection honouring the greatest mystery writer and the most famous detective of them all seems to me an eminently suitable undertaking for a large public library such as ours.

But many casual visitors to the collection do find its existence odd. They wonder why Toronto has such a thing, more in an enquiring spirit than a hostile one. Does the author have a connection with the city? Not really–he passed through more than once and lectured here on spiritualism in his later years. Did a local collector donate it? No, though the initial purchase was not expensive.

THE GENESIS

The events that led to the collection's founding had more than a little to do with the complete reorganization of the library at that time. Toronto had long had a large central library with both reference and circulating divisions, which had been housed in a dignified Carnegie building since 1909. In the late 1960s, it was decided to make the library completely reference and move it to a new site where the two major subway lines cross. This central and accessible location, and the striking building (designed by Raymond Moriyama) that was erected, were a great success and have led to an enormous increase in the use of the reference library.

The city had been growing furiously for the previous quarter century (and still is, for that matter). A 1909 library was no longer suitable and the 1960s were a period when public money was readily available for cultural and educational projects. The library set up subject departments, which began buying extensively to meet the new all-reference mandate.

Among these new departments was Literature, which was contemplating the disappearance of its major activity, the circulation of fiction. There would still be students, doing research for literary essays, but a public library is not for students only. So, consciously or unconsciously, the department was looking for something new.

Across the street from the old library was an antiquarian bookseller with whom the library frequently did business. One day in 1969 he phoned to say that he had acquired some five hundred novels, mostly mysteries, in an estate sale. These books were not really his specialty and were taking up space, so if the library would buy them all, they could have them for $1,000, or two dollars per book. Since these were pre-war editions, this was a bargain, even in 1969.

So two librarians from the Literature Department visited the shop, inspected the books, and decided to buy them. Conan Doyle was the major author represented, with about two hundred books. It was apparently on the way back to the library–there must have been a remarkably long wait at the traffic lights or perhaps they stopped off for a coffee and a cigarette–that the librarians came up with the idea of using these two hundred books as the nucleus of an Arthur Conan Doyle collection. One of them, Cameron Hollyer, became the collection's first curator; he was there when the idea was conceived, cherished it until it was born two years later, and looked after it for the next twenty years, bringing it to a healthy maturity.

These two librarians informed the head of their department that they had purchased the material and what they thought could be done with it. She caught their enthusiasm and promised to speak to the library director, John Parkhill. When she did, she found him more receptive to the suggestion than she had anticipated, since he had already been approached from another direction. A second customer had entered the shop and shown interest in the same material. He was told it had been sold and to whom. He then marched across the street to see the library's Director. The second customer was yet another librarian, Donald Redmond, from the Douglas Library at Queen's University in Kingston, Ontario, and a good friend of both John Parkhill and Sherlock Holmes. To our Director, Mr. Redmond said something along the lines of, "Well, you've bought these books, so now you've got to do something with them. You should start an Arthur Conan Doyle Collection and keep up with the field." It must have seemed that this endeavor was meant to be!

THE FOCUS

The Literature Department was authorized to start a special collection devoted to Sir Arthur Conan Doyle. The scope was and is to collect, in book form or in any medium to which they have been adapted, editions of the works of Conan Doyle and others who have used his characters, along with bibliographies, indexes, criticism, and any other supporting material that is deemed appropriate. The interest and support of administration meant that funding was available for large purchases and for the necessary staff time. Another advantage was that from the time it opened, it was apparent that the "Sherlock Holmes" collection was of interest to the press, and it has continued to be a frequent feature in articles about the library. The presence of Donald Redmond was also fortunate, not only in his advice to the director, but in his knowledge of the world of Sherlockian societies and publications–knowledge not shared by anyone on staff at the time, but which is a requirement for anyone looking after such a collection.

THE FIRST PURCHASE

No sooner had the books arrived from across the street than Mr. Redmond forwarded a catalogue from a British dealer, with a strong recommendation that we buy the collection offered, which we did. The first purchase was important in giving rise to the idea of starting the collection, but this second one, built up by Harold Mortlake, was important in itself. It consisted of some nine hundred items for about $7,500, amounting to 1,500 pieces of material. For instance, *The Strand Magazine* was counted as one item, but it came in a large number of bound volumes. The Mortlake Collection contained many of Conan Doyle's first and other early editions from England and the United States, including not only the Sherlock Holmes stories but his other works of fiction. Conan Doyle wrote in most of the popular genres–adventure, horror, science fiction, ghost stories, and historical fiction, as well as mysteries. The historical fiction, which the author regarded more highly than his mysteries and which was very popular for a long time, has fallen out of favour, with the exception of the Brigadier Gerard stories set during the Napoleonic Wars. Sherlock Holmes has always been in print, of course, and so has *The Lost World*, the first man-meets-dinosaur novel.

THE EVOLVING COLLECTION

We have continued to buy different editions of Conan Doyle's works, new and old, elegant and ugly, carefully produced and also the umpteenth rendition of misprints and murky illustrations reproduced from long-ago originals. It is interesting that in recent years Oxford and Penguin have produced properly edited and annotated texts; our author seems to be assuming "classic" status.

We also buy simplified versions for adults learning English and even more simplified versions for children. I myself see no reason to introduce the Hound of the Baskervilles to tiny tots, but we have an edition designed to do just that! Some children's books are more pictures than text, and we also acquire comic books, aimed at both children and adults.

Only in 1891 did American law grant nonresident foreigners copyright protection, so there are editions of Conan Doyle's earliest works from many American publishers. These are known as pirate editions, which is a little harsh, since they were legal, though unauthorized, and brought the author no financial benefit. It is due to this state of affairs that an American collector amassed some three hundred editions of *The Sign of Four*, which we later acquired.

The Strand Magazine is of great importance in Conan Doyle's career. He had written many short stories which had appeared in other magazines, as well as several novels, including two short ones featuring Sherlock Holmes, whose success had been no more than modest.

In 1891, the first year of *The Strand*'s existence, Conan Doyle began publishing the first series of Sherlock Holmes short stories. It is generally agreed that (with the exception of *The Hound of the Baskervilles*) the best Sherlock Holmes fiction is found in the short stories. The reappearance of a few characters (Holmes, Watson, the policeman Lestrade) and a setting (the rooms at 221B Baker Street), though by now a commonplace device, was at the time new and intriguing. Conan Doyle was at his best in these circumstances. His best historical fiction, the Brigadier Gerard stories, are of the same type. The appearance of the Sherlock Holmes stories in *The Strand* marked a huge increase in the fame and fortune of their author. Both he and the magazine prospered greatly, and for the rest of his career much of his work, including all the later Sherlock Holmes stories, made its first appearance there.

Some years after the Arthur Conan Doyle Collection was established, Cameron Hollyer acquired a number of Conan Doyle's letters to the editor of *The Strand*. Some of these business letters are entertaining. A reader had claimed that Holmes would not really have been able to tell which way a bicycle was going from its tracks, but Conan Doyle has experimented with his own bicycle and yes, you can tell. On another occasion the unhappy author says he had carefully built up his story to a surprise climax–and it has appeared in the magazine with an illustration of his great surprise right at the beginning of the story.

Another part of the collection's first large purchase (the Mortlake Collection) consisted of a large number of non-Conan Doyle Sherlock Holmes stories dating from the early part of the twentieth century and which were published in many languages across Europe, from Portuguese in the west to Russian in the east. They were completely unauthorized and are remarkably sensational literature, with covers showing Holmes being menaced by crocodiles or masked men in torture chambers and other dangers seldom encountered in Victorian England.

We have followed up the initial purchase in two ways. We buy material in other languages, mostly European but with some Asian as well, notably Japanese. There are many translations and adaptations of Conan Doyle and a good deal of original material about Sherlock Holmes written in Japanese. We also continue to buy other people's fiction based on our author's characters. Parodies began to appear as soon as Holmes gained fame in *The Strand*, and for many years now those authors who believe there cannot be too many Sherlock Holmes stories have been adding to their number, which continues to grow annually. If an author feels that there is too much Sherlock, he takes as his chief character Sherlock's lazy brother Mycroft, or Irene Adler (who outwitted Sherlock), or the landlady, Mrs. Hudson. An oddity of the last decade has been the appearance of Conan Doyle himself as a fictional character in works by several authors, with varying degrees of success. Prose fiction is not the only medium in which Conan Doyle's characters appear, of course. There are plays, movies, and television versions, and we acquire their texts, programmes, and tapes.

The Mortlake Collection and the ongoing acquisitions in the areas it covered are all primary material. Secondary material was the focus of our second big purchase; this belonged to a Torontonian, Judge S. Tupper Bigelow, who had been collecting books, pamphlets, and magazines about Sherlock Holmes for the previous twenty years. An exhibit of material from his collection a few years earlier had perhaps played a part in the librarians' getting the idea of acquiring a collection of their very own.

Bigelow's collection was purchased at the same price as the Mortlake one. There was little overlap, and they complemented each other perfectly. Judge Bigelow had also created a card index to the contents of his collection, to enable him to find articles on such subjects as Dr. Watson's middle name, the location of his wound, and the number of his wives, to list three matters about which people have been arguing happily for the last eighty years and will apparently continue doing so for the next eighty.

Here, too, we have continued to buy the continuing stream of material dealing with our author and his works. The judge's useful index was kept up until the end of 2002 by Donald Redmond, since such an undertaking is far too time-consuming for anyone to be paid to do it. These two men were both active in the Sherlockian world, which I will describe a little, since our collection cannot be understood otherwise.

THE SHERLOCKIAN WORLD

The formation of societies to celebrate, discuss, and publish material about authors is a common phenomenon and Sherlockian societies are true to form in holding conferences and in sometimes producing papers and books of scholarly quality. But these societies are not devoted to an author but to a character. For instance, there is an Arthur Conan Doyle Society, but it is much younger than many of the Sherlockian societies and much less popular. The Sherlockian societies are given to "the game," a form of mock scholarship based on the premise that the Holmes stories are basically factual accounts narrated by Dr. Watson. The societies did not originate this. It began as a form of highbrow entertainment by a number of writers, of whom Dorothy L. Sayers is the most famous. She wrote several essays on Sherlockian problems, settling to her own satisfaction which university Holmes attended and why, given that the reader is told that the man's name is John H. Watson, his wife calls him James. There are any number of inconsistencies and anomalies in the stories and much ingenuity has gone into tidying them up.

The United States has the most Sherlockian societies and for many years they were a largely American phenomenon. The societies are mostly offshoots, or scions, of the Baker Street Irregulars of New York, the first of them, and which has been publishing *The Baker Street Journal* since 1946. The Sherlock Holmes Society of London is another venerable institution, but in recent years other societies have sprung up in other parts of Britain. There had been two Sherlock Holmes societies in Toronto prior to the founding of our collection but both were defunct. In

1972, the year after the collection opened, the still-flourishing Bootmakers of Toronto was launched. The reference to their name is to a clue in *The Hound of the Baskervilles*, in which Sir Henry Baskerville's missing boot has a label: "Meyers, Toronto." The Bootmakers and the Arthur Conan Doyle Collection have enjoyed a symbiotic relationship over the years. There are also societies in non-English-speaking countries, above all in Japan. The list of current societies numbers two hundred and seventy-six, nearly two hundred of them American.

Sherlockian societies hold meetings, sponsor conferences, and publish journals and pamphlets and, less often, books. Some Sherlockians are inspired to feats of scholarship. An annotated edition of the complete Sherlock Holmes stories is in process of being published; this one, unlike the Oxford and Penguin editions mentioned earlier, adds "the game" to its annotations. Nor is it the first such edition. But the earlier edition with Sherlockian annotations is over thirty years old, and the present editor has somewhat different interests; there is plenty of room for both of them. Sherlockian writers have brought their varied professional knowledge to bear on the stories–legal, medical, and historical. Others combine hobbies and produce Sherlockian cookbooks and songbooks, studies of the firearms used, and instructions for knitting Sherlockian motifs.

There are also Sherlockians who are inspired to become publishers. Only a small quantity of Sherlockian material is published by commercial presses and only occasionally is any money made. Most of the writing and publishing is a labour of love. It has been truly remarked that never has so much been written by so many for so few!

Societies also produce and sponsor Sherlockian artwork, crafts, and memorabilia. There are reproductions of paintings and drawings, figurines, dolls, coffee mugs, keychains, T-shirts, and anything else that tickles the fancy of the sponsoring body. We try to acquire everything in print, but we are selective in our purchases from the great outpouring of Sherlockian realia.

Many Sherlockians are collectors and, happily for the collecting librarian, in addition to the notices of new material in society journals, there are two monthly newsletters, one American (*Scuttlebutt from the Spermaceti Press*) and one British (*The District Messenger*), which do nothing but list new things for sale with prices and sources, and note upcoming events such as conferences, plays, movies, and television programmes of interest. The authors of these newsletters rely on other Sherlockians for details, not only of items of obvious relevance, but for references in books and magazines on other subjects which have been serendipitously discovered. No one can cover all fields, so the Sherlockian public is alerted when someone comes across Holmes in a book on indexing or investment strategies, or finds a travel magazine article which mentions *The Hound of the Baskervilles* in a feature on Dartmoor.

Years ago, Sherlockians playing the game used to be more fundamentalist in their attitude to Conan Doyle and dismissed him as "Watson's literary agent." Currently they are more relaxed, and the Sherlockian sources note reprints of his non-Sherlockian fiction, as well as criticism and biographies (of which there have been a surprising number, considering our man's respectability) and mentions of him in magazines, such as an article on Conan Doyle's Edinburgh in a magazine about Britain and one on his early promotion of Alpine skiing in Switzerland in a skiing magazine.

There is an enormous amount of Sherlockian activity on the Internet, including some very large and lively discussion groups. My favorite site is http://www.sherlockian.net, which has much information, along with links to more sites than seem possible, including a list of societies and people with things for sale.

THE FACILITIES

The Arthur Conan Doyle Collection was housed for a short time in an unused office in the old library building, which in addition to the bookshelves was furnished with an old table, chairs, and rugs, as well as a mantelpiece purchased from a wrecking company. All these furnishings were moved to the new building and reassembled in a custom-built, climate-controlled room on the fifth floor, where we exist as a small reproach to the modernity of the rest of the building and guiltily hide the computer terminal behind a pillar. The room has a friendly, old-fashioned atmosphere and has some comfortable upholstered chairs where browsers can settle with their selections from the shelves, in a manner unusual for a special collection.

Over our mantlepiece are original drawings by Sidney Paget, who illustrated the stories in *The Strand*, and Frederic Dorr Steele, who illustrated their American appearance in *Collier's*. Both men have influenced the public's image of Holmes. Paget provided the deerstalker, and his illustrations were a strong influence on the appearance of the

Granada television series with Jeremy Brett. The Paget drawing was bought, as were all our expensive purchases, in the collection's early days. Our two drawings by Dorr Steele were generous donations from a local collector. The American impression of Holmes was greatly influenced by this artist and by the actor William Gillette, the first to play Holmes and to play him so often that Gillette became identified with the character. Gillette contributed a curved pipe, but the preposterous calabash seems to have originated in comic skits. The lean frame and bony features with a deerstalker and pipe (and probably a magnifying glass) that constitute the idea of Holmes is used time and again by cartoonists and advertisers, whose work is also of interest to us.

HIGHLIGHTS

The printed item that is the pride of our collection, as it would be of any Doylean/Sherlockian collection, is the 1887 *Beeton's Christmas Annual.* Sherlock Holmes made his debut here in the short novel *A Study in Scarlet.* This popular annual potpourri of light reading matter was not an outlet that conferred any prestige on items appearing there, but the author had been trying to place this novel for quite some time. As he later recounted, one publisher told him "the market is flooded at present with cheap fiction," so he was perhaps relieved to get it published at all. *Beeton's* was a paperback, intended to be read over the holidays and used to light the fire afterwards. In spite of a large print run, very few survive, and we are happy in our possession of a good bright copy.

TRANSITIONS

By the time Cameron Hollyer retired in 1991, he had built up a splendid collection. By the later 1980s the money for acquisitions had been greatly reduced and has further diminished since then. Public institutions just do not have the resources of "the good old days." Along with the decrease in the supply of money, there has been a great increase in the price of our author's works, especially Sherlock Holmes–even more so than in antiquarian books generally. How fortunate it is that the collection's first curator laboured to such good purpose while the sun was shining!

When I took over the collection on Hollyer's retirement, I was working as a book selector and reference librarian in the Literature Department and had also been a member of the Bootmakers of Toronto for several years. My specialty was Victorian literature, and I had been an avid mystery reader since my teens. Since older mystery fiction was a specialty of the Literature Department's general collection, I had taken the opportunity to read a great deal of it. I never thought I'd be boasting on a job application of all the hours I'd spent reading mysteries, which family and friends had assured me was time wasted. Indeed, I thought so myself, but you never know what may come in useful.

The palmy days of the seventies are very different from my own. I buy mainly current material, the prices of which are usually modest. I buy some older editions and the occasional first edition, filling in the few gaps in the holdings of a collection now numbering over 10,000 items. Yet it was in my time that the collection acquired its most valuable item. This is the manuscript of *Angels of Darkness*, an unfinished play handwritten by Conan Doyle in five notebooks. It is a very early work using the same American material about Mormons which forms part of *A Study in Scarlet*. Indeed, on the title page the original title was *A Study in Scarlet*, but it has been crossed out and the present title substituted. Holmes does not appear, though there is a character called Dr. Watson. The play was finally published in 2001 by the Baker Street Irregulars. This manuscript was bequeathed to us by Anna Conan Doyle, widow of Sir Arthur's son Adrian, who visited the collection in its early days and obviously remembered her visit with pleasure. We do get quite a number of donations. Most are small, but their cumulative value is considerable. Some individuals and societies give us their journals and pamphlets on a regular basis, year after year, and their generosity is greatly appreciated.

There are Conan Doyle manuscripts in a number of distinguished libraries, but when this collection was founded it was the first of its kind. Since then there have appeared two related collections devoted to Sherlock Holmes, one in the Marylebone Library in London and another very large one in the library of the University of Minnesota at Minneapolis. We, though, have a Conan Doyle collection and gather material about him, his life, and activities. As well as fiction, he wrote on history, spiritualism, and topics of the day, including true-life crime when he thought there had been miscarriages of justice. It must be admitted, though, that without Holmes, Conan Doyle would be a dim figure known only to specialists in the literature of the period when the nineteenth century met the twentieth.

THE VISITORS

The collection is housed on the same floor as the language lab and books for adult learners of English, of whom there are many. Toronto is the most ethnically diverse city in North America, with a huge proportion of immigrants. Some of them are curious enough to drop into the Arthur Conan Doyle Room. Many do not know who he is, but only a couple of people have not heard of Sherlock Holmes, though sometimes they have to pronounce the name over a few times for library staff to recognize it. He is the Great Detective, bringing reason to bear on crime and belonging to what seems, probably only in retrospect, a more stable and secure age. The world of London, greatest of cities of its time, shrouded in fog with horses drawing hansom cabs clip-clopping through its streets, has a fascination extending beyond the English-speaking world of whose cultural baggage it is a part.

This fascination would have surprised Conan Doyle, since as is well known, after four volumes he disposed of Holmes by throwing him over a cliff locked in mortal combat with Professor Moriarty. Public demand prompted publishers to offer sufficient incentive to resurrect him, but as time went on Conan Doyle's heart was less and less involved with the frivolities of fiction. Up to the First World War his output was overwhelmingly fiction, but after it he published little fiction. He had not given up writing; in 1918 he published *The New Revelation*, the first of many books and pamphlets promoting the cause of spiritualism, much to the dismay of his publishers and his public. From a biographical point of view, though much less so from a literary one, this is an interesting phase of his life, and one that we cover in the collection, not merely with Conan Doyle's own works, but other books about spiritualism and some family papers on the subject. Printed biographical studies of Conan Doyle are made more interesting by our also having some personal material. I am very fond of several sets of family snapshots that we possess, ranging in time from his honeymoon with his second wife (a Mediterranean cruise in 1907) to a visit with his wife and children to the southern hemisphere in 1920. Of particular interest to us are those photographs taken during his visit to Canada in 1914.

THE FRIENDS

In 1996, the library set up a Special Collections Department. The connection with the Literature Department was lost, but it has been more than offset by our becoming part of a larger group devoted to the care of rare and fragile materials. A significant stage in the collection's life was the founding of the Friends of the Arthur Conan Doyle Collection in 1997, with the aim of promoting the collection and raising funds for it. They have sponsored a number of lectures since then and arranged outings and co-sponsored a 2001 Doylean/Sherlockian conference in Toronto, activities which have certainly raised the collection's profile. Membership in the Friends is not limited to southern Ontario. We have Friends, not only from across North America, but from even further afield, attesting to the international respect the collection has gained. A newsletter, *The Magic Door*, keeps all members in touch with developments in the collection and activities sponsored by the Friends. Recent donations have included a number of items once owned by Conan Doyle, including a personal account book and major support for the purchase of about thirty books from his personal library. As the Friends prosper, so do we. Their existence and support is of great importance to the collection.

CONCLUSION

A little over thirty years has passed and the Arthur Conan Doyle Collection has become a well-established part of the library. With its position among the other special collections and with the support of its new Friends group, it is well placed to continue to prosper. The Collection brings information and pleasure, not only to Sherlockians, but to a wide range of people interested in the late Victorian world, as well as to the casual drop-in visitor who, in the centre of a modern city, enjoys a quiet moment in a room devoted to a bygone age.

The Adventure of the Unopened Box: Building the Sherlock Holmes Collections at the University of Minnesota Libraries

Timothy J. Johnson

SUMMARY. The article traces the historical development and description of significant acquisitions that comprise major portions of the Sherlock Holmes Collections of the University of Minnesota Libraries Special Collections. Beginning with the formation of the Norwegian Explorers, a local scion society of the Baker Street Irregulars of New York, in 1948, the article presents the intertwined nature in the development of this local interest group and the growth of the Holmes Collections. Various strategic acquisitions methodologies, such as donor relations, exhibitions, scholarly publications, and conference development are presented as part of the narrative. *[Article copies available for a fee from The Haworth Document Delivery Service: 1-800-HAWORTH. E-mail address: <docdelivery@haworthpress.com> Website: <http://www.HaworthPress.com> © 2004 by The Haworth Press, Inc. All rights reserved.]*

KEYWORDS. Sherlock Holmes, Special Collections, University of Minnesota, donor relations, acquisitions

---

Timothy J. Johnson, MA, MATS, is Associate Librarian and Curator, Special Collections and Rare Books, University of Minnesota, Twin Cities Campus, Suite 111 Elmer L. Andersen Library, 222–21st Avenue South, Minneapolis, MN 55455.

[Haworth co-indexing entry note]: "The Adventure of the Unopened Box: Building the Sherlock Holmes Collections at the University of Minnesota Libraries." Johnson, Timothy J. Co-published simultaneously in *Collection Management* (The Haworth Information Press, an imprint of The Haworth Press, Inc.) Vol. 29, No. 3/4, 2004, pp. 121-141; and: *Managing the Mystery Collection: From Creation to Consumption* (ed: Judith Overmier, and Rhonda Harris Taylor) The Haworth Information Press, an imprint of The Haworth Press, Inc., 2004, pp. 121-141. Single or multiple copies of this article are available for a fee from The Haworth Document Delivery Service [1-800-HAWORTH, 9:00 a.m. - 5:00 p.m. (EST). E-mail address: docdelivery@haworthpress.com].

Available online at http://www.haworthpress.com/web/COL

doi:10.1300/J105v29n03_10

THE ADVENTURE BEGINS

In 1993, a fourteen-member planning committee, consisting of authors, collectors, professors, librarians, and curators, produced an eleven page long-range plan for the Sherlock Holmes Collections of the University of Minnesota Libraries.[1] The long-range plan opened with a summarized history of the collections.

> The Sherlock Holmes Collection was begun in 1974 with the purchase of the small but notable James Iraldi collection by a grant from the McKnight Foundation. The remarkable Philip H. Hench collection was given to the university in 1978. It consists of approximately 1800 books and 1500 issues of periodicals, as well as unique material of Sir Arthur Conan Doyle, William Gillette, the famous portrayer of Holmes on the stage, and Frederic Dorr Steele, the preeminent American illustrator of the adventures. The Hench collection is the largest of its kind in an American research library, and it has been a magnet that has drawn to the university a number of other gifts, such as the Frederic Dorr Steele Memorial Collection in 1986, and the Edith Meiser scripts and broadcast recordings in 1987, the actress and writer who first adapted the adventures for radio, beginning in 1930. The library and papers of the late Vincent Starrett were purchased in 1988, with the help of the John E. Andrus III Charitable Trust. Starrett was a prolific author and journalist, a notable bibliophile, and the celebrated Sherlockian who wrote the famous sonnet "221B" and *The Private Life of Sherlock Holmes.* The Howard Haycraft collection, consisting of his working library and papers, came to the university by bequest in 1992. Haycraft wrote the classics *Murder for Pleasure* and *The Art of the Detective Story*, the first comprehensive histories and analyses of the detective story. A number of other collections have been given to the Sherlock Holmes Collection, as well as assemblages of material by collectors of Sherlockiana.
>
> John Bennett Shaw, of Santa Fe, New Mexico, has built the largest collection in the world relating to Sherlock Holmes. He began collecting Sherlock Holmes in 1937, at the age of twenty-three, and today is still collecting vigorously. His library holds 9000 books; thousands of magazines; photographs, films, recordings, and tapes; art and craft works; toys and games, articles of clothing, etc. He

has agreed to turn over his great library to the university in October 1993.[2]

This excerpt is a bare-bones account of the acquisitions history of the Holmes Collections. What follows is an attempt to put meat on the bones, or as Holmes himself observed in "The Reigate Squires," "It is of the highest importance in the art of detection to be able to recognize, out of a number of facts, which are incidental and which vital. Otherwise your energy and attention must be dissipated instead of being concentrated."[3]

THE CURIOUS OCCURRENCE OF THE NORWEGIAN EXPLORERS

One vital fact that concentrates our attention in the case of the Holmesian collections is the curious occurrence of the Norwegian Explorers.[4] It is almost a certainty that nothing which followed would have been possible were it not for a 1947 lunch at the University of Minnesota Campus Club. Here, on an April midday, five prominent faculty members–all with a shared Sherlockian interest–decided to form a scion society of the New York-based Baker Street Irregulars.[5] Although the origin of the name for this local society–the Norwegian Explorers–is shrouded in mystery, both its Scandinavian character and original membership firmly bound its activities to the University.[6] Its first meeting, as reported in the pages of *The Baker Street Journal*, was held on a stereotypical Minnesota night. "On a bitter cold evening, January 23rd [1948] (21 degrees below zero), seven loyal Sherlockians foregathered at the Covered Wagon (in memory of John Ferrier) to drink the canonical toasts and discuss appropriate topics from the Master's life and work."[7] Toasts and topics have continued to mark the livelihood of the Explorers through the last five decades, as has Sherlockian research and scholarly work. In 1951, historian Theodore C. Blegen, with the assistance of Emerson G. Wulling and his Sumac Press, published *The Crowded Box-Room.* A year later Sumac Press issued Blegen and University Librarian Errett Weir McDiarmid's *Sherlock Holmes: Master Detective.*

These early activities of the Explorers caught the attention of Dr. Philip S. Hench, Chief Rheumatologist at the Mayo Clinic in Rochester, Minnesota. Hench, who received the 1950 Nobel Prize in Physiology and Medicine (along with Dr. Edward Kendall and Dr. Tadeus Reichstein) joined the Explorers in the early 1950s. Over the next few years Hench and other Explorers worked on a Holmesian project of international scope that put them in contact with another important group, The Sherlock Holmes Society of London. On June 25, 1957 members from Minnesota and London gathered at the funicular station at the Reichenbach Falls in Switzerland to unveil a plaque which read: "Across this dreadful cauldron occurred the culminating event in the career of Sherlock Holmes, the world's greatest detective, when on May 4, 1891 he vanquished Prof. Moriarty, the Napoleon of crime." During this same eventful year McDiarmid was invested in the Baker Street Irregulars as "The Bruce-Partington Plans" and the Explorers published their third book, *Exploring Sherlock Holmes*, with Sumac Press.

By the mid-1960s there was some question on whether or not the Explorers would continue their Sherlockian activities. McDiarmid, now Director of the Graduate School Fellowship Office, was on leave in Chile to help the University of Concepcion establish their graduate programs. Hench, who had retired from the Mayo Clinic in 1957, but continued his pursuits with the Explorers, died in 1965. Four years later Blegen was gone. But the early 1970s saw a renewed interest and new members, and it is here that the history of the Holmes Collections intersects with that of the Norwegian Explorers.

THE JAMES C. IRALDI COLLECTION

On May 2, 1974, members of the Explorers received an announcement of the "acquisition of a distinguished Sherlock Holmes Collection by the University of Minnesota Library." Austin McLean, Curator of Special Collections, and the members of the Explorers were instrumental in this first acquisition. The announcement continued:

> Through a gift from the McKnight Foundation, the University of Minnesota Library has been able to acquire the interesting collection of Sherlockiana collected by Mr. James C. Iraldi of New York. In addition to early editions of the adventures, the collection includes numerous memorabilia, photographs, clippings, etc. The Collection will be available for display to members of the Norwegian Explorers.[8]

On the same day Bryce Crawford, faculty member in Chemistry, submitted the following resolution to the University of Minnesota:

WHEREAS the University of Minnesota Libraries have, through the alertness of the staff, the helpfulness of friends, and the generosity of the McKnight Foundation, acquired a sound collection dealing with the affairs of Mr. Sherlock Holmes and Dr. John Hamish Watson; and

WHEREAS the Norwegian Explorers, as the resident scion society with canonical jurisdiction in and for the cities of Minneapolis and St. Paul, rejoice in this acquisition and congratulate the University and the community of Sherlockian scholars in their good fortune, and

WHEREAS the said Norwegian Explorers wish to signalize their desire to be helpful and supportive in the maintenance and development of this irregular resource; and

WHEREAS for many years Errett Weir McDiarmid has served the Norwegian Explorers as the Sigerson of that body, and the University of Minnesota Libraries in divers ways, demonstrating stimulating originality, canny resourcefulness, generous wisdom, and sound canonical scholarship;

THEREFORE BE IT RESOLVED that the Norwegian Explorers petition the University of Minnesota Libraries to designate this newly acquired collection, together with such further acquisitions as may properly accrue to it,

THE ERRETT WEIR McDIARMID COLLECTION
OF SHERLOCK HOLMES[9]

Given the absence of any official response, one wonders what the reaction of University Librarian Ralph Hopp was to this petition. In any event, the Libraries did not name the collection after McDiarmid. But the resolution underscored the scion society's support for the collection and the desire for its continued growth. As the fiftieth anniversary of the Explorers notes, "the growth of the resources of the Library and the involvement of the Explorers are so intertwined as to be inseparable."[10]

THE JOHN BENNET SHAW COLLECTION

Eighteen months later, in the autumn of 1975, John Bennett Shaw was invited to deliver a department-sponsored lecture at the University.[11] Shaw's address, "The Cult of Sherlock Holmes," provided an upper-Midwest audience with a panoramic description of the Holmesian landscape. Towards the end of his presentation, Shaw made some library-related observations.

> I should mention the collections. You have here in your University Library the McDiarmid collection of Holmes material, which is quite good. There's a remarkable collection at the Metropolitan Central Library in Toronto. Originally, most of it belonged to Judge S. Tupper Bigelow, a Baker Street Irregular. I have what is probably the largest of all research collections, with ten or twelve thousand Holmes items. I have a room that was built just to house my collection, and I must report that it's almost full and I don't know what I'm going to do.[12]

One might imagine the number of bibliographic ears that perked up on hearing this last remark. It is not too difficult to believe that this marked the beginning of thought in more than a few minds to bring Shaw's collection to Minnesota.

Eight years later, in July 1983, Shaw was invited back to the University as part of a two-day conference focused on the dramatic side of Holmes. The event was co-sponsored by the University and the Norwegian Explorers and in a pre-conference press release the Sante Fe collector was described as "a witty and popular lecturer who owns what is thought to be the world's largest collection of Sherlock Holmes books, articles and artifacts."[13] Shaw's wit and popularity were evident in his lecture on the various theatrical and cinematic portrayals of the world's most famous consulting detective. A "live" portrayal–in the form of a simulated radio drama–was offered by Dave Moore and Don Shelby, both from the local CBS affiliate WCCO.

Radio presentations were an important aspect of this conference, and to accentuate that importance Edith Meiser was also invited to attend. From 1930 to 1943 Meiser had written, adapted (and in some instances augmented) Sherlockian cases for radio. Her broadcast scripts were acted out by the likes of Richard Gordon, Louis Hector, Reginald Fortune, Basil Rathbone, Nigel Bruce, John Stanley, Alfred Shirley, and William Gillette. Meiser, along with John Bennett Shaw, discussed "Adventures on the Air" as part of the proceedings. Andrew Malec, along with other members of the Special Collections staff, created an exhibit to complement the conference. Entitled "Molding the Image: William Gillette as Sherlock Holmes," the exhibit featured material from the Hench Collection.[14] It seems clear that the invitations to both Shaw and Meiser to participate in the conference were part of an ongoing desire to help them keep Minnesota in mind as each contemplated the disposition of their collections. This sense is confirmed in a letter sent by Austin McLean of Special Collections and E. W. McDiarmid to Dr. Willard Thompson, director of Summer Session at the University. McLean and McDiarmid wrote:

> Your support last July of the visit here by John Bennett Shaw, the eminent lecturer on Sherlock Holmes, has fostered a remarkable turn of events. He was very pleased with the large and appreciative audience for his public lecture in the Mayo Auditorium. He also had an opportunity to examine the Hench Collection of Sherlock Holmes in Special Collections of Wilson Library, which impressed him considerably, even though he holds the largest Sherlock Holmes collection in the world. Later he expressed interest in the possibility of Minnesota acquiring his collection after his death. We have nearly completed negotiations with him, and are seeking outside funding to be able eventually to obtain his collection.
>
> For this important reason, and to strengthen our good relations with him, we would like to invite him here again, for a public lecture, probably in July. At this time the Sherlock Holmes traveling exhibit, drawn from the Hench Collection and being designed and mounted by the University Gallery, will have here its first showing. We believe that Mr. Shaw would be a significant and popular attraction for the Summer Session . . .
>
> We would like to invite Ms. Meiser here also this summer, in July, to speak about the writing and broadcasting of the Sherlock Holmes stories.[15]

McLean and McDiarmid were setting the lines and marking the site for future Holmesian developments.

THE MARY KAHLER AND PHILIP S. HENCH COLLECTION

Four years after the arrival of the Iraldi Collection, the University Libraries acquired the Mary Kahler and Philip S. Hench Collection of

Sherlock Holmes and Arthur Conan Doyle in December 1978. In the late summer and early fall of 1979, the University Libraries and its Department of Special Collections and Rare Books celebrated the acquisition by means of an exhibit. At the exhibit opening on July 18, local CBS news anchor Don Shelby offered some remarks on "Holmes Today: An Investigative Reporter." Mr. Shelby would be instrumental in a later acquisition for the collection and in promoting financial contributions to support the collections. In the exhibit catalog, written by Andrew Malec, there is a description of the Hench Collection and the impetus behind its development that dates back to the doctor's activities in Switzerland. The description is worth quoting at length.

> Dr. Hench's interest in the Reichenbach project stimulated his collecting enterprise. Though he had assembled Doyle publications through the years, the bulk of the collection was acquired in the late 1950s and early 1960s. It consists of approximately eighteen hundred books, fifteen hundred issues of various periodicals, photographs, illustrations, manuscripts, and various sorts of memorabilia–all relating to Arthur Conan Doyle. The collection relates preponderantly to Sherlock Holmes, but Doyle's other works, particularly his non-Sherlockian fiction, are also well represented.
>
> Among the unique Holmesian items in the collection there are two pages from the original manuscript of *The Hound of the Baskervilles*. Mounted and framed with the pages is an original drawing by Frederic Dorr Steele (1874-1944) illustrating the scene described by Doyle. Steele is generally recognized as the best of the early American illustrators of the Sherlock Holmes tales. The collection holds eleven other original illustrations by Steele, as well as a great quantity of his correspondence relating to his Sherlockian art work.
>
> The career of William Gillette, especially his portrayal of the great detective, is well documented in the Hench collection, which includes letters, Gillette's own scrapbooks and his photograph album containing notable theatrical personalities of his day.
>
> The chief strength of the collection is its numerous editions of the Sherlock Holmes stories. The first British appearances of most of the tales are present in a complete run of *The Strand*, and many of

> the initial American publications are represented by such periodicals as *Harper's Weekly*, *Lippincott's*, and *Collier's*.
>
> Nearly a thousand books in the collection are first and other editions of the Holmes stories, including all British first editions and all but two of the American firsts. There are four copies of the very rare *Beeton's Christmas Annual*, 1887, containing the initial publication of *A Study in Scarlet*. Also, there are a great number of translations of the adventures, in such languages as Czech, Dutch, French, Gaelic, Danish, Greek, Italian, Turkish, and Japanese, showing that Holmes and Watson are truly international figures. . . .
>
> It was a notable achievement for Dr. Hench to assemble such a distinguished collection in such a short time, but he did not build it alone. Mrs. Hench was an active participant, and she gave her husband many of the most important items in the collection as gifts.[16]

While it was a notable achievement, it was not a new activity for the doctor and his wife. The Hench household had already engaged itself in building another world-class collection. Housed at the University of Virginia, "The Philip S. Hench Walter Reed Yellow Fever Collection is an extensive compilation of correspondence, notes, reports, printed materials, photographs, negatives, and artifacts spanning a period of almost one hundred years. This array of items occupies seventy-two linear feet of shelf space and 147 boxes in the Department of Historical Collections and Services, The Claude Moore Health Sciences Library, University of Virginia."[17] This collection, combined with the wealth of Doyle and Holmes materials at Minnesota, is testament to a truly amazing life.

GROWING A SHERLOCKIAN COLLECTION AND THE FREDERICK DORR STEELE ARTWORK

Conferences, exhibits, and publications continued as the main vehicles for promoting the growing Sherlockian collection at Minnesota and attracting new donors. September 1984 saw another conference, this one under the guise "The Adventures of Sherlock Holmes in Minnesota." Sponsored by the Norwegian Explorers, the Minneapolis Public Library, the St. Paul Public Library, the University of Minnesota, and the Libraries' Department of Special Collections and Rare Books, the conference featured over two dozen speakers. Once again, John Bennett Shaw was a participant and was joined by his wife, Dorothy. Her work–a miniature reproduction of Holmes' dwelling at 221B Baker Street–was on display during the conference. Australian architect Derham Groves, working to a much larger scale, offered his rendition and dreams for a future home for the collections–the Sherlock Holmes Centre. The ever resourceful Andrew Malec produced another exhibit and accompanying catalog entitled "The Other Master: Frederic Dorr Steele" as a part of the conference.[18] Malec noted that many of the exhibition items came from the Mary Kahler and Philip S. Hench Arthur Conan Doyle Collection, but he also noted a gratefulness "to the Steele family for the loan of a number of other valuable materials." Additional thanks were provided to other individuals and institutions for items donated or loaned for the exhibit. The ground was being laid for the next acquisition.

Nineteen eighty-five saw Holmes traveling through the upper-Midwest on another adventure. Curator of Special Collections Austin McLean, along with Malec and E. W. McDiarmid, helped plan, prepare, and promote a traveling exhibit of Sherlockian material. The enterprise, known on the road as "Investigating Sherlock Holmes," was organized by the Touring Exhibitions Program of the University of Minnesota's Art Museum and funded in part by the National Endowment for the Humanities (N.E.H.).[19] Items for the exhibit were drawn from the Hench Collection, with additional materials supplied by J. Randolph Cox and Malec from their private collections. Lyndel King, director of the Art Museum (now the Weisman Museum) and members of her staff were instrumental in making the exhibit a reality. Dr. C. Paul Martin, who would become the first president of the Norwegian Explorers (following their incorporation in 1986), viewed the exhibit at Southwest State University in Marshall, Minnesota. Other venues for the exhibit included: the Minnesota Valley Regional Library, Mankato State University, Jackson County Library, Dacatah Prairie Museum, Duluth Public Schools, North Branch Area Library, Grand Rapids Public Library, LaCrosse Public Library, Bemidji Community Art Center, Wabasha Public Library, Rochester Public Library, Northland Community College, and the Owatonna Arts Center. According to the final report sent to the N.E.H., "Investigating Sherlock Holmes" toured from May 1985 through December 1988 to a total of 18 sites throughout Minnesota and to 2 sites in neighboring states (Aberdeen, South Dakota and

LaCrosse, Wisconsin), reaching a total of 63,785 viewers during that period.[20] While the final report mentioned a number of benefits that accrued to both the University Art Museum and the Libraries, for our purposes here we must quote the most notable gains for the collections:

> *Investigating Sherlock Holmes* has contributed to the growth and fortification of Holmes materials held by Special Collections. The son and daughter of illustrator Frederick Dorr Steele, who attended a Holmes conference at the University in 1984, subsequently donated their father's artwork to the collection because they were impressed with the visibility the materials would receive here. John Bennett Shaw, who holds the largest private collection of Holmes materials, has chosen Special Collections and Rare Books as the repository for his collection, a gift that will greatly expand the depth and scope of these materials. He is periodically sending materials now, with the remainder to come here after his death. And another major collection, the holdings of the late Vincent Starrett, the pre-eminent American Sherlockian scholar, have [sic] been donated to the collection.[21]

The Steele Collection arrived in 1986, a gift from the artist's children. In March of that year, a letter from one of Steele's daughters had arrived on Andrew Malec's desk in Wilson Library. The letter immediately caught his attention.

> The reason for this letter, Andy, is that I feel a responsibility toward preservation of what I have here of F.D.S. letters, etc. . . . So, Andy, I have been remembering the care showed by you and the Library to preserve every scrap of Sherlockiana, and I'm wondering if that is not the place for this 'treasure trove'. . . We all three took great pleasure in the fine job you made of your F.D.S. booklet, which elicits nothing but praise from friends and family. Also we appreciated the rare combination of tact and enthusiasm you have shown in dealing with us in the family.
>
> Besides, not to be too solemn about all this–we enjoy and marvel at your letters!
>
> So, Andy, coming at last to the point of this letter: would you like to have these relics? No strings attached![22]

Malec, in a reply to Steele's daughter, said: "As you can imagine, I have been most excited since I read your letter of March 17th . . ."[23] Meanwhile, Austin McLean informed the Libraries' head of collections about the prospective gift and requested travel expenses to allow Malec to visit Steele's daughter. The visit occurred in early May and by the end of the month McLean was writing the family a letter of thanks for the gift that had been delivered to Minneapolis. During the annual birthday festivities in New York the following January, members of the Baker Street Irregulars (BSI) and the Adventuresses of Sherlock Holmes (ASH) received a pleasant little book.[24] The extended brochure, by Malec, was a celebration of the collection. "This brochure has been published in recognition of the establishment of the Frederic Dorr Steele Memorial Collection in the University of Minnesota Libraries, given by Mrs. Anne Steele Marsh, Mrs. Zulma Steele Grey, and Mr. Robert G. Steele. One thousand copies printed, of which 325 are presented to the Baker Street Irregulars and the Adventuresses of Sherlock Holmes, on 9 January 1987, by John Bennett Shaw, BSI, Senior Fellow, University of Minnesota."[25]

THE EDITH MEISER COLLECTION

Additional goodwill came to the Libraries with the purchase of the Edith Meiser Collection in 1987. Four years earlier, while Special Collections was working with Shaw on the details for his collection, McLean and McDiarmid reported the following to Thompson:

> Our negotiations for the Shaw collection have been agreeably complicated by the prospect of acquiring yet another important Sherlock Holmes collection. Edith Meiser, though known mainly for her acting career, also wrote the radio scripts for the Sherlock Holmes stories that began to be broadcast in the 1930s. Her collection of original scripts, tapes, and other material is unique. The Meiser collection is being sought by private collectors and institutions, but Ms. Meiser insists that her collection shall go to the institution that acquires the Shaw collection.[26]

Thus, with the collection development site lines firmly established and the foundation securely laid, the Libraries and Shaw continued the win-win proposition of library building. Special Collections enlisted the willing help of Shaw in acquiring the Meiser records. An inventory of the collection was received from New York and passed on to Santa Fe. Shaw responded that the

> . . . listing of the Meiser holdings arrived yesterday. I spent some time then and more today on it and there are some things over which I drool–such as unpublished Holmes Play, Vaudeville script and some of the records. Damn, I hope you get it all . . . It would be fun getting these things so they could be properly listed by De Waal and the shows heard by Sherlockians on cassettes. And with Hench and Shaw this would cover another area which we have not too much. I wish you luck.[27]

Two years later, Special Collections was still working on bringing Meiser's dramatic material to the Midwest. Shaw wrote to encourage the effort.

> I do hope we can continue to work with Ms. Edith Meiser for securing her marvelous radio-Holmesian collection. The letter she sent you just recently is, I think, a break-through. I would like to talk with you about it before I leave for New York–early in the morning of January 8th. Of course I will talk to her about it and if you give me some concrete thoughts I will pass them on.[28]

The breakthrough took another two years to achieve, but was well worth the wait.

THE VINCENT STARRETT COLLECTION

The following year, 1988, saw the arrival of Vincent Starrett's collection to Minnesota. The relationship between Starrett and Minnesota goes back to at least the founding of the Norwegian Explorers in 1948. In April 1948, Starrett wrote to Dr. Stanley Pargellis at the Newberry Library:

> Last February you wrote me about a Minneapolis chapter of the B.S.I. (The Norwegian Explorers) who wanted us to visit them and speak to them. I didn't reply because (a) I was busy, and (b) didn't see how under the sun I could get up to Minneapolis anyway. This is still my fix, but your letter has been lying around reproaching me for weeks. Please thank McDiarmid and express my regrets, if you will.

As with Starrett himself, there was some question on whether or not his collection would ever come to the Twin Cities. More than a little convincing and argument was needed with library administrators before the purchase was approved. And, as with the Meiser Collection, John Bennett Shaw took an active role.

In the Spring of 1986, McLean wrote to Michael Murphy, the literary executor of the Starrett estate.

> Yesterday I was talking with John Bennett Shaw and he suggested that I write you about Sherlockian activities at the University of Minnesota, and send you several of our recent publications, including the one on the proposed Sherlock Holmes Centre. . . . Last week Zulma Steele Grey offered to donate her large collection of letters, drawings, etc. of her father, Frederick Dorr Steele. And as you probably know, the great library of John Bennett Shaw eventually will come to Minnesota. I believe that you are looking for a home for the Vincent Starrett Collection. Please consider the University of Minnesota as a possible institution.[29]

Unfortunately, Murphy died before the transaction could be consummated, but his widow was still keen on keeping the collection intact and selling it to an institution. McLean, as part of his lobbying the library administration, informed the head of the Collections Division that a Boston dealer was acting as agent in the sale and was

> . . . offering it to us [Minnesota] first, because we have the leading Sherlockian resources in America. I don't know whether people in Chicago know about the availability of the Starrett collection, but I expect that Newberry, U. of Chicago, or some other place would snap it up. . . . This is an extremely important collection for Minnesot[a]. We must get it, somehow.[30]

Administrative responses were not encouraging.

> It is fair to say that none of us is enthusiastic about it. . . . I have several basic problems with the proposal. There is the purely tactical matter of paying for such a collection. . . . More fundamentally than these tactical issues, however, I simply do not see the importance of this collection for the University Libraries. . . . I would encourage you, instead, to turn your collection development attention to other, more programmatically central areas.[31]

McLean fought on. He followed with a second memo to the head of collections that outlined the acquisitions history of the Holmes collections, beginning with the Hench Collection. "The Hench Collection has drawn to it a number of notable gifts, and some purchases have been made."[32] After describing the importance and wealth of the Hench Collection, he moved to Shaw. "The main reason he [Shaw] was interested in Minnesota was the Hench Collection–it holding extremely rare books or unique material that he could never possess."[33] From Shaw he moved to Steele and Meiser, the heat of his argument affecting his typing skills. "This year were [sic] have acquired to [sic] very important collections. The family of Frederic Dorr Steele–the famous American illustrator–gave their material here. . . . The other collection is on its way here from NYC. It is the scripts and broadcast recordings made by Edith Meiser . . ."[34] Having outlined the collections, McLean shifted his argument to those who used the collections, in essence bringing up the heavy artillery of well-known researchers and published authors to pound home the point. He capped off this portion of the lobbying campaign by mentioning the successful traveling exhibition and his proposed means of purchasing the collection. Still, the head of collections was not convinced. "Even if we wanted his collection–and I am not sure we do–it seems to me beyond our means."[35] But there were two signs for hope. First, Shaw was willing to defer payment on his collection. And, second, the director of the Humanities/Social Science Libraries at the University would be consulted. His response, given certain conditions on price and fund-raising, was that "we may be able to do it."[36] By April McLean had convinced library administrators on the importance and value of the collection; the purchase was approved.[37]

THE HOWARD HAYCRAFT COLLECTION

The acquisition of the Howard Haycraft Collection in 1992 encompasses nearly the entire history and development of the Sherlock Holmes Collections and predates–in terms of the relationship between Haycraft and the University–the purchase of the Iraldi Collection which marked the formal beginning of the collections. Haycraft, a 1928 graduate of the University of Minnesota, informed University Librarian E. B. Stanford in early 1971 of his "interest in exploring arrangements to place my collection of mystery and detective fiction in a university library where it would be properly housed and used for study and research in the future."[38] Stanford, who was soon to be on leave, turned the matter over to McLean in Special Collections. McLean corresponded with Haycraft within weeks and suggested a visit to Haycraft in New York. By March McLean was thanking Haycraft for the wonderful visit, lunch at the Players Club, and a chance to view the collection. At the same time, McLean offered a number of helpful suggestions to Haycraft on how a will or other formal agreement might be written as it pertained to the donation of the collection. Mention was also made that "because of the strength of our holdings in related fields encompassed by the Hess Collection, we are very much interested in developing an equally important collection in mystery literature."[39] Within another two weeks, Haycraft responded with "many thanks for your prompt and helpful letter . . . a copy of which I have sent to our attorney for guidance in drawing my new will."[40] Haycraft also provided the name and address of his legal firm, along with that of the attorney handling his will "for your files." Howard Haycraft died on November 12, 1991. The following August the University's office of general counsel communicated the terms of the will to McLean and the Libraries. Besides books, periodicals, and papers, the bequest included $2,000 for the preservation and maintenance of the collection.

THE JOHN BENNETT SHAW COLLECTION

The activities and interests of John Bennett Shaw and his world-famous collection are interwoven into this entire narrative and it is appropriate that we end with a few additional anecdotes of a Shavian nature.[41] In 1982, Bryce Crawford, now a professor and using the letterhead of the Molecular Spectroscopy Laboratory at Minnesota, wrote to McDiarmid about the future of the Shaw collection. The letter is a wonderful testament to the ongoing relationship between the University and the Norwegian Explorers (with Crawford as a founding member).

> The points raised by John Bennett Shaw do indeed catch my interest, and perhaps even excitement. I believe that our follow-up should be reasonably prompt. By that I don't mean we should fall all over ourselves, but that we should proceed to indicate to John that the possible ultimate marriage of his collection with ours is very appealing to us: and that we would like to explore this possibility further. To this end I think it is rather important that someone toddle down to New Mexico to spend a day with John and to discuss possibilities and potential and appropriate provision of a pro-

> gram which would lead comfortably to this end. If you yourself cannot go down this fall, I would urge you and Austin to use some of our funds to send Austin down to New Mexico on this mission of developing further understanding with John Bennett Shaw.
>
> To me the object now is to present to Shaw the idea–as persuasively and convincingly as possible–that his valuable and beloved collection would indeed be well placed with us; that it would be looked after by a responsible institution with knowledgeable and responsible officers in charge of such special collections; and that the net result would be the formation of the unquestioned first and greatest collection of its kind, in an institution where it would receive proper care, with appropriate access provided for scholarly work. Austin is the university library officer in charge of special collections, and a very impressive individual in that capacity, clearly knowledgeable about book matters and special collection matters, and by no means a neophyte with regard to the peculiarities of Holmesiana. . . .
>
> So I urge that this be done. I don't think an airplane ticket for Austin would be too expensive . . . In fact I'd rather like to go along and join him myself; as you know I love that southwest country. But I don't think I would add anything in terms of the purpose of such a visit.[42]

McLean made the trip towards the end of the year and it paid dividends. In a post-Christmas note Shaw said that "I lean even more to Minnesota for eventual depository for the collection but am boggled at how to do it–appraisal, terms, and so on."[43] By the time of the Holmesian birthday festivities in January, Shaw was busy talking to anyone with the expertise on how to make the thing happen. On his return from New York, Shaw reported that

> I have spent much time thinking and talking about the possible future at Minnesota for my beloved library. . . . I have talked about the matter some with Mr. Hollyer at the Toronto Library, with my long-time friend and [t]ax [a]dvisor, and with my lawyer. . . . Before I go on with thoughts about this let me recount a most interesting talk I had. I lunched with Edith Meiser who has the wonderful bunch of things she did for Radio–scripts, discs and so on. She ran into a problem with giving it (to an isolated Western University) as

> a tax break. I suggested that she sell it to Minnesota. . . . Then she stunned me by saying she felt her collection should go when mine went, and to the same place.
>
> So I am serious about the matter. What I want and you must help formalize this idea, is that after my death [the] University of Minnesota takes possession of the entire Holmes collection . . . [44]

The correspondence and the visits between New Mexico and Minnesota continued. A decade later, in the fall of 1993, Shaw wrote to University Librarian Thomas Shaughnessy about the state of affairs.

> As you know I have been collaborating with the Library's Special Collections and Mr. Austin McLean for more than a decade on The Sherlock Holmes–A. Conan Doyle Collection. And as I am certain that you know I entered into an agreement with The University, dated 14 February 1983, that my Holmes-Doyle library would be transferred to the University upon the occasion of my death.
>
> However, due to the fact that on 10 October this year I will become 80 and as my wife and I plan to move into a small house/apartment I would like assent from you that I transfer my library to The University according to the terms of the 1983 agreement but while I am living.[45]

Shaughnessy agreed to the change and the transfer occurred. On an early November morning library personnel unloaded the moving van with its ten tons of books, periodicals, memorabilia, puzzles, pipes, and memories. A year later, on October 2, 1994, Shaw died. The University of Minnesota Libraries formally dedicated the collection the following autumn.

CONCLUSION: THE ADVENTURE CONTINUES

This, in essence, is still a bare-bones account of the acquisitions history of the Sherlock Holmes Collections at the University of Minnesota Libraries. The adventure of the unopened box does not end with the arrival of the Shaw materials. Collections large and small still arrive. Recent accessions include the David Hammer papers and Eve Titus manuscripts.

A very supportive Friends group has been formed and its quarterly newsletter highlights items from the collections and trumpets new arrivals. A development campaign is now underway to create an endowed curatorship, named in honor of McDiarmid. And the box has been opened. In December 2002, the Library completed a three-year cataloging project funded in part by a generous gift from the Hubbs family. Over 15,000 book and serial titles are now available through the University's online catalog. But mysteries still remain. The large volume of audio-visual materials and personal papers remain to be cataloged. Holmes himself would be pleased with the collection's growth and its increased access and use. But he would also urge us on. As he remarked in the case of "The Illustrious Client," "I am accustomed to have mystery at one end of my cases, but to have it at both ends is too confusing."[46]

ENDNOTES

1. Committee members were: Peter E. Blau (Washington, DC), Joseph B. Connors (Minneapolis, MN), Pj Doyle (Minneapolis, MN), Richard Lancelyn Green (London, England), David Hammer (Dubuque, IA), Cameron Hollyer (Scarborough, Ontario), Jon L. Lellenberg (Washington, DC), E. W. McDiarmid (St. Paul, MN), Austin J. McLean (Minneapolis, MN), Jennie C. Paton (Statesboro, GA), John Bennett Shaw (Santa Fe, NM), Doris Skalstad (Minneapolis, MN), R. Dixon Smith (St. Paul, MN), Thomas L. Stix (Norwood, NJ).

2. "A Long-Range Plan for the Sherlock Holmes Collection, University of Minnesota," April 12, 1993, p. 1.

3. Michael Hardwick, *The Complete Guide to Sherlock Holmes* (New York: St. Martin's Press, 1986), 87.

4. Although used interchangeably, "Holmesian" is more commonly employed in the U.K., Commonwealth countries, and Europe whereas "Sherlockian" is a particularly American description. But anyone "playing the game" gladly embraces both terms.

5. The five were: Wallace Armstrong (Physiological Chemistry), Theodore C. Blegen (Dean of the Graduate School), Bryce L. Crawford (Chemistry), Errett Weir McDiarmid (University Librarian), and E. W. Ziebarth (Speech).

6. Blegen was an historian with an interest in Norway and immigration from that country. He was an active and instrumental member of the Norwegian American Historical Association, so the mystery surrounding the name of the scion society may be solved if Blegen's interests and activities are considered.

7. In Julie McKuras and Richard J. Sveum, M.D., *The History of the Norwegian Explorers* (Minneapolis: The Norwegian Explorers, 1998), 6.

8. McKuras and Sveum, 15.

9. McKuras and Sveum, 15-16.

10. *Ibid.*, 16.

11. Shaw, by then residing in Santa Fe, New Mexico, was one of the most recognized and respected Sherlockians in the world. If some collector had any doubts on the disposition of any item, Shaw put them at ease with his advice: "Don't throw it away. Send it to me." His collection included any possible manifestation of the Sherlockian image, from carved bars of soap and jigsaw puzzles to rare first editions.

12. John Bennett Shaw, "The Cult of Sherlock Holmes," in Bryce L. Crawford, Jr. and Joseph B. Connors, eds. *Cultivating Sherlock Holmes* (LaCrosse, WI: Sumac Press, 1978), 25.

13. McKuras and Sveum, 18.

14. The exhibit catalog may be viewed at http://special.lib.umn.edu/rare/wg.pdf.

15. Austin A. McLean and E. W. McDiarmid to Dr. Willard Thompson, March 8, 1983.

16. Andrew S. Malec, *Arthur Conan Doyle: An Exhibit from the Mary Kahler and Philip S. Hench Collection, July 18-September 30, 1979* (Minneapolis: University of Minnesota Libraries, Department of Special Collections and Rare Books, 1979), 8-12. The Malec catalog may be viewed online at http://special.lib.umn.edu/rare/acd.pdf. As of December 2002, the Collections include stories in seventy-one languages.

17. For more information on the Hench Yellow Fever Collection, go to the collection Web site at http://yellowfever.lib.virginia.edu/reed/.

18. Andrew Malec. *The Other Master: Frederic Dorr Steele* (Minneapolis: Special Collections, O. Meredith Wilson Library, University of Minnesota, 1984). The catalog may be viewed online at http://special.lib.umn.edu/rare/fds2.pdf.

19. Andrew Malec, *Investigating Sherlock Holmes* (Minneapolis: University Art Museum, 1985). The booklet may be viewed online at http://special.lib.umn.edu/rare/inv.pdf.

20. "Final Performance Report, Investigating Sherlock Holmes: A Touring Exhibition," 3.

21. *Ibid.*

22. Zulma S. Grey to Andrew Malec, March 17, 1986.

23. Andrew Malec to Zulma Steele Grey, April 2, 1986.

24. It is widely held, by those playing "the Game," that Holmes is still alive and keeping bees in Sussex, thus his birthday on January 6 is a time for high celebration. Holmes longevity is attributed, in part, to the fact that no obituary has ever appeared in *The Times*, and thus there is no need to celebrate a death–only a birthday will do.

25. Andrew Malec, *The Frederic Dorr Steele Memorial Collection* (Minneapolis: Special Collections and Rare Books, University of Minnesota Libraries, 1987).

26. Austin A. McLean and E. W. McDiarmid to Dr. Willard Thompson, March 8, 1983.

27. John Bennett Shaw to Austin McLean, November 1, 1983. De Waal refers to Ronald B. De Waal, a librarian who, since the early 1970s, had been busy creating Sherlockian bibliographies. His work includes *The World Bibliography of Sherlock Holmes and Dr. Watson* (1974), *The International Sherlock Holmes* (1980), and *The Universal Sherlock Holmes* (1994).

28. John Bennett Shaw to Austin McLean, December 30, 1985.

29. Austin J. McLean to Michael Murphy, April 1, 1986.

30. Memo from Austin McLean to Frank Immler, December 11, 1986.

31. Memo from Frank Immler to Austin McLean, December 18, 1986.

32. Memo from Austin McLean to Frank Immler, December 23, 1986.

33. *Ibid.*

34. *Ibid.*

35. Memo from Frank Immler to Austin McLean, January 6, 1987.

36. Memo from Joe Branin to Austin McLean, March 16, 1987.

37. Lest we leave the wrong impression, there are collections that have "gotten away." One of the most recent examples is that of a very significant collection of Doyleana which has found its way to the Newberry Library. The donor, a professor of cardiovascular and thoracic surgery at Rush Medical College, was repeatedly approached by Minnesota, but the pull and attractiveness of the world-renowned Chicago institution was just too much. Happily, the donor and Minnesota remain on friendly terms.

38. E. B. Stanford to Howard Haycraft, January 25, 1971.

39. Austin J. McLean to Howard Haycraft, March 4, 1971. The Hess Collection–part of the Children's Literature Research Collection at Minnesota–includes story papers, dime novels, series books, Big Little Books, pulps, and comic books from the 19th and 20th centuries. At this point, both McLean and Stanford were thinking of the Haycraft materials in relation to existing children's literature and book illustration collections held by the University Libraries.

40. Howard Haycraft to Austin J. McLean, March 15, 1971.

41. A depiction of events surrounding the acquisition of the John Bennett Shaw Collection would most likely require an entirely separate article. Given the restraints and the previous mention of Shaw we trust that the reader will excuse the paucity of information at this point.

42. Bryce Crawford, Jr. to E. W. McDiarmid, October 5, 1982.

43. John Bennett Shaw to Austin McLean, December 27, 1982.

44. John Bennett Shaw to Austin McLean, January 20, 1983.

45. John Bennett Shaw to Thomas W. Shaughnessy, September 22, 1993.

46. Hardwick, *The Complete Guide to Sherlock Holmes*, 194.

Mysteries in a Law Library: The Law in Popular Culture Collection at the University of Texas School of Law

Marlyn Robinson
Rhonda Hankins

SUMMARY. The Law in Popular Culture Collection (LPOP) at the Jamail Center for Legal Research at the University of Texas at Austin houses some 4,000 works of fiction, most of them legal mysteries, and over 600 movies that have an association with the law or lawyers. The LPOP collection includes works of high and low culture and offers unique insights into the public's perception of the lawyer as well as the lawyer's perception of the public and the legal system. This article, an interview with the originator and curator of the LPOP collection, discusses the beginnings of the collection, the philosophy of the collection, and the practicalities of maintaining the collection. *[Article copies available for a fee from The Haworth Document Delivery Service: 1-800-HAWORTH. E-mail address: <docdelivery@haworthpress.com> Website: <http://www.HaworthPress.com> © 2004 by The Haworth Press, Inc. All rights reserved.]*

Marlyn Robinson, BA, MSLIS, is Reference Librarian, Tarlton Law Library, University of Texas School of Law, 727 East Dean Keeton Street, Austin, TX 78705. She created and now maintains the Law in Popular Culture Collection. Rhonda Hankins, BA, MIS, is Senior Administrative Associate, Tarlton Law Library, University of Texas School of Law, and a master's candidate at the University of Texas Graduate School of Information.

[Haworth co-indexing entry note]: "Mysteries in a Law Library: The Law in Popular Culture Collection at the University of Texas School of Law." Robinson, Marlyn, and Rhonda Hankins. Co-published simultaneously in *Collection Management* (The Haworth Information Press, an imprint of The Haworth Press, Inc.) Vol. 29, No. 3/4, 2004, pp. 143-160; and: *Managing the Mystery Collection: From Creation to Consumption* (ed: Judith Overmier, and Rhonda Harris Taylor) The Haworth Information Press, an imprint of The Haworth Press, Inc., 2004, pp. 143-160. Single or multiple copies of this article are available for a fee from The Haworth Document Delivery Service [1-800-HAWORTH, 9:00 a.m. - 5:00 p.m. (EST). E-mail address: docdelivery@haworthpress.com].

Available online at http://www.haworthpress.com/web/COL

doi:10.1300/J105v29n03_11

KEYWORDS. Mystery, thriller, legal, law, Jamail Center, Tarlton Law Library, LPOP, Law in Popular Culture

November 4, 1937

Mr. Ira P. Hildebrand
Law B. 106

Dear Judge Hildebrand:

A week or so ago the General Library furnished the Law Library with a small collection of popular books as a service being furnished to branch libraries of The University system for popular reading for students making more use of those branches than of the Main Building. Through Miss Hargrave I learned that you found some objections to this material and that it has been returned. I am sorry that our selection was unsatisfactory.

The whole scheme has been framed on the assumption that students do not spend their time exclusively in reading textbooks and assignments and that, if the University Library does not make some small effort to supply them with reading material of a popular and interesting character, they will read the movie magazines, *True Confession*, and other low grade literature of this sort.

It may well be that we have miscalculated the reading interests of Law students and I shall be very glad to buy from General Library funds fifteen or twenty volumes selected by the Law School as a substitute for those we had first sent to you. I shall be glad to know your reaction to this proposal.

Yours very truly

Donald Coney
Librarian

***

November 5, 1937

Mr. Donald Coney
Librarian
University of Texas
Austin, Texas

My dear Mr. Coney:

Thanks to you for thinking of the Law Library when you decided to furnish small collections of books to the department libraries of the University. For 30 years I have tried to impress on our students that their law work should consume every moment of the time while they are in the Law School. For this reason, I do not want any attractive books to lead them astray "from the beaten path." For this reason I think attractive reading books should not be placed in the Law Library. The law faculty meets the first Thursday in each month and I will present this matter to our faculty at our next meeting and write you again. If the other members of the faculty think I am incorrect in my conclusion, I will be glad to inform you to that effect.

Yours very sincerely,
Ira Hildebrand
Dean, Law School

TIMES CHANGE

The Tarlton Law Library at the University of Texas School of Law now has "attractive books" in an attractive setting and students describe it as a favorite place in the Law School. From its beginnings as a small part of a light reading collection to its position as a highly-respected scholarly resource, the Law in Popular Culture Collection has grown to provide a realistic portrait of the image of the lawyer over several centuries and several continents. Rhonda Hankins, master's candidate at the University's School of Information Science, asks co-worker Marlyn Robinson, the collection's creator, how it all came about.

RH: First, give us a quick and dirty overview of the collection.

MR: The collection consists of works of fiction in all genres, as well as humor, plays, comics, and feature film and television series videos. The primary criteria for inclusion are that it must either have a lawyer as a central character or have been written by a lawyer. In this way, the collection reveals both the public's perception of the lawyer as well as the lawyer's perception of the public and the legal system. As you might guess, courtroom dramas and legal thrillers predominate, but there are also many works in which the practice of law has little or nothing to do with the plot. No judgments are made as to quality and works of both high and low culture are included. There are novels by Dickens and Shakespeare, Max Brand and Mary Higgins Clark; videos range from *Anatomy of a Murder* and *Witness for the Prosecution* to *Body of Evidence* and *Cowboy Counsellor*. Not only are these films and books used in the classroom, for scholarly research, and for pleasure, but they also provide an opportunity for members of the legal profession to understand how others see them. There are now approximately 4,200 volumes and 650 movie titles in the collection.

RH: What is the significance of this collection?

MR: This collection is unique. There is a tradition among law libraries to have works on law and literature, emphasizing the works of Shakespeare, Scott, Trollope, and other so-called literary authors. There was a good deal of interest among practitioners and professors around the turn of the last century, with a number of publications on the subject.[1] In 1921, John Wigmore published his definitive "One Hundred Legal Novels" in the *Illinois Law Review*. He compiled the list because "it is certain that the lawyer must, like other men, for his pastime and mental ease, abandon himself now and then to the thrall of fiction. He will not read all the novels–even all the good ones; he will probably not read many. He must select. Let him, then, select those which will mean something to him as a lawyer, will have a special interest for one of that elect profession with all its traditions, its memories, its secrets of the craft."[2] He believed that "the novel–the true work of fiction–is a catalogue of life's characters. And the lawyer must know human nature. He must deal understandingly with its types, its motives. These he cannot find–all of them–close around him; life is not long enough, the range is not broad enough for him to learn them by personal experience before he needs to use them. For this learning, then, he must go to fiction, which is the gallery of life's portraits."[3] Law libraries used this list as a guide for buying law-related fiction and some took Wigmore's advice that contemporary works should be included as well as the classics. The 1953 New York University catalog of the law collection includes *The Law and Lawyers of Pickwick* (1894) and the 1944 thriller *Leave Her to Heaven*. The law and literature movement lost momentum and then died out for many years until it was resurrected in the mid-1980s by Richard Weisberg,[4] law professor at Yeshiva University in New York City. Soon after, the huge successes of Scott Turow and John Grisham convinced publishers that the lawyer novel was once again a profit center and the trade market skyrocketed. Since *The Firm* was published in 1991, there have been around 200 legal novels, mostly legal thrillers, released per year. Although academic law libraries can be counted on to have classics like *To Kill a Mockingbird* or *Anatomy of a Murder*, only a few buy modern fiction and even then, few titles are purchased. In contrast, approximately one-third of the American Bar Association-approved schools have movies in their libraries. But none of them house books and movies together and absolutely no one has made an effort to collect on the scale that we have. Ours is a one-stop shop for any scholar who wants to research either the lawyer/author or the image of the lawyer in film, classic literature, modern novels, legal humor, drama, or poetry.

RH: What inspired you to start this collection? When? How did you present this idea to management? What arguments do you think were the most persuasive?

MR: What inspired me? Dorothy's ruby slippers. Seriously, I first clicked with popular culture studies when I learned that the red shoes used in MGM's *The Wizard of Oz* were deemed culturally significant enough to be on display in the Smithsonian Museum of American History. My academic background is in history, and those studies traversed the time periods when history was taught strictly as a political subject and later as a culturally personal subject–from kings, wars, and governments to architecture, folklore, entertainment, food, religion, clothing, and lifestyle; in other words, from the mighty to the mundane, but equally relevant.

The collection previously existed as parts of two discrete collections in the Library. We had a Popular Reading Room which housed law-related mysteries, general novels, and other light reading and the Media Collection, which included all our microforms and videos, as well as a small but growing number of law-related feature films. The mystery collection came about partly due to the interests of the late Professor Charles Alan Wright, one of the country's foremost authorities in constitutional law and a member of our faculty for over forty years. He was very fond of legal mysteries, reviewed them in *The Practical Lawyer*, and the Library purchased those he recommended. He was a stickler for accuracy, e.g., once pointing out that the light coming from a window in the Old Bailey could not have crossed the defendant's face since the real window was on the other side of the room. The Library's current director, Roy Mersky, also enjoys mysteries, and so, by the time I started working here in 1986, the library already owned several hundred titles. I took over the work of adding to that collection both because I did most of the trade and university press book selection and because I was a long-time mystery reader.

At that time, it was something of an academic library "sin" to house two radically different formats together. But, several years later, when the director suggested that we might move the law-related novels from the overflowing Popular Reading Room to the room formerly inhabited by a computer lab, I began to lobby for a special collection on law and popular culture, combining the books and videos. It took nearly a year to convince management that this would be beneficial to the library, mostly because there were other potential uses for that space. I argued that this collection would make our library unique, that the placement of the room was perfect (a potentially very attractive and very visible component of our main floor), and that it would be economically advantageous–*i.e.*, provide national exposure, give our students a sense that we cared about them, and it would be inexpensive to maintain.

Coincidentally, the Association of American Law Schools had scheduled their midwinter meeting in January 1992 in San Antonio, a mere one hundred miles from here. By then we had a nice little collection of around 125 movies, and Mr. Mersky decided that we should have a mini-conference on the lawyer and popular culture as a sort of post-AALL dessert. We quickly put together a two-day event. Dr. Ray Browne, founder of the popular culture movement, was our keynote speaker, and panelists' topics ranged among Perry Mason's influence on Italian courtroom architecture, white-slave-trade movies, law in 1930s westerns and Gilbert and Sullivan operettas (with musical accompaniment), and a slide show of legal film posters. The turnout and enthusiasm was such that Mr. Mersky realized that it would be worth our time and effort to create a truly outstanding new feature for the library. In 1993, we moved the relevant books from the Popular Reading

Room and feature films from Media into their new space on our main floor.

RH: How on earth did you begin to assemble this collection? At that time, were there any other such collections that you used as a model for this one?

MR: We already had a collection of around 1,000 law-related novels and one hundred-plus movies, most of which had been acquired since the late 1980s, so there was a base on which to build. However, the concept of combining the study of law with popular culture was absolutely new ground. Popular culture itself was still a relatively new academic discipline[5] and there had been only a few publications on its connection to law.[6] If in the late 1980s the subject was considered off-the-wall to general academics, it was considered even more far-fetched and useless to the pedagogically conservative law faculty around the country. If not for the imaginative thinking of Mr. Mersky, who could see its potential and trusted my judgment, this collection would not exist. Most of my several decades of library experience had been spent in special collections of one sort or another and now I had to think of this simply as another special collection, apply those general principles, and more or less make up the rules for what should go in it.

RH: How much is this collection used? What is its percentage of the Library's circulation? What constituencies use this collection the most? What videos get checked out the most? Who are the most popular authors?

MR: Last fiscal year (9/01-8/02) 2,200 items were checked out, representing approximately eight percent of the Library's total circulation. That number contrasts dramatically with the cost, which is miniscule. LPOP (the official RLIN location id) materials cost .04% of the book and serials budget for that time period, a slight increase from previous years because additional funds were allotted for the first acquisitions of DVDs. The movies circulate far more than the books because our largest constituency is law students. They are looking for a quick study break and seldom have the time and energy for even light reading when they are required to read hundreds of pages for class each day. The top video "renter"–no surprise–is *The Paper Chase* (390 check-outs to date), followed by *My Cousin Vinny*, *A Fish Called Wanda*, *The Godfather I & II*, *True Colors*, *All the President's Men*, and *Bonfire of the*

Vanities, all of which have had more than 150 check-outs. University staff members are the biggest users of the book collection. In this case, best-selling authors are best-circulating authors: John Grisham, Scott Turow, and Patricia Cornwell among the Americans, John Mortimer and Anne Perry among the English.

RH: Any in-house opposition to your getting a slice of the budget pie? How much did you get? Has that percentage increased, decreased, or remained the same over the years?

MR: The LPOP collection takes such a minute percentage of the annual budget that staff and faculty opposition does not arise. It is also a given that when budget dollars are low those purchases come to a screeching halt, to be picked up at a later time when we are little more flush. The annual expenditure has averaged around $4,000, with lows of $2,000, and highs of $6,000. We have spent less in the past few years because we no longer make major expenditures for out-of-print items, but that is primarily due to lack of expansion space.

RH: What percentage of your time at work is devoted to maintaining this collection?

MR: Probably fifty percent if I count the time I spend doing something else as well. I do some of the Web work during slow times at the reference desk. I select LPOP titles from some of the same review sources I select university or trade titles from, another task also done while I'm at the reference desk so it's multi-layered multi-tasking. However, working on the collection always takes a backseat to reference questions, research for faculty, or special projects.

RH: What were your original collection goals? Your collection development policy and selection criteria?

MR: "The average American's understanding of our legal system is both reflected and shaped by our popular culture. Best sellers, movie theaters, and prime time television have long been inundated with images of lawyers, whether as savior-like heroes, despicable villains, or complex human beings. The goal of this collection is to provide as broad a picture as possible of the image of the lawyer in the United States and British Commonwealth." This is the opening statement of the current collection development policy. It was worked out over several years' time, with minor and major changes.

The first amendment to the original, unwritten, and unfocused policy established a geographic boundary. I decided to limit the materials to those arising from the British and United States common law tradition. There was no particular reason for that other than that it made sense to limit it to our own curricula.

The second one was actually a matter of circulation policy. While part of the Media Collection, the films were under lock and key, did not circulate, and could be viewed only in the Media Room. Knowing that usage would increase enormously, I successfully argued that we had to let them circulate because otherwise we could be in violation of copyright. The videos are "home use only" and restricting usage to a public space could be interpreted as an illegal practice. They now circulate but only to law school students, staff, faculty, or other University faculty so that wear and tear is kept to a minimum.

The first major change was to limit the collection to materials depicting the lawyer, as opposed to law in general. That is to say, this would be a "lawyer in popular culture," not "law in popular culture" collection. In the first place, lawyers (and law faculty) see law in everything. We could potentially be subject to faculty whim requiring us to buy any novel or film about murder, divorce, tax, landlord/tenant disputes, or fishing rights and we would clearly be setting ourselves up to run into problems justifying the use of library funds. Some of the early purchases, when it was a "law in popular culture" collection, reflected this lack of focus; e.g., the Marx Brothers *The Cocoanuts*, which is about Florida land scams. Secondly, at that time, the lawyer's image was a political hot potato. George Bush and Dan Quayle nearly made a campaign plank out of the 750,000 litigation-crazy, tasseled-loafer-wearing trial lawyers during the 1992 presidential election.[7] There had been several high-profile killings in courtrooms and law firm offices.[8] The American Bar Association established a commission to improve the public's perception of the profession.[9] At the same time, although there had been a number of articles on the subject[10] and a few law schools offered courses on law in film or literature, there were no facilities to actually study the phenomenon. The general consensus among lawyers was that the image was bad and that no one should give the topic serious attention because that would simply verify the consensus. When I broached the idea to our director, he visibly winced but agreed that it made sense. Again, we would have a collection that was both unique and highly attractive to scholars.

Lastly, my original concept of the collection was that it would not be a stultifying "law and literature" collection but that it would be restricted to contemporary, popular works. The next step was to decide to include both "high" and "low" culture and to welcome the law and literature works. This largely came about because of my research into the novels of Wilkie Collins, one of the earliest mystery writers and a member of Lincoln's Inn, who often included lawyers and serious legal issues in his plots.[11] Learning about nineteenth century reading culture made me realize that Collins's popularity at that time equaled Grisham's today and that we have merely deified and stratified the authors of that century as "literature" when in fact, they were writing the "trash novels" of their time. It also formed the basis for the decision to add lawyer/poets to the collection.

RH: Have there been any other changes in the collection development policy and reality over the years? That is, have you gotten more into mass market paperbacks and away from more literary works à la Wilkie Collins?

MR: We have not turned away from literary works at all. I recently ordered a copy of the collected works of Washington Irving after discovering that he had been licensed as an attorney. We got into mass market paperbacks simply because publishing and marketing has changed over the years. Many authors now start in paperback and only move into hardcover after proving their sales capability to the publisher. Another sign of the times is the fairly recent inclusion of lawyers in religious or romance novels, an almost entirely mass market industry. I have to admit that one of our catalogers thought we had reached bottom when she had to spend time on original cataloging for a book with a Fabio look-alike on the cover.

RH: What are some of the different types of legal mysteries? Which authors might other libraries consider acquiring?

MR: This question is both interesting and problematic because law stories, like law films, are usually a hybrid or subgenre of fiction, e.g., comedy, western, romance, crime fiction, science fiction. Mysteries are a subgenre of crime fiction, which also includes detection and espionage. Subsets of the mystery are caper, cozy, classic whodunit, forensic, hard-boiled, historical, military, police procedural, political, psychological, sci-fi, special subject (e.g., sports, cats, cooking, bibliomystery), and suspense or thriller. The term legal thriller, which is used much more widely than legal mystery, possibly appeared in print for the first time in a *Washington Post* book review,[12] but did not come into common usage until the mid-1990s.[13] Most readers see it as a subgenre of the mystery although it probably should be a subgenre of detective stories since the protagonist is most often a lawyer/detective *à la* Perry Mason. Moreover, the legal thriller may not be a thriller at all but a cozy, historical, caper, or political mystery.

However, to simplify matters, we will consider it a hybrid and for readers who have not yet been bitten by the legal thriller bug I can suggest authors who write primarily in the legal category as well as some who cross multiple genre lines: *Caper*: Carl Hiassen, Elmore Leonard, Donald Westlake; *Classic whodunit*: Sarah Caudwell, Anthony Gilbert, Erle Stanley Gardner, Cyril Hare, Emma Lathen, Sara Woods; *Cozy*: Carolyn Hart, Margaret Maron, Elliott Roosevelt, Margaret Truman; *Forensic*: Patricia Cornwell, Jeffrey Deaver; *Hard-boiled*: James Cain, James Ellroy, George Higgins, Andrew Vachss; *Historical*: Bruce Alexander, Edward Marston, Anne Perry; *Humor*: John Mortimer; *Minority detective*: Michael Nava, Margaret Coel, Christopher Darden; *Political*: David Baldacci, Richard North Patterson, Christopher Buckley; *Private eye*: Stephen Greenleaf, William Tapply, Sara Paretsky; *Regional*: Tony or Sophie Dunbar, D. W. Buffa, Paul Levine; *Romance*: Bettina Krahn, Al Tarvin; *Sci-fi* : Kate Wilhelm.

I think of the true legal thriller as a story that combines elements of the mystery or detective story with the courtroom drama. For a "best" list I refer to a more knowledgeable person than I: Jon Breen. The second edition of his *Novel Verdicts* lists the following top legal thrillers: Jay Brandon, *Defiance County*; Henry Cecil, *Settled Out of Court*; Michael Connelly, *The Concrete Blonde*; William Coughlin, *Shadow of a Doubt*; Al Dewlen, *Twilight of Honor*; Warwick Downing, *The Water Cure*; Robert Fish, *A Handy Death*; E. S. Gardner, *The Case of the Careless Kitten*; John Grisham, *A Time to Kill*; Cyril Hare, *Tragedy at Law*; William Harrington, *Which the Justice, Which the Thief*; Evan Hunter; *The Paper Dragon*; Edgar Lustgarten, *A Case to Answer*; Steve Martini, *Prime Witness*; Ellery Queen, *The Glass Village*; Robert Traver; *Anatomy of a Murder*; Scott Turow, *Presumed Innocent*; Carolyn Wheat, *Mean Streak*.[14]

RH: With the plethora of mystery novels being published these days, how do you decide what to get and what to skip?

MR: Before the law in popular culture collection was even a gleam in my eye, I had made a great contact in Otto Penzler, owner of The Mysterious Bookshop in New York City. We wanted reading copies (i.e., cheap) of law-mysteries for the Popular Reading Room collection and he periodically shipped us a box or two of books, usually with a nice find of which I would not have been aware. Among them was the first female-lawyer-detective novel, LeRoy Scott's *Counsel for the Defense*, published in 1912. I had absolute faith in his judgment, and he was invaluable in providing us with Golden Age mysteries. Eventually I organized a want-list using Jon Breen's *Novel Verdicts: A Guide to Courtroom Fiction*[15] and with the help of a local dealer tracked down many of the non-mystery titles we lacked. By the time we moved into the room, we had a very well-grounded historical collection. Now I buy everything I can identify and can afford in a given fiscal year. It's easier and cheaper to buy books while they are in print than to discover later that we should have had something and then have to make a greater effort to find an out-of-print copy.[16] I make no judgment as to relative worth of a book in terms of its quality and freely admit that some of these books are really badly written.

RH: When did you start adding videos and why?

MR: We started buying movies in 1987. When I came to work here we had selection by committee–a weekly meeting where the professional staff looked over publishers' flyers and chose materials to purchase. Our director knew that another law library had begun to dabble in films and at one of those meetings he declared "We should buy movies!" Everyone said "Right! *Judgment at Nuremberg*! *To Kill a Mockingbird*! *Anatomy of a Murder*!"–then looked blankly at each other because they couldn't think of any other titles. It was gut instinct for all of us that buying law-related movies for classroom use made perfect sense.[17] Shortly thereafter, we discontinued the committee system and professional staff did book selection according to their specialties. Since I was responsible for the fiction collection, I was also given charge of the law films. I had no idea how to track down relevant titles and the first few years were happenstance orders from the occasional video catalog. Our first purchase was *Rashomon* in 1987, but it wasn't until 1991 that we bought more than a few titles a year, simply because the home video market had not yet expanded very much. In 1990, we found a guide in Reynard Strickland's article, "Bringing Bogie out of the Court Closet: Law and Lawyers in Film."[18] It was only when WestLaw added *Magill's Directory of Cinema* to their databases that I had a working research tool, and shortly after that I discovered the American Film Institute's decennial catalogs. By 1994, I had a film want-list that filled seven fat looseleaf binders with over 3,000 titles.

RH: What periodicals do you read regularly to keep up with reviews?

MR: *Publisher's Weekly, Library Journal, TLS, New York Times Book Review, Chronicle of Higher Education, London Review of Books*, publishers' and vendors' catalogs.

RH: How do you decide which vendors to buy books from? Do you negotiate with vendors?

MR: That isn't up to me at all. Our acquisitions department performs the mechanics of ordering and operates independently of the staff who choose books for purchase. They use two major vendors for trade publications: Strand Bookstore in New York City, where we get a fifty percent discount, and Baker & Taylor, where we have a state contract. On occasion, I want a book that is out of print and they use one of the big online services like Bookfinder.com to find the title. We get the films from Baker & Taylor or directly from a catalog if it is only available from there. We do not buy used videos or from e-Bay–because of concern about possible bootleg copies.

RH: How has selection and acquisitions changed over the years? Is it getting easier or harder?

MR: Both are easier thanks to the Internet and electronic ordering services. In terms of books, it is less time-consuming for the selectors to get the relevant information that our acquisitions department needs to create an order and determine a vendor. We have online access to *Books in Print, Book Review Digest*, and other bibliographic databases. They can immediately determine if a vendor has a title in stock. We also have the services of the big out-of-print databases like Bookfinder.com and Alibris.com. It helped too, when the major wholesale vendors recognized the market for videos in libraries. For both the LPOP books and films, ordering is now more centralized.

RH: Any lessons learned the hard way in terms of collection development or acquisitions policy?

MR: This wasn't learned "the hard way" but it is definitely important to have a written collection development policy. It gives one a footing either to defend purchases or decide not to buy something. I've had to educate new associate directors who question the "trash" I buy. If the policy is in print and *ergo*, approved, it's easier for them to accept. When a faculty member wants us to buy a movie which does not fit our criteria I can at least argue that they can rent it for a one time-showing or buy it themselves if they intend to reuse it. (Our faculty have special research funds that they can use for travel or book purchases.) It also always helps me stand the course when changes are suggested, e.g., a recent idea that we should have Texas-related movies.

RH: When did you launch the Web pages for LPOP? Do you do all the html programming yourself or do you depend on a Webmaster? How did you learn that stuff?

MR: The Library Web page was launched in 1994 and the only real content on it was the current year's Fifth Circuit cases and the LPOP filmography, which had been available as a printed document for several years. The filmography was put up by our Webmaster and a student assistant who put it into a Perl script database. Neither of them knew Perl so one read the instructions from the manual while the other typed it in. I did the html mark-up for everything that has been added since. The public services staff had a mystifying half-day course in html code from the University data center but after reading articles on Web design I figured out what Web editors were and got a free version of HotDog. When the company dropped the version I'd been using, I taught myself how to use Composer, Netscape's very simple Web editor. It is as much as I need since the pages are almost entirely text and I try to keep them as easy to load as possible. I've also used Front Page for some image work, but mostly just type in the code myself. Because I make so many additions and changes I'm the only staff member outside of our Webmaster and head of technical services who is authorized to upload to our server.

RH: Which of the LPOP Web pages get the most hits?

MR: That is somewhat difficult to say because of the way the UT counter analyzes hits. We do know that overall the legal narrative e-text pages[19] get the most hits. Within that there are several resources which receive the majority of hits, all for different reasons. The suspense novella *The Devil and Daniel Webster* is commonly used for high school and college courses and it gets 300+ hits a week. It's in print, but not cheap. It's easier for teachers to link to our page, and much easier on students' pocketbooks. The true crime collection, *The Complete Newgate Calendar*,[20] is also quite popular. It's an excellent resource for courses on legal history, trials and literature, criminal justice, and English history and linked to by numerous course pages, historical societies, and bibliographic metasites. We have several criminal trial narratives on the site: the Australian Tichborne Claimant, Frank James, William Penn, Abraham Lincoln's *Trailor Murder Mystery*, and the Tweed political ring, as well as several collections. On occasion, one of these will get an anomalous and unexplainable number of hits. For example, one week we had over 600 hits to the Tichborne case, in another nearly 500 to "The Ordeal of Philip Stanfield" in *12 Scots Trials*, and every few months we get hundreds of hits to the *Newgate Calendar*'s chapter on the thirteenth century Scottish cannibal Sawney Beane.

RH: How do you envision expanding the LPOP Web pages in the future?

MR: I am currently in the process of adding a guide to TV lawyers, both in easily recognized "law" shows such as "Perry Mason" or "The Practice," and in any series which included a lawyer as a major character. Nonfiction "People's Court"-type shows, a genre which goes back to the very beginnings of television, are also included. That project is nearly complete and the next major addition will be old time radio. There were a number of mystery/lawyer-detective radio shows, such as "Perry Mason," "Mr. District Attorney," and "The Whisperer." I haven't worked out the scope, but it will be similar to the television listings, and will also include actual sound recordings. Beyond that, I intend to add more historical trials and early legal mystery fiction to the "Legal Narratives" page.

RH: What mistakes have you made and what did you learn from them? Anything you'd like to redo (i.e., advice to others)?

MR: STORAGE. We got locked into book/display cases which look very nice, but are very expensive and do not display videos or DVDs efficiently. Once the videos and books were brought together into the same space, the new bookcases had to match the pre-existing video display cases, and later on, expansion was predicated on whether there was money for new shelving. Additionally, other physical formats were not considered. We should be collecting ephemera but presently are not, because we have nowhere to put posters, law games, etc. Also, the collection is housed in a limited physical space, a room that cannot be expanded. We certainly did not foresee how large the collection would become. Anyone considering having a mystery collection would likely also have a multi-format collection of books, film, audio, possibly graphics and ephemera, and I would strongly suggest that they look at what other libraries have done.

RH: To conclude my questions, has the collection been a success and why?

MR: The librarian's most important job is to anticipate users' needs, to know what they will need before they even know they have a need. Legal educators are generally a conservative lot, but eventually they do catch on to new methods. With a growing number of professors questioning the Socratic and casebook method of teaching, with more of them coming into law schools with interdisciplinary backgrounds, and finally with the academic acceptance of popular culture in the classroom, it was inevitable that there would be a need for this kind of collection. At the same time, legal scholars were turning to storytelling, both as theory and as a way to teach trial technique, to look at the client, to read judicial opinions, and as a teaching method. The result has been that we have had visiting researchers from all over the world, provide subject matter for other University classes, act as a resource for instructors who teach law and film or literature, and have even been reporters' "experts" for the occasional newspaper or magazine article. I hate to say it, but we built it and they came.

REFERENCES

1. See, e.g., William Emile Doster, *The Conflict Between Literature and Law: An Oration Delivered before the Assembly of the Harvard Law School, March 18, 1859*, Cambridge, MA: Allen and Farnham, Printers, 1859; Irving Browne, *Law and Lawyers in Literature*, Boston: Soule and Bugbee, 1883; Thomas Alexander Fyfe, *Charles Dickens and the Law*, Edinburgh: W. Hodge & Co., 1910; John Marshall Gest, *The Lawyer in Literature*, Boston: Boston Book Co., 1913.

2. John H. Wigmore, A List of One Hundred Legal Novels, 17 *Illinois Law Review* 26, 27 (1922), also available at http://www.law.utexas.edu/lpop/etext/wigmore.htm.

3. *Id.*, at 31.

4. See e.g., Richard Weisberg's, *The Failure of the Word: The Protagonist as Lawyer in Modern Fiction*, New Haven: Yale University Press, 1984 or *Poethics: And Other Strategies of Law and Literature*, N.Y.: Columbia University Press, 1992.

5. Dr. Ray Browne founded *The Journal of Popular Culture* in 1967 and the Popular Culture Association in 1969. His efforts in the Department of English at Ohio's Bowling Green State University led to the inception of the Department of Popular Culture as an M.A. Program in 1973, followed a year later by an undergraduate program. In 1977 the school offered a Ph.D. in American Culture and in 1987 popular culture became a specialization in that program. Since those programs began many other universities have offered courses in popular culture, many of them modeled after similar courses at Bowling Green.

6. See, e.g., Donald G. Baker, The Lawyer in Popular Fiction, 3 *Journal of Popular Culture* 493 (1969); Maxwell Bloomfield, Law and Lawyers in American Popular Culture: An Essay in Law and American Literature, in *Law and American Literature: A Collection of Essays* 125, N.Y.: Knopf, 1983; Francis M. Nevins, Law, Lawyers, and Justice in Popular Fiction and Film, *Humanities Education* 3 (May 1984); Anthony Chase, Lawyers and Popular Culture: A Review of Mass Media Portrayals of American Attorneys, 1986 *American Bar Foundation Research Journal* 281 (1986); Lawrence Friedman, Law, Lawyers and Popular Culture 98 *Yale Law Journal* 1579 (1989); Robert Eli Rosen, Ethical Soap: L. A. Law and the Privileging of Character, 43 *University of Miami Law Review* 1229 (1989). For a comprehensive bibliography on the images of lawyers in popular culture, see Marlyn Robinson, The Lawyer in Popular Culture: A Bibliography, available at http://tarlton.law.utexas.edu/lpop/lpopbib2.htm.

7. Text of President Bush's Speech Accepting the Republican Presidential Nomination, *Facts on File Digest*, Aug. 20, 1992, p 606 A1.

8. Joan Cheever, The Deadly Practice of Divorce, *National Law Journal*, Oct. 12, 1992, p. 1 [recounting seven incidents of men distraught over divorce proceedings opening fire in courthouses across the country in 1992, killing two lawyers and three judges, wounding three lawyers, three sheriff's deputies and two court clerks]. Jennifer Warren, Grudge over Soured Deal May Have Led to Rampage, *Los Angeles Times*, July 3, 1993, p. A1 [recounting an incident of a client who went berserk in a San Francisco law firm, killing eight people and wounding six before taking his own life].

9. Ann Pelham, Under Fire, ABA Hires PR Expert; Message to the Public: Lawyers Aren't So Bad, *Legal Times*, Nov. 23, 1992, p. 1.

10. *Supra*, note 6.

11. Marlyn Robinson, From Collins to Grisham: A Brief History of the Legal Thriller, 22 *Legal Studies Forum 21* (1998), also available at http://www.law.utexas.edu/lpop/legstud.htm.

12. Curt Suplee, Attorney with a New Writ: Ron Liebman's Legal Thriller–Summary Statement of the Law, *Washington Post*, Dec. 27, 1983, B1, reviewing Liebman's first novel *Grand Jury*.

13. The full text articles in the Lexis News library were considered a relevant sampler. A search was run for "legal thriller" with the following results: Seventy-four hits from 1980-1992, 359 hits through 1993, 688 hits through 1994, 998 hits up to 1995, 4,733 hits through 2002.

14. Jon Breen, *Novel Verdicts* xi, Lanham, Md., Scarecrow Press, 1999.

15. Jon Breen, Novel Verdicts: *A Guide to Courtroom Fiction*, Metuchen, N.J., Scarecrow Press, 1984, now available in its second edition (1999).

16. The hardcover first edition of *A Time to Kill* was published by Wynwood Press in 1989 and is currently available from a dealer for $2,500. (Listed on Bookfinder.com 1/8/2003.) Its original price was $18.95. *The Wall Street Journal* reviewed *The Firm*, resulting in huge sales for Doubleday. *A Time to Kill* was barely reviewed at all, and Grisham was reduced to selling copies out of his car trunk to independent bookdealers.

17. In fact, two bibliographies of potentially useful law films had already been published. See, Roger C. Cramton, *Audiovisual Materials on Professional Responsibility*, Chicago, ABA Section of Tort and Insurance Practice, 1987 and Paul J. Mastrangelo, Lawyers and the Law: A Filmography, 3 *Legal Reference Services Quarterly* 31 (1983), 5 *Legal Reference Services Quarterly* 31 (Winter 1983).

18. Reynard Strickland, Bringing Bogie out of the Court Closet: Law and Lawyers in Film, *The Gargoyle, University of Wisconsin Law School Forum* 4 (Spring 1990).

19. Available at http://www.law.utexas.edu/lpop/etext/.

20. *The Complete Newgate Calendar*, London: Privately printed for the Navarre Society, 1926. The original series of this work, by R. Sanders, was published in five volumes in 1760 and narrated notorious crimes from 1700 till then. Later series were issued from about 1820 as the *Newgate Calendar*, and the *New Newgate Calendar* appeared weekly in 1863-65. There was also an *Annals of Newgate* by the Rev. M. Villette and others in 1776.

Mystery and the Romance Reader

Tracy Allen

SUMMARY. Mystery fiction and romance fiction share many common elements often including the same readership. Romance readers consume vast numbers of books not all of which are romances. Similarly mystery readers often enjoy that most intense form of romance: romantic suspense. In the last decade, authors such as the phenomenally popular Janet Evanovich have pleased large numbers of romance and mystery readers by combining elements of each genre along with a distinct style and voice. The reasons why individual readers, who might classify themselves as primarily romance or mystery fans, find pleasure in other genres comes down to a myriad of appeal factors. Matching readers with books they will enjoy, no matter what "official" category they occupy, is a very satisfying job. *[Article copies available for a fee from The Haworth Document Delivery Service: 1-800-HAWORTH. E-mail address: <docdelivery@haworthpress.com> Website: <http://www.HaworthPress.com> © 2004 by The Haworth Press, Inc. All rights reserved.]*

KEYWORDS. Janet Evanovich, romantic suspense, romance fiction, reader's advisory work, booklists

---

Tracy Allen is on the staff of the Las Vegas Clark County Library District. She was formerly Reader Advisory Librarian, Anoka County Library, Blaine, MN.

Address correspondence to: Tracy Allen, 2135 Cactus Pine Court, Las Vegas, NV 89135.

[Haworth co-indexing entry note]: "Mystery and the Romance Reader." Allen, Tracy. Co-published simultaneously in *Collection Management* (The Haworth Information Press, an imprint of The Haworth Press, Inc.) Vol. 29, No. 3/4, 2004, pp. 161-178; and: *Managing the Mystery Collection: From Creation to Consumption* (ed: Judith Overmier, and Rhonda Harris Taylor) The Haworth Information Press, an imprint of The Haworth Press, Inc., 2004, pp. 161-178. Single or multiple copies of this article are available for a fee from The Haworth Document Delivery Service [1-800-HAWORTH, 9:00 a.m. - 5:00 p.m. (EST). E-mail address: docdelivery@haworthpress.com].

Available online at http://www.haworthpress.com/web/COL

doi:10.1300/J105v29n03_12

INTRODUCTION

Romances are relationship stories. They give us a powerful impression of people falling in love and committing themselves to one another, often at the speed of light. The format demands that within so many pages a couple will meet, face some sort of conflict, and find each other in the resolution. It is a very speedy process that satisfies the needs and demands of the average romance reader. However, there is another part of that same reader that relishes a relationship that develops slowly, a relationship in which the details are doled out in tiny snippets between depictions of day-to-day activity and the common crime spree. Any individual may read many different genres for many different reasons. Sometimes romance readers are also mystery readers because, in addition to enjoying the mystery format, they are hooked on getting those little details of a relationship spread out over volume after volume. The mystery structure simply provides the requisite conflict–repeated *ad infinitum*–on which to build a story that can then be decorated with small details of the detective's personal life.

Romantic suspense is another animal entirely. Romantic suspense is romance in the extreme. In the modern romantic suspense story, a couple will meet, face some sort of conflict involving danger and crime, and find each other in the resolution. Romantic suspense is an intense form of romance because the conflict is quite literally centered on trust. Can the heroine really trust the man for whom she is beginning to have feelings? The question often takes one of two forms: Can he truly protect her or is he going to kill her? In a typical romance the heroine is in danger of breaking her heart if she chooses badly (although she never does). In typical romantic suspense she is in danger of losing her life.

Reader's advisory work is about grasping the myriad of appeal factors associated with a work of fiction. Systematic organization demands that we find some way to group similar items into large discernable categories. As acquisitions librarians, we cannot spend the resources it would take to establish a special section for mystery stories featuring steamy romance and sarcastic heroines. We must, for practicality's sake, simply file these works under mystery, even though steamy sex and funny heroines are the very appeal factors that might entice readers of romance. They also may be the very appeal factors that provide the best reading experience of all for a reader who enjoys both romance and mystery for many different reasons. Janet Evanovich's Stephanie Plum series has made the point that there are millions of romance readers who will be equally pleased with the right sort of mystery. These are the readers who are attracted to the slow motion relationship story. For these readers the actual solving of the puzzle, the questioning of witnesses and gathering of clues, which apparently constitutes the purpose of the story, is simply the frame on which the interesting relationship details are strung. By the same token, there are devoted mystery readers who are delighted by the women-in-jeopardy, life-threatening crime story that is built around the central relationship core of romantic suspense. In the case of romantic suspense, the appeal can be great for mystery lovers looking for restored order out of the chaos caused by crime because the story ends with the ultimate value in societal order: monogamous commitment.

The logical question then becomes: Where do these books fit into a standard genre system and how do we get the books to readers based on appeal rather than simply genre definition? I'd like to try to answer this question by analyzing three different types of stories: romantic suspense, mysteries with romance elements, and stories in the Janet Evanovich style. All three types have in common, to a greater or lesser degree, the combination of crime and romantic love. Included at the end of this chapter are extensive lists illustrating titles appropriate to each category.

ROMANTIC SUSPENSE

Modern romantic suspense has strong roots in the Gothic tradition, which emphasized women overcoming threatening situations and asserting their own strengths. "Woman in jeopardy" is an apt description of romantic suspense because the plot so often turns on the real peril in which the heroine finds herself. Stalked by serial rapists and murderers, the focus of a madman's obsession, framed and/or blamed for murders and other crimes, her family threatened, the romantic suspense heroine has some key differences compared to the amateur sleuth and professional investigator of mystery fiction. Despite the puzzle element that the two types of story share in common to varying degrees, the women of mystery fiction are not threatened personally. When they do experience danger, it is of the wrong place, wrong time variety or is a hazard of the profession, but it is rarely any different from what their male counterparts would suffer. However, it is important to note that modern "woman in jeopardy" stories may differ from romantic suspense by a focus on the woman in jeopardy reclaiming her own safety or pursuing answers to questions that threaten her independence, such as in Mary

Higgins Clark's *On the Street Where You Live*. In this particular book, the love interest appears on only a few pages and develops no close relationship with the heroine until the denouement. The term *romantic suspense* today refers almost exclusively to romance novels in which the fundamental themes of trust and redemption are taken to the farthest extreme, usually because of eminent danger. Romance fiction embraces all sorts of sub-genres from light comedies and regencies to stories of deepest despair, but no matter what form a romance takes, the central themes of trusting another person with your soul, and in the case of suspense, with your very life, remain fast. The Romance Writers of America have two simple rules for identifying a romance: Is the focus of the story the development of a relationship between the heroine and hero, and are they happily together in the end? When we speak of arranging fiction by assigning varieties to one main area or another, e.g., mystery or romance, this sort of fundamental definition can be crucial. If you are holding a story of suspense where two characters

- are thrown together from the start in order to confront some personal threat (usually to the female),
- are sometimes suspicious of one another being the cause of the trouble at hand,
- experience a growing sexual attraction they cannot deny despite an equal dose of fear or suspicion, and
- overcome danger and acknowledge that they belong together forever,

then what you have is a romance despite any and all mystery trappings. It is important to note as well, for purposes of identification, that romantic suspense heroes come in two basic forms. The original is the Byronic model; dark, brooding, and dangerous he sometimes frightens the heroine, and may appear to be the hidden source of her danger. He often has been accused, even convicted (all wrongly as it turns out), of serious crimes in his past. In the end, the heroine must trust herself and him in order to survive and in so doing accepts that he is her soul mate. This process is part of the "taming" and redeeming of the uncivilized hero that demonstrates the heroine's victory. The second sort of hero is the sympathetic man in a position of authority forced by circumstances to suspect the woman to whom he simultaneously finds himself attracted.

A perfect example of modern romantic suspense and this second type of hero can be found in Linda Howard's newest book, *Dying to Please*. Thompson Cahill is a police detective who encounters Sarah Stevens just after she's single-handedly stopped a couple of thugs robbing her employer. Sarah works as a special butler for a judge who also needs a bodyguard. Cahill meets her again under more adverse circumstances when her employer is murdered. Against his better instincts, Cahill is attracted to Sarah and must force himself to put aside those thoughts until her innocence is established. Once it is, Sarah and Cahill become quite close, working together to overcome personal issues regarding trust and independence. When Sarah's new employers are also murdered, Cahill momentarily feels betrayed as the thought creeps in that Sarah may have used their relationship to cover her identity as a murderer. Sensing his reservations, Sarah is devastated by the ruin of her life and Cahill's betrayal. The trust issues come to a head in a moment of hot angry sex when he tries to make it all up to her, but only leaves her feeling more alone. Sarah is soon kidnapped and molested by the real killer who has become obsessed with her. In the end her ultimate healing from the attack and from Cahill's betrayal comes as they make love in the last scene of the book.

Another example of the best in modern romantic suspense comes from Katherine Sutcliffe who made her name as an historical romance writer. *Darkling I Listen* is the powerful story of Hollywood bad boy Brandon Carlyle who has come home to Texas after being released from prison. The whole world, including himself, is convinced Brandon recklessly caused the death of a young porn star while he was in an alcoholic daze. Brandon has other problems: A dangerous stalker has found him and so has a beautiful tabloid reporter. Even as she helps him out of some tight spots and their attraction grows, the reporter, Alyson James, hides her identity from Brandon. As they fall in love, Alyson must consider if she can trust someone with Brandon's mean past, and Brandon must decide if he can really love someone who has lied to him. They also have to survive the stalker and a pretty nasty local sheriff. Told with all the trappings of mysterious suspense and danger, *Darkling I Listen,* maintains a consistent theme throughout the novel. This archetypal romantic suspense theme, intensified by its application to the hero and the heroine, is one of finding peace with the trust of a true soulmate.

MYSTERIES WITH ROMANCE ELEMENTS

The conventions for romance fiction clearly require a happily ever after ending. Even though the reader is always given a happy conclusion, she actually sees very little of the "ever after part." This is one reason why family series are so popular. With each new couple's story, one gets glimpses of the lives of former heroes and heroines. The enjoyment of continuing details is something the romance reader finds in mysteries with romance elements.

Almost every mystery series includes something of the detective's personal relationships, which often develop at a snail's pace over the course of many books. It is the slow development and the multitude of obstacles that appeals to romance readers who enjoy the romance in this different format. Amidst the standard clue finding and witness interviewing, many authors sprinkle in small doses of heart-rending romance. For example, in Laurian Berenson's series, amateur sleuth Melanie Travis has been slowly growing closer to Sam Driver. At one point they decide to marry, but then he leaves town. The next book, *Once Bitten*, begins as Melanie explains she is dealing with the pain one breath at a time. Over the course of the book a body and a murderer are found, but it is the ending that packs the emotional punch. In the very last pages Melanie opens her door to find Sam standing outside. The book ends as she reminds herself to breathe "in, out. In, out" (p. 281). Mystery writers also have the freedom to wreak the ultimate emotional devastation: They kill off lovers.

The J. D. Robb In Death series is perhaps the single best example of a mystery series completely infused with romance. The series chronicles the cases of police lieutenant Eve Dallas. It is set in New York City sixty some years in the future so in addition to everything else the stories are rich with futuristic details and some world building. Eve's husband, Roarke, is a former hoodlum turned zillionaire businessman whose empire had some shady beginnings. Eve meets Roarke in the course of the first book when he falls under suspicion for the crime she is investigating. Although they are often termed romantic suspense, the use of the term just doesn't fit this series. First, it is a series and, as I have noted, romantic suspense–by virtue of being romance–has a one couple per book convention to maintain. Secondly, the series is so much a part of the police procedural tradition that the mystery side of the story always gets a crucial share.

Robb is a pseudonym for best-selling romance author Nora Roberts, created to accommodate her very prolific style. Roberts stands strong in her position as a romance writer, and the huge success of this series surely owes something to the appeal she has for romance readers. More than any other mystery series, romance readers consistently claim the In Death books as favorites. The popular romance Web site *All About Romance* (http://www.likesbooks.com) does a yearly poll of reader favorites. Eve Dallas has won hands down as favorite feisty (read tough) heroine for several years. She was only supplanted this year by another Roberts' heroine but may well return since Eve has the advantage of continual eligibility with each new book. Perhaps even more telling is the fact that Eve and Roarke had won as best couple for five years in a row, only falling to honorable mention status this year. Interestingly, the In Death series is also quite popular with male readers for whom the appeal would seem to lie in the traditional mystery qualities of the series. Eve Dallas is one heck of a hardboiled heroine. Her tragic childhood and natural surliness combine to create a tough cop for whom doing the job right and "standing for the dead" is the only reason for existing. Adding something more to Eve's life is where the romance, and ultimately the theme of the series, comes into play. Although married by the third book, Eve and Roarke's relationship is far from the fully realized sort of entity one finds at the end of a romance novel. Between the two of them they have layers of emotional issues to address. The series is actually a beautiful rendering of a romance in slow motion with each episode bringing Eve and Roarke slightly closer to a true melding of soul mates. The balance of each individual story favors the crime solving elements, but the romantic relationship taken throughout the entire series strikes the perfect note for romance readers, and for those readers who like both elements, the appeal is perfect.

Charlaine Harris' Lily Bard books are another mystery series that has the possibility of very strong appeal for romance readers and lovers of mysteries with romance elements. In this case the problem might be exposure as the books are not marketed at all to romance readers, and this is a fine example of a suggestion of a library acquisition that could win accolades for both reader's advisory and acquisitions librarians. The series is much darker than one might assume, especially given the comical cozy look of some of the paperback edition covers. The heroine is Lily Bard, who cleans houses for people in Shakespeare, Arkansas. Lily came to Shakespeare to rebuild some sort of life in the aftermath of her kidnapping and rape by a motorcycle gang. There is so much emotional depth to these stories that the mystery often seems superfluous, a fact which can have great appeal for some readers. With the first book, Lily begins to open up to others a little, and by the third she begins a tentative relationship with a private detective whose past is nearly as tragic as hers. They marry in secret, trying to protect the fragile bonds they've formed. The most recent book, *Shakespeare's Counselor*, deals with Lily and Jack losing a baby they didn't know was on the way. The scene depicting the miscarriage and its aftermath is worthy of the best romance novel.

Lily Bard also illustrates another important point: A strong heroine enthralls romance readers. One delightful example is a sweet miss named Taylor from Julie Garwood's *Prince Charming*. Taylor has married for convenience and escape to America in order to rescue her nieces. Lucas, her new husband, is discovering just what a strong, truly prepared woman she is. His equally rough friend remarks on meeting Taylor, "She's got a gun in her pocket. She always carry one?" (p. 217). Lucas just shrugs it off, already having accepted that his wife is no traditional Victorian lady.

There is a little Kinsey Millhone in every romance heroine, and many a romance reader is drawn to the mystery section because of writers like Marcia Muller and Sue Grafton who pioneered the truly alpha female detective. The appeal of the tough female detective also explains the tremendous popularity among romance readers of a series that is neither romance nor mystery. This is the Anita Blake Vampire Hunter series. Anita is a unique detective, solving all sorts of paranormal crime while balancing her love triangle with a vampire and a werewolf. The stories are overwhelmingly sensual and violent with Anita being responsible for much of the damage inflicted.

THE EVANOVICH PHENOMENON

If romantic suspense is about trust and mysteries are about creating order from chaos, the Stephanie Plum series is about making personal peace with absurdity. This hugely popular series illustrates the importance of recognizing appeal factors like no other work does. It appeals to romance readers, but it isn't romance. It appeals to mystery readers, although many hard-core mystery fans claim it is really more comic adventure than true mystery. When *One for the Money* debuted in 1994, there was a buzz in the romance community, especially the fledgling online sites. This book was a treasure: funny, steamy, smart, and oh, yeah there's some crime. Evanovich began by writing romances, many for the Loveswept line. Her romances often included features we've come to expect from the Stephanie Plum series: cars meeting with disaster, sarcastic heroines, and spunky old ladies with large handbags. With the invention of Stephanie Plum, Evanovich technically moved over to the ranks of mystery writer, but more than any other writer making that switch, she brought romance fans with her. However, Evanovich didn't just write a mystery with a lot of romance or romantic suspense with a lot of comedy. She didn't even construct a hybrid using bits of various genre conventions. What she did was create a story world where Stephanie in all her hair fluffing, hamster owning, junk food eating, and self-deprecating zaniness is the center of reason, and all those characters circling around her are odd in comparison. Stephanie is Everygirl, who understands that in the midst of a crisis French fries and new shoes are essential. The reader is meant to solidly identify with Stephanie and is thus encouraged to appreciate the absurdity of life where a former discount lingerie buyer becomes a bounty hunter with a gun in her cookie jar. The stories are not romance, not only because they are a series, but also because Stephanie doesn't have a happy ending in sight. The romance elements come in the form of steam and sizzle. The sexual tension Evanovich creates is worthy of the best romance in terms of style. The function, however, unlike a romance, is not to reveal Stephanie's one true soul mate, but rather to throw one more curveball of absurdity into Stephanie's life. The attempts she and Joe Morelli make at getting the deed done are interrupted at crucial moments for several books before there is any romantic consummation. Joe Morelli is a card-carrying romance hero. The problem is that Stephanie just can't bring herself to be a romance heroine. For one thing she has the hots for another guy. Enter Ranger, bounty hunter extraordinaire and the object of reader lust across the nation. Stephanie is also not your average cozy amateur sleuth. She may be the queen of being in the right place at the wrong time, but the danger she encounters is quite real and very gritty. People die grisly deaths. People are tortured and maimed. The first person narrative is a humorous paradox linking Stephanie and all her mishaps to the grim world of dozens of hard-boiled detectives that came before her.

Some people read Evanovich because they like humorous amateur mysteries. Some people read Evanovich because they like women detectives. Many people read Evanovich because they want to follow the twists and turns of Stephanie's sizzling love life. I have had patrons in entirely different areas of the stacks overhear my recommending Evanovich and then try her adventures for themselves. They come back later raving about these books they never would have thought they'd like. The big question is what to recommend to Evanovich fans who want "more just like that." There are actually two parts to the answer. First, of course we as librarians must determine what "that" means to the individual reader. If the reader wants more humorous mysteries, we go in that direction. If they want humorous romance, we go in another.

The "If You Like Janet Evanovich" list that I created for Anoka County's Web site is divided by appeal factor. As you can see, the appeal runs the gamut from serious, tough female leads to the fluffiest of comic romance, any of which might please your average Evanovich reader. The first part of that list features titles that most closely resemble the Stephanie Plum series in style and content, which brings me to the second part of the answer. We can try to identify those books written in the wake of Evanovich's popularity, appealing purposefully or not, to the same general characteristics of sizzle, comedy, and crime combined. The second list of Evanovich readalikes features some books marketed as mysteries, such as the Sierra Lavotini series, and some, such as *Welcome to Temptation*, marketed as romance. What they have in common is a style and plot that closely parallels an Evanovich story. There are smart, sarcastic heroines who find themselves in some sort of criminal situation. There is sizzling sex written in the romance novel style. There are many kooky secondary characters. There is also a greater or lesser degree of success at hitting the exact same notes that make Evanovich so popular. The most successful at emulating Evanovich is Nancy Bartholomew, whose Sierra Lavotini series manages to duplicate almost all of the appeal factors found in Evanovich's series while clearly maintaining its own style.

In addition to capturing the Evanovich sassiness, Charlaine Harris's Sookie Stackhouse series also trades in on the appeal of vampire plots. Romance readers have long been fans of a good vampire story. This particular series is getting positive feedback on several romance reader Web sites. Harris herself told me that they are selling better than any of her other books. Jennifer Apodaca's first book in the Sam Shaw series, *Dating Can be Murder,* shows great promise. The humor is laugh-out-loud, and the characters include the heroine's grandfather, two sons, and a beer drinking dog, all of whom rush to help out with the investigations. The love interest is a gorgeous security expert who calls Sam "babe" and wants to test drive her newly purchased chest.

Also worth noting is Suzann Ledbetter's Hanna Garvey series. Hannah begins the series as the new manager for a luxury retirement community. The cast of vivacious and kooky seniors provides all sorts of investigative support. Hannah's love interest is the local sheriff seven years her junior. The two of them have every bit as much trouble as Stephanie and Morelli at consummating their relationship.

Janet Evanovich's success clearly illustrates the way certain stories can have appeal for many different types of readers. Readers are comfortable with a system that organizes books by genre because they think "their" books are in a predictable place, and that's a good foundation. But the fine points of reader advisory service demand a little specialization in order to join readers with books they will love, books which just might be living in different parts of the library. The reader advisory librarian is a tour guide whether in person or with the production of a good, Web-based booklist which can be used by patrons and other staff alike. The lines between mystery and suspense and romance are blurring, especially as publishers try to reach fans of all types. For both acquisitions and reader's advisory librarians, the first step in keeping up with reader demand is to understanding why stories labeled mysteries might appeal to the reader of romance. The second step is acquiring and publicizing those novels that appeal to both sets of readers. The following lists will assist in those two processes.

The Lists

A note about the following lists: For the most part I have kept my selections to books published in the last few years. I created the "If You Like Janet Evanovich" list for Anoka County library, and it appears on the Web site http://www.anoka.lib.mn.us. The other lists were created especially for this article. I would like to thank the members of Fiction-L listserv and co-workers at the Rum River branch of Anoka County Library for their suggestions.

Romantic Suspense

Adair, Cherry. *Kiss and Tell, Hide and Seek, In Too Deep*
Albert, Michele. *Getting Her Man*
Andersen, Susan. *Exposure, Obsessed*
Anderson, Linda. *Secrets of Sadie Maynard, When Night Falls*
Bach, Lauren. *Slow Hands, Lone Rider*
Barton, Beverly. *Every Move She Makes, What She Doesn't Know*
Brown, Sandra. *The Crush, Envy, Alibi*
Cameron, Stella. *Cold Day in July*
Castillo, Linda. *The Perfect Victim*
Coffey, Jan. *Twice Burned, Trust Me Once*
Cohen, Paula. *Gramercy Park*
Cresswell, Jasmine. *Third Wife, The Refuge, The Conspiracy*
Dare, Justine. *High Stakes*

Davis, Dee. *Dark of the Night, After Twilight, The Promise, Just Breathe, Midnight Rain*
Erickson, Lynn. *On Thin Ice, On the Edge*
Forster, Suzanne. *Husband, Lover, Stranger, The Morning After*
Garwood, Julie. *Heartbreaker, Mercy, Killjoy*
Graham, Heather. *Night of the Blackbird, Hurricane Bay*
Harper, Karen. *The Stone Forest, The Baby Farm*
Henderson, Dee. The O'Malley Family series
Howard, Linda. *Dying to Please, Mr. Perfect, Open Season, Now You See Her, Dream Man*
Jackson, Lisa. *Hot Blooded, Cold Blooded*
Jerott, Michelle. *Her Bodyguard*
Joyce, Brenda. *The Chase*
Kane, Andrea. *No Way Out, Run for Your Life*
Krentz, Jayne Ann. *Smoke and Mirrors, Lost and Found, Deep Waters, Silver Linings, Eye of the Beholder, Flash,* Eclipse Bay trilogy
Lee, Miranda. *Hearts of Fire, Secrets and Sins*
London, Cait. *When Night Falls*
Lowell, Elizabeth. The Donovan family series, Rarities, Inc. series
Martin, Kat. *Hot Rain*
Marton, Sandra. *Raising the Stakes*
McCall, Dinah. *White Mountain*
McKenna, Shannon. *Behind Closed Doors*
McKinney, Meagan. *Still of the Night*
Michaels, Barbara. (multitudes of titles, which tend towards gothic)
Myers, Helen. *Final Stand, Dead End*
Quick, Amanda. *With this Ring, I Thee Wed, Wicked Widow*
Robards, Karen. *To Trust a Stranger*
Roberts, Nora. *Carnal Innocence, Hidden Riches, Divine Evil, Villa, Three Fates*
Sala, Sharon. *Snowfall*
Sawyer, Meryl. *Closer than She Thinks, Unforgettable*
Skye, Christina. *My Spy, Going Overboard*
Smith, Taylor. *Deadly Grace*
Stewart, Mariah. *Voices Carry, The President's Daughter*
Stuart, Anne. *Still Lake, Shadows at Sunset*
Sutcliffe, Katherine. *Darkling I Listen*
Taylor, Janelle. *In Too Deep, Can't Stop Loving You*
Wainscott, Tina. *Now You See Me, Unforgivable*
Young, Karen. *Kiss and Tell, Someone Knows*

Romantic Mysteries

In the listings below, the significant other is indicated in brackets. Note how often this person is affiliated with law enforcement. The series with particular appeal for romance readers are in bold. Where the couple are equal partners in the investigations and the focus of the story, the union is indicated with a bold face "and." The levels of romance vary greatly from very subtle to very prominent.

Albert, Susan Wittig. China Bayles series [Mike McQuaid (police)]
Andrews, Donna. Meg Lansdown series [Michael Waterston]
Berenson, Melanie. Travis series [Sam Driver]
Brown, Rita Mae. "Harry" Haristeen–Mrs. Murphy series [ex-Fair Haristeen]
Burke, Jan. Irene Kelly series [Frank Harriman (police)]
Conant, Susan. Holly Winter series [Steve Delaney]
Craig, Phillip R. Martha's Vineyard series–J. W. Jackson (ex-police) [Zee (wife extraordinaire)]
Crombie, Deborah. Scotland Yard Superintendent Duncan Kincaid and Sergeant Gemma Jones series
Daheim, Mary. Bed and Breakfast series–Judith McMonigle [Joe Flynn (retired police)]
Daheim, Mary. Emma Lord series [various]
Davis, Nageeba. Maggie Kean series [Sam Villari (police)]
Day, Dianne. Freemont Jones and Michael Kossoff–private investigators (historical San Francisco)
Deaver, Jeffery. *Devil's Teardrop*–Documents analyst, former FBI agent Parker Kinkaid **and** current FBI agent Margaret Lukas
Douglas, Carole Nelson. Irene Adler series [Godfey Norton (barrister)] (Victorian era)
Douglas, Carole Nelson. Temple Barr [love triangle]
Fowler, Earlene. Benie Harper [Gabe Ortiz (police)]
Gardner, Lisa. *The Third Victim*, *The Next Accident*–Rainie Connor (PI) **and** Pierce Quincy (FBI)
Gellis, Roberta. Magdalene de la Batarde series [Sir Bellamy of Itchen] (medieval London)
Gerritsen, Tess. *The Surgeon*, *The Apprentice*–Jane Rizzoli homicide detective
Glass, Leslie. NYPD Detective April Woo and lover/colleague Lt. Mike Sanchez

Hager, Jean. Iris House series–Tess Darcy [Luke Fredrik]

Harris, Charlaine. Lily Bard series [Jack Leeds], Aurora Teagarden series [various]

Hart, Carolyn G. Death on Demand series–Annie Laurence [Max Darling]

Hawley, Michael A. *Double Bluff*

Henry, Sue. Alaska Mystery series–Alex Jenson and Jessie Arnold

Hoag, Tami. *Ashes to Ashes*, *Dust to Dust*

Jance, J. A. Sheriff JoAnna Brady [Butch Dixon]

Johansen, Iris. Eve Duncan series [Joe Quinn (police)]

Joyce, B. D. Francesca Cahill **and** police commissioner Rick Bragg (historical New York)

Kellogg, Marne Davis. Federal Marshall Lilly Bennett [Richard Jerome]

Kingsbury, Kate. Lady Elizabeth Hartleigh **and** Earl Monroe (American officer) (WWII England)

Krich, Rochelle. Detective Jessie Drake series [various]

Lehane, Dennis. Patrick Kenzie **and** Angela Gennaro series (PIs)

Lippman, Laura. Tess Monaghan series [Crow (musician)]

MacLeod, Charlotte. Sarah Kelling and Max Bittersohn

Maron, Margaret. Judge Deborah Knott series [various]

Matthews, Alex. Cassidy McCabe series (Zach Moran–reporter)

McCrumb, Sharyn. Elizabeth MacPherson series

Muller, Marcia. *Point Deception*

Munger, Katy. Casey Jones series [various]

O'Shaughnessy, Perri. Attorney Nina Reilly [Paul Van Wagoner (PI) and ex-Jack McIntyre]

Pearson, Ridley. Lou Boldt, John LaMoia, and Daphne Mathews [changing partners, very dark]

Pence, Joanne. Angie Amalfi series [Paavo Smith (police detective)]

Peters, Elizabeth. Vicky Bliss series (John Smythe–art thief), Amelia Peabody series [Radcliffe Emerson (archeologists)] also numerous single titles such as *Legend in Green Velvet*

Pickard, Nancy. Jenny Cain series [Geof Bushfield (police)]

Picoult, Jodi. *Salem Falls*

Quick, Amanda. *Slightly Shady*, *Don't Look Back*–Lavinia Lake *and* Tobias March–Private Investigators, Regency England

Robb, J. D. Detective Eve Dallas and Roarke

Roberts, Gillian. Amanda Pepper series [C. K. MacKenzie (police)]

Rowland, Laura Joh. Samurai Sano Ichiro series [wife Reiko] (17th century Japan)

Shelton, Connie. Charlie Parker series [Drake (pilot)]
Slaughter, Karin. Dr. Sara Linton **and** Police Chief Jeffrey Tolliver (**divorced** with complicated relationship up for further exploration)
Smith, Julie. Skip Langdon series [Steve Steinman (filmmaker)]
Speart, Jessica. Rachel Porter series [Jake Santou (police)]
Stabenow, Dana. Kate Shugak series [various love interests], Liam Campbell series [Wy Chouinard (pilot)]
Swanson, Denise. Scumble River Mysteries, Skye Denison
Talford, Amy. *Dying to Meet You*
Taylor, Kathleen. Tori Bauer [various]
Thompson, Victoria. Gaslight series Midwife Sara Brandt **and** Detective Sergeant Frank Malloy (turn of century New York)
Van Wormer, Laura. Sally Harrington series [DA Doug Wrentham]

Strong Women Detectives

Barnes, Linda. Carlotta Carlyle series
Barr, Nevada. Anna Pigeon series
Benjamin, Carol Lea. Rachel Alexander and Dash series
Duncan, Sharon. Scotia MacKinnon series
Evans, Liz. Grace Smith
Grafton, Sue. Kinsey Millhone series
Jance, J. A. Sheriff JoAnna Brady series
Lanier, Virginia. JoBeth Sidden series
LaPlante, Linda. Lorraine Page series
Munger, Katy. Casey Jones series
Muller, Marcia. Sharon McCone series
O'Connell, Carol. Kathy Mallory series
Reichs, Kathleen. Temperance Brennan series
Robb, J. D. In Death series–Lt. Eve Dallas
Rogers, Chris. Dixie Flannigan series
Seranella, Barbara. Munch Mancini series
Stabenow, Dana. Kate Shugak series
Tan, Maureen. Jane Nichols series

If You Like Janet Evanovich

There is nothing quite like Janet Evanovich's Stephanie Plum Bounty Hunter series. The hilarious sarcasm, the steamy romance, the strange relationship Stephanie has with crime-solving all combine to make a unique reading experience. What follows are some suggestions, grouped by type, to fill the months between Evanovich releases.

Top Picks

Andrews, May Kay. *Savannah Blues*. Written under a pseudonym by an established mystery author, this book is a riot of quirky characters, rich detail, light romance, and murder.
Apodaca, Jennifer. Samantha Shaw Series
Bartholomew, Nancy. Sierra Lavotini Series. Sierra is a stripper in Florida with a hunky cop for a boyfriend and a psychotic, but helpful neighbor.
Green, Chloe. Dallas O'Connor Series

Independent Crime-Solving Women with a Sarcastic Bent

Evans, Liz. Grace Smith Series
Harris, Charlaine. Lily Bard Series
Hayter, Sparkle. Robin Hudson Series
Henderson, Lauren. Sam Jones Series
Kellog, Marne Davis. Marshall Lilly Bennett Series
Lippman, Laura. Tess Monaghan Series
Munger, Katie. Casey Jones Series
Strohmeyer, Sarah. Bubbles Yablonsky Series
Taylor, Kathleen. Tory Bauer Series

Hilarious Romantic Suspense with a Mystery Type Adventure

Anderson, Susan. *Baby Don't Go, Be My Baby, Baby I'm Yours*
Bond, Stephanie. *I Think I Love You, Our Husband Got Your Number*
Crusie, Jennifer. *Crazy for You, Getting Rid of Bradley, Tell Me Lies, Faking It, Fast Women, Welcome to Temptation*
Heller, Jane. *Name Dropping, Sis Boom Bah*
Howard, Linda. *Mr. Perfect, Open Season*
Ledbetter, Suzann. Hannah Garvey Series
Michaels, Kasey. *Can't Take My Eyes Off of You*

Steamy Romance with a Mystery Type Adventure

Anderson, Linda. *The Secrets of Sadie Maynard, When Night Falls*
Andersen, Susan. *Exposure, Obsessed*

Howard, Linda. *Kill and Tell, Now You See Her, All the Queen's Men, Dying to Please*
Lowell, Elizabeth. *Amber Beach, Jade Island, Pearl Cove, Midnight in Ruby Bayou, Moving Target, Running Scared*
Roberts, Nora. *Divine Evil, Carnal Innocence, Hidden Riches*
Tan, Maureen. *AKA Jane, Run Jane Run*

Really Funny Romance

Note: Evanovich herself started out writing these kinds of humorous romances. Try these authors.

Carroll, Leslie.
Gibson, Rachel.
Ireland, Liz.
Michaels, Kasey.
North, Hailey.
Ortolon, Julie.
Phillips, Susan Elizabeth.
Ridgway, Christie.

Particularly Funny Mysteries

Block, Lawrence. Bernie Rhodenbarr Series
Sanders, Lawrence. Arch McNally Series

Serious Alpha Female Detectives

Barnes, Linda. Carlotta Carlyle Series
Duncan, Sharon. Scotia MacKinnon Series
Grafton, Sue. Kinsey Millhone Series
Lanier, Virginia. Jo Beth Sidden Series
LaPlante, Linda. Lorraine Page Series
Robb, J. D. In Death Series (Eve Dallas)
Rogers, Chris. Dixie Flannigan Series
Seranella, Barbara. Munch Mancini Series
Stabenow, Dana. Kate Shugak Series

In the Evanovich Style

Andrews, Mary Kay. *Savannah Blues*
Andersen, Susan. *Baby, I'm Yours, Be My Baby, Baby Don't Go*
Apodaca, Jennifer. Sam Shaw series

Bartholomew, Nancy. Sierra Lavotini series
Bond, Stephanie. *Our Husband, Got Your Number, I Think I Love You*
Boyd, Paula. Jolene Jackson series
Crusie, Jennifer. *Welcome to Temptation, Fast Women, Faking It,*
Graves, Jane. *I Got You Babe, Wild at Heart*
Green, Chloe. Dallas O'Connor series
Harris, Charlaine. Sookie Stackhouse series
Hayter, Sparkle. Robin Hudson series
Heller, Jane. *Female Intelligence, Sis Boom Bah, The Secret Ingredient*
Henderson, Lauren. Sam Jones series
Hughes, Charlotte. *Hot Shot, A New Attitude*
Ledbetter, Suzann. Hannah Garvey series
Levine, Laura. Jaine Austin series
Martin, Nancy. Blackbird Sisters series
McBride, Mary. *Still Mr. and Mrs.*
Michaels, Kasey. *Maggie Needs an Alibi*
Neri, Kris. Tracy Eaton series
O'Grady, Leslie. Wanda Miranda LaFortuna series
Rubino, Jane. Cat Austen series
Strohmeyer, Sarah. Bubbles Yablonsky series
Trocheck, Kathy Hogan. Callahan Garrity series
Winters, Jill. *Plum Girl*

Murder, Mystery, and Mayhem: The Development of a Mystery Book Discussion Group

Elizabeth Arneth

SUMMARY. Describes a two-year period in which a book discussion group proposal evolved into a viable forum for interesting monthly discussions of a variety of mysteries. *[Article copies available for a fee from The Haworth Document Delivery Service: 1-800-HAWORTH. E-mail address: <docdelivery@haworthpress.com> Website: <http://www.HaworthPress.com> © 2004 by The Haworth Press, Inc. All rights reserved.]*

KEYWORDS. Mystery book discussion groups, Cyrus H. Booth Library

THE GENESIS

We were coming to the end of a discussion group based on books that represented the sixties, and as people began to walk out, one of the

Elizabeth Arneth, MSEd, is a retired high school English teacher and dean. She serves as a trustee on the Library Board of the C.H. Booth Library, Newtown, CT, and also as a board member of the Friends of Connecticut Libraries.

Address correspondence to: Elizabeth Arneth, 4 Settlers Lane, Sandy Hook, CT 06482.

[Haworth co-indexing entry note]: "Murder, Mystery, and Mayhem: The Development of a Mystery Book Discussion Group." Arneth, Elizabeth. Co-published simultaneously in *Collection Management* (The Haworth Information Press, an imprint of The Haworth Press, Inc.) Vol. 29, No. 3/4, 2004, pp. 179-187; and: *Managing the Mystery Collection: From Creation to Consumption* (ed: Judith Overmier, and Rhonda Harris Taylor) The Haworth Information Press, an imprint of The Haworth Press, Inc., 2004, pp. 179-187. Single or multiple copies of this article are available for a fee from The Haworth Document Delivery Service [1-800-HAWORTH, 9:00 a.m. - 5:00 p.m. (EST). E-mail address: docdelivery@haworthpress.com].

Available online at http://www.haworthpress.com/web/COL

doi:10.1300/J105v29n03_13

women in the group began to talk about how much she would miss getting together. At that point, I said something like, "Well, how would you feel about mysteries?"

And that was the beginning of my friendship with Marion Wood, and also the beginning of a very popular mystery discussion series because both of us turned out to be aficionados who had a lot in common and soon came to enjoy working together. But from the very beginning we thought it was important not to present ourselves as experts, (we weren't), but as just enthusiastic fans who thought other people might want to join us in exploring the genre.

THE LAUNCH

We started off by going to lunch with the director of adult programming for the Cyrenius H. Booth Library in Newtown, Connecticut, where all the programs were to be held. It is important that you have a supportive connection who knows how to obtain books and to handle publicity, as well as how to trouble-shoot any other problems. Kim Weber has become a wonderful friend who has supported everything we have suggested and then attended all the meetings plus brought all the refreshments. Kim is in charge of ordering the books we used, either from a wholesaler at a forty percent discount or obtaining them through interlibrary loan. The books have to be readily available in paperback and once they arrive, they are stored in a special section of shelves devoted to this project. Another member of the team is Mary Maki who also happens to be the President of the Friends of the Booth Library. This group has donated money to offset some of the expenses incurred by the library. Mary has also become involved in the planning and helps run the discussions. The four of us are very compatible and work very well together, which has been a blessing.

THE BOOKS

We chose female detectives as our first topic because we felt women mystery writers were something we wanted to explore. Upon hindsight this might have been a mistake because no men ever came to any of the programs except for Marion's husband, who also is a mystery lover. However, the lack of male participation in any of the book discussion groups at the library is curious–men tend to show up at programs based on history, non-fiction, or travel, but not mysteries.

The first grouping of authors included Agatha Christie, Patricia Cornwell, Nevada Barr, and Janet Evanovich, who were chosen because they created a broad range of female sleuths. Organizing according to a theme was also very helpful. The second theme in the series was titled "Mysteries in the American Landscape," and it encouraged us to look at how important setting was in the story line, e.g., Florida for Hiassen, the Midwest for Lillian Braun, and the Southwest for Hillerman. Our last series was called "Partners in Crime" and it enabled us not only to discuss the partners in the mystery for a particular evening: We could also compare and contrast them to previous characters, such as comparing Robert Parker's Spenser and Hawk to Janet Evanovich's Stephanie Plum and Ranger.

STRATEGIES FOR THE MEETINGS

Once the books were chosen, we met a week before each program to decide what questions to ask based on our reading of the books. We also developed an agenda that helped keep us on track so that we would stay within the time constraints (we met from 7:30 p.m. to 9:00 p.m. every third Tuesday once the program began). Biographical sketches of the authors were presented first, accompanied by handouts listing other works written by them. The biographies were usually compiled from information supplied by Google or Ixquick on the Internet, and they turned out to be very significant in helping to explain choices authors made about their characters, plots, and settings. For example, Nevada Barr comes from a family of strong, independent women; her mother is a pilot. Robert Parker's unusual living arrangements and difficult marriage were obviously incorporated into *The Catskill Eagle*, a book written at a time when he was separated from his wife. The sketches took no more than two minutes, but they generated a great segue into discussions because the members would immediately comment on the connections between the lives of the authors and their works.

My primary responsibilities were to generate a wide variety of questions, and lead the discussions, and I would make notes while reading the books, then use a variety of resources to develop different approaches. For example, when we needed to establish some basis for how women detectives handled crime *vis a vis* how their male counterparts functioned, mystery guides such as *Deadly Women* edited by

Grape, James, and Nehr, or *Detecting Women 2*, edited by Willetta L. Heising, proved to be invaluable. Topics such as sexual relationships, handling violence, the use of weapons, even their relationships with criminals became intriguing sources for conversation. Once certain behaviors had been identified, this established a rubric that enabled us to compare and contrast different characters as the series moved along. At one point we compared and contrasted Kay Scarpetta with Anna Pigeon in terms of their common traits: being middle aged, cynical, disappointed in love, and having a very close relationship with a female relative.

Logistically, there are some issues with which to contend even when you have an agenda. It is important to keep people on track, but they love to tell their stories, so you need to use a firm but gentle approach to keep anyone from dominating the situation. Sometimes this is easier said than done. At our very first meeting based on Agatha Christie's *The Body in the Library*, a woman began a tirade about how much she disliked the book, especially since Miss Marple seemed to hate men. All the techniques you can use to try to get someone to move on did not work; luckily she finally ran out of steam before I had to ask her to leave. Not exactly an auspicious beginning, but fortunately she never returned (I did ask Marion to speak to her about the behavior because she was an acquaintance). The rest of the women must have enjoyed the evening in spite of it all because they all returned for the next gathering.

You also never know who might show up on a particular night. One time we were discussing Rozan's *Bitter Feast* and enjoying a tea party to celebrate how many cups of tea Lydia Chin tasted in the course of the novel, and in the midst of it all, this strange woman wandered into the room. She told us she had not read the book, but that the program sounded interesting so she thought she would stop by. As Kim continued to serve the tea, the mysterious stranger regaled us with this long, rambling dissertation on an experience she had drinking tea. She was affable, however, and soon fell quiet (actually at that point she appeared to be nodding off), and we were able to move on. Another time we were debating Carl Hisassen's *Sick Puppy*, and out of the blue one woman asked, "Don't you think the dog acts as a *deus ex machina*?" There was dead silence until I explained the Shakespearean allusion, but it did give us pause. That is what makes the whole thing so much fun: You never have any idea about how things are going to turn out depending on who shows up. One thing we have learned to do after all this time is to trust the group. Once they feel comfortable with each other, they are perfectly capable of running the discussions themselves with very little direction from us. At the end of one meeting, I reviewed the fifty questions that I had prepared and never mentioned and was delighted to discover the group had covered most of them.

PUBLICITY

Perhaps the most amusing activity, besides actually running the discussions, has been devising publicity photo opportunities. The *Newtown Bee*, our local paper, is noted for having the same sort of pictures running from week to week. You know the type of pictures: people standing in front of a building, people sitting on a couch, people handing each other checks, etc., so we decided to do something different in order to attract attention. Since our very first book choice was Agatha Christie's *The Body in the Library*, after much thought we decided to do the obvious. One of us would be the body in the library, and the other one would be the detective hovering over the corpse, magnifying glass in hand. Not particularly original, but what made it so funny is that my partner is much smaller than I am, and it wound up that she wore my raincoat and slouch hat, while I played the stiff. She looked like a midget playing a sleuth, but people got a kick out of it. Carl Hiassen's *The Sick Puppy* presented us with another challenge because we thought a dog would be an appropriate prop, but no one could figure out who had an amenable black Labrador. Luckily, the Director of Adult Programming at the library happened to know a woman with a very agreeable, albeit huge, black and tan coon hound named Shadow. After obtaining special permission to bring an animal into the library, we had a lot of laughs with Shadow, who would hold a pose indefinitely while being offered a piece of a hot dog. Straw hats, Hawaiian shirts, a plastic blow up palm tree, and sunglasses rounded out the equipment that time. By this time, the photographer was beginning to shake her head over what we would decide to do next. For *Sing It to Her Bones* by Marcia Talley it appeared that a skeleton would have to be found. I remembered that my physical therapist had one, and he was happy to let us use it with the stipulation that we couldn't move it because the framework was fragile. Since the novel is set in Annapolis, USNA sweatshirts, a model of a sailboat, and a USNA baseball hat for our bony friend made for another interesting photograph. By this point, we figured we had already outdone ourselves, but then *Catskill Eagle* by Robert Parker turned out to be the perfect choice for a picture since it opens with a jail break, but where to find the appropriate set of bars? My partner suggested we try a local bank that had a vault. The Vice President happened to be a friend, and he said he could arrange it. Someone located an eagle hand puppet and we thought we were in business until we accidentally got locked in the vault, and no one had a key to the gate because it was never closed! The three of us had to sit on the floor of the vault while bank employees frantically searched through four boxes of keys until the right one was found twenty minutes later. We did manage to fill the time by talking about the press release and a recent article in *The New York Times* about Parker's unusual living arrangements with his wife. Perhaps the highlight of this experience was seeing the expression on the photographer's face.

Besides the pictures in the *Bee*, the library's Adult Program Director used a variety of methods to publicize the series. She would have special flyers printed and placed in various prominent places in the library as well as different stores and businesses all over town. Bookmarks would also be made with a list of the books that would be read as well as the dates and times we would be meeting. Kim also designed postcards with the booklist on them, and then mailed them to the participants. The publicity resulted in us having around ten to fourteen women at each discussion group.

READERS AND AUTHORS

The last part of this paper is devoted to discussing our relationship with Marcia Talley and Kate Charles, two mystery authors who came to speak to the group, and in the course of their presentations answered many of the questions posed in previous conversations that we could not resolve without the personal input of the authors themselves.

Many things just seemed to happen serendipitously while we were putting on these discussion groups. Last year, the young woman who handles adult programming was visiting a friend in Nashua, New Hampshire when she happened to go to a book signing. It was there that Kim met Marcia Talley, who has written several books about Hannah, a breast cancer survivor who lives in Annapolis with her husband and who keeps running into dead bodies. Hannah turns into an amateur detective because of her experiences, and Marcia just published the third book in the series. At any rate, Marcia and Kim struck up a conversation, and soon Marcia had volunteered to come to Newtown to make a presentation on how to write a murder mystery. She had dinner with us and proved to be a delight. Marcia also didn't ask for any money, but we gave her an honorarium anyway. Her PowerPoint presentation on her second novel was absolutely fascinating, and very informative to boot. Everyone had a great time.

This past November, Marcia was making a book tour and once again suggested that she and her friend, Kate Charles, would be happy to create a conversational format in which the two of them would ask questions about each other's work. Kate Charles lives in England and writes mysteries centered around the Anglican church and all the intrigues that surround the inhabitants who live in a small village. Her series is based on a character named David Middleton-Brown and his girlfriend, Lucy.

Their discussion at the library was enthralling, and they were so happy to meet people who had not only read their books, but asked interesting, intelligent questions about them. The issues they brought up were widely ranging. Kate was asked what was the weirdest place she had ever placed a corpse. That query led to a story about how she had visited Walsingham many times and began to wonder if the ongoing violent confrontations between Catholics and Protestants over the authenticity of the shrine would ever lead to murder.

This questioning led to her writing *The Snare of Death.* Since each one of her chapters starts with a psalm, someone asked her how she was able to find the most appropriate psalm for a particular chapter. Kate told us that she had put the entire "Book of Psalms" into her computer, and then cross-indexed each one. Another technique she related is that all of her characters have a complete biography written for each one of them before she begins writing the narrative, and she keeps track of them with various lists. Another thing she is adamant about is choosing the correct names for her characters. She makes sure that they are true for the time periods she writes about in order to add to the authenticity of the setting. There are no outlines for any Charles book; she said the entire story develops organically in her brain. One time she woke from a deep sleep and had the complete story line in her head. This vision became *Cruel Intentions*. Another person asked her about the use of digitalis in her novel *Evil Angels Among Them*. Kate had made the acquaintance of a famous toxicologist at a gathering, and she asked him what would speed up or slow down the effects of digitalis that is administered in a pill form that looks exactly like artificial sweetener. He replied that gin would speed up the reaction, but tea would slow it down. She used both reactions in her story.

Marcia writes very differently than Kate does. She outlines everything and keeps notes on what is happening as the story develops. Marcia keeps notebooks filled with ideas from articles in the paper, material presented at conferences, or just something someone might have said in passing. Since she lives in Annapolis, she travels around the area scouting various sites that might become part of a story line. She recently was in the Baltimore area in a small town (perhaps Charlestown?) taking notes on different buildings and gardens. Many times she will mix and match details she has observed on her field trips, e.g., put a different railing on a house, or change a location, etc. This time she was looking at a garden when a woman came out of the house to ask what she was doing. It turned out later that she was worried that Marcia might be a census taker. At any rate, she invited Marcia into her home and was happy to show her the garden that was eventually incorporated into a story line. Because Marcia's novels center around Hannah, the challenge is to keep making her more interesting as her character develops. Since Marcia and Hannah are both cancer survivors, Marcia said she always makes sure to interject some aspect of recovery into the opening sequences. To keep Hannah from becoming boring, Marcia is continually adding new family members and friends to the mix, as well as changing location. Marcia, like Kate, also has her poison expert known as the Poison Lady. This woman has an encyclopedic knowledge of pharmacopoeia and is always happy to talk about it with Marcia. Marcia told of an inspiration she got for a scene in a mystery she is presently writing. She was visiting the John Paul Jones shrine at the United States Naval Academy, and she began to speculate what might happen if a midshipman was found murdered there. Marcia then asked Admiral Larson, a good friend and a past USNA superintendent, what would the procedures be if a body were found in the crypt. The admiral made a few phone calls and really upset a young lawyer on the academy staff who didn't quite understand that the admiral was thinking hypothetically. When it came to the issue of authenticity, Marcia said it pays to keep an open mind about any information that might come her way; e.g., it just recently came to her attention that if there was an accident on the Bay Bridge, it would not be handled by a state trooper, or a local police officer because the Bay Bridge has its own police force. You never know when that factoid might be woven into a story line. Marcia loves to tell funny stories, and one of them concerned some female fans of her mysteries who made it a point to track down every single scene in the stories. The only problem is, some of the places they allegedly found had been created in Marcia's imagination.

Marcia also talked about the book she edited that was recently featured in *The New York Times Book Review*. It is titled *Naked Came the Phoenix*. This is a collaborative novel written by mystery writers who had been featured on "The New York Times Best Seller List," such as

Nevada Barr and Faye Kellerman. The ladies had a great time trying to set each other up with a chapter that then had to be continued by a different writer. Marcia said there were problems with continuity; for example, the funniest story was about a character who seemingly drowns in one chapter, only to be miraculously resurrected by CPR in the next. Marcia said she would make sure the next time that when she killed someone, he was going to stay dead! Some of the proceeds from this book will be donated to breast cancer research. Because it has been so well received, Marcia is already thinking of another collaborative mystery titled *Naked Came the Griffin. Phoenix* was set in a health spa, but this one will be located in a gated community where all sorts of awful things happen.

We ended this special evening with the Head Librarian taking us for a tour of the library that ended up in the attic allegedly inhabited by the ghost of Mary Hawley, a benefactor of Newtown who donated money to build the library, the town hall, and Hawley School. We all wondered if Mary Hawley and all of the strange stories about her might one day wind up in a novel written by either Marcia or Kate. This was an unbelievable experience that truly was a fitting ending for two years of mystery book discussions. And if life imitated art, this would be the perfect place to end this paper. However, we have been brought back by popular demand, and will begin the next series in April that will feature Dana Stabanow, Deborah Crombie, Sujata Massey, and Thomas Perry–authors selected after reviewing the results of a survey we handed out. The mystery continues . . .

REFERENCES

De Andrea, William, ed. *Encyclopedia Mysteriosa*. New York: Prentice Hall, 1994.

Grape, Jan, Dean James and Ellen Nehr, eds. *Deadly Women*. New York: Carroll and Graf, 1998.

Greenberg, Martin H., and Bill Pronzini, eds. *The Ethnic Detectives*. New York: Dodd Mead, 1985.

Heising, L. Willetta, ed. *Detecting Women 2*. Dearborn: Purple Moon Press, 1996.

Oleksiw, Susan, ed. *A Reader's Guide to the Classic British Mystery*. Boston: G.K. Hall, 1998.

Paretsky, Sara, ed. *A Woman's Eye*. New York: Delacorte Press, 1991.

Pronzini, Bill, ed. *Gun in Cheek: An Affectionate Guide to the "Worst" Mystery Fiction*. New York: The Mysterious Press, 1982.

Smith, Marie, ed. *Ms Murder*. New York: Citadel Press, 1989.

Thomson, Douglas H., ed. *Masters of Mystery*. New York: Dover Publications, 1978.

A Brief History of Scholarly Study of Detective Fiction, with Particular Attention to the Detective & Mystery Fiction Area of the Popular Culture Association

Mary P. Freier

SUMMARY. Academic study of detective fiction is an outgrowth of several things: the study of popular culture, women's studies, ethnic studies, and gender studies. It has become a legitimate area of study for academic scholars. The Popular Culture Association and American Culture Association's Detective & Mystery Fiction Area has been an important part of the legitimizing of the field, giving scholars a forum in which to present and discuss ideas and scholarly journals in which to publish.

KEYWORDS. Mystery fiction, detective fiction, literary criticism, Popular Culture Association, American Culture Association

---

Mary P. Freier is Reference & Instruction Librarian, Laurence McKinley Gould Library, Carleton College, One North College Street, Northfield, MN 55057.

[Haworth co-indexing entry note]: "A Brief History of Scholarly Study of Detective Fiction, with Particular Attention to the Detective & Mystery Fiction Area of the Popular Culture Association." Freier, Mary P. Co-published simultaneously in *Collection Management* (The Haworth Information Press, an imprint of The Haworth Press, Inc.) Vol. 29, No. 3/4, 2004, pp. 189-196; and: *Managing the Mystery Collection: From Creation to Consumption* (ed: Judith Overmier, and Rhonda Harris Taylor) The Haworth Information Press, an imprint of The Haworth Press, Inc., 2004, pp. 189-196. Single or multiple copies of this article are available for a fee from The Haworth Document Delivery Service [1-800-HAWORTH, 9:00 a.m. - 5:00 p.m. (EST). E-mail address: docdelivery@haworthpress.com].

Available online at http://www.haworthpress.com/web/COL

doi:10.1300/J105v29n03_14

THE ACADEMY AND DETECTIVE FICTION

Although detective fiction has co-existed with "serious" fiction for some time, academic attention to detective fiction by literary scholars is a relatively recent development. Academic study of detective fiction is an outgrowth of several things: the study of popular culture, women's studies, ethnic studies, and gender studies. The study of detective fiction has also been very responsive to the development of the genre itself.

Academics have been traditionally fond of mystery fiction; indeed, they have often been guilty of writing it. Dorothy L. Sayers, for example, paved the way for other academics to write their own mysteries, such as Amanda Cross (Carolyn Heilburn). But academics traditionally thought of mysteries as something that they read and wrote for pleasure, as opposed to the literature about which they taught and wrote. Academics also tended to focus critical study on the literary canon: those works which, it was believed, had stood the test of time due to their superior qualities. Or, so the evidence seemed to show.

A search of the *Modern Language Association International Bibliography* demonstrates that very little attention was paid to detective fiction before 1970; it is difficult to search for books and articles on the general subject because there were no descriptors for genre fiction assigned to entries at this time. Searching the "Subject Author Index" for items about Raymond Chandler shows that 248 are indexed; however, only six of them were written before 1970 *(MLA International Bibliography).*

No dissertations on detective fiction were written in any departments during this period, as revealed by a search of *Dissertations Abstracts (ProQuest Digital Dissertations)*. However, there were some stirrings of professional interest in the genre at this time. A very few critics attempted to analyze traditional literary canonical works as if they were detective fiction. The works of Dashiell Hammett and Raymond Chandler, who both got their starts in the most un-literary pages of *Black Mask*, were being scrutinized for their hardboiled view of reality and detection *(MLA International Bibliography)*. This attention was in part due to the well-known film versions of their works, but some interest was also generated by the contrast of their works with that of writers such as G. K. Chesterton and Sayers, whose theological inclinations made it easy for critics to interpret their detective fiction as commentary on the nature of good and evil and even of God. The "mean streets" of

Chandler and Hammett were relatively amoral and godless places, and their writings seemed to require an entirely different reading.

However, there were other reasons for the lack of academic attention to detective fiction in the 1960s. "Publish or perish" was beginning to be heard more often, and few academic journals were interested in scholarly studies of detective fiction or in scholarly studies of other genre fiction. If a professor could not get work published in a scholarly journal or by an academic press, s/he could hardly expect to be granted tenure and promotion. Many of these journals and presses were committed to the study of the literary canon, and members of their editorial boards were likely to share this commitment.

However, other events were occurring in academia in the 1960s and 1970s, and these things were very much to the benefit of scholarly attention to detective fiction. Oddly enough, politics furthered the case of the detective novel. The literary canon itself came under attack in the sixties, and English departments were forced to examine questions about why the authors of the literary canon were so overwhelmingly white, male, and dead. Critics began to examine writers who, although they had written bestsellers, were long forgotten. Many of these writers were women, and many were people of color. Often they supported themselves and their families by writing potboilers, works whose major motivation was the money that they would generate. Potboilers seldom got much academic critical respect, although they sometimes received popular acclaim and often became bestsellers. But the academic critics began to re-discover these writers and began to examine the potboilers themselves. And, they began to see research possibilities in studying these previously unworthy pieces of writing. Mary Roberts Rinehart was a perfect example of a popular novelist whose work had been ignored by academic critics; her novels have never gone out of print, and her popularity as a writer and celebrity was immense during her lifetime. Academic literary critics, however, had seen no need to write about her career or her writing.

ENTER THE POPULAR CULTURE ASSOCIATION

The study of popular culture for its own sake also began to pick up momentum, and, in 1971, the first academic conference devoted to popular culture was held, sponsored by the newly-formed Popular Culture Association (PCA) (Browne 2002). One paper on the subject of detective fiction appears in the program for the 1967 meeting of the Popular

Culture Association. In a session on "Popular Literature," Arnold R. Hoffman of Adrian College presented a paper on "Crime and Culture in Mrs. Rinehart's Fiction" (Browne 2002).

CREATION OF THE DETECTIVE & MYSTERY AREA

The PCA continued to promote the study of detective fiction. When it first created areas in 1974, Detective & Mystery Fiction was included (Browne 2002). As the conference has grown, the Detective & Mystery Area has also blossomed. Detective novelists have often been speakers at the conference, and the 2003 meeting featured both Sara Paretsky and Stuart Kaminsky *(Popular Culture Association and American Culture Association 2003 National PCA/ACA Conference, New Orleans Marriott, April 16-19, 2003)*. Although the PCA is an academic conference, its participants have chosen their field of study out of love, or, in some cases, their work in detective fiction is an avocation, rather than their primary job responsibility. Thus, PCA participants have never lost their sense of enjoyment of detective fiction as popular literature. While one is less likely to hear readings and discussions by mystery novelists at PCA as compared to BoucherCon, one is more likely to hear an article or book in its embryonic stages, and, if some conversations are to be believed, to hear future authors of detective fiction discuss the direction of both the form and content of the detective novel.

Some explanation of the PCA meetings is in order. The meetings are academic conferences, but with a major difference. Most of the people attending the conference are presenting their scholarly works. Scholars in popular culture studies are a relatively recent phenomenon, and, when the PCA was first being organized, it was not unusual for scholars in these areas to be told that their studies were not worth pursuing, not because of the quality of their scholarship or writing, but because of the subjects. An early concern in the PCA was that no field of study suffer from such discrimination, and the tendency for the PCA is not to reject papers, although some authors will receive some suggestions for improvement.

The Detective & Mystery Fiction Area is not juried; the Area Chair accepts all proposals submitted to the area, unless the proposal actually belongs in another area of the PCA. The Area Chairs handled all of the receipt and acceptance of proposals and are also responsible for organizing the various (in all of its meanings) papers into coherent panels. Needless to say, some panels are more coherent than others. People attending the sessions are never discouraged from leaving after the one paper in which they are interested has been presented, and they are also never discouraged from appearing late to hear only some of the papers on the panel. In order to facilitate such coming and going, the Detective & Mystery Fiction Area has always adhered to three rules in the presentation of their panels: (1) no paper will be allowed to take over twenty minutes to read; (2) all papers will be read in the order in which they appear in the program; and (3) all discussion will be held until after all the papers in the panel have been read. These rules have allowed for spirited discussion and argument and have also ensured that all presenters get a fair chance to present their papers. Another, possibly unenforceable, rule of the Detective & Mystery Fiction Area is that the presenter must never reveal the identity of the murderer during the paper: Because the scholars attending these sessions are also aficionados, the notes that they are taking often include lists of the authors whose novels they want to read or the names of particular novels, and knowing the murderer's identity might destroy the pleasure in the reading of a detective novel.

Maintaining the joy of their field of study has always been important to the members of this Area. There are, as there are at all academic conferences, informal discussions at local restaurants and watering holes. But the Detective & Mystery Fiction Area also organizes its own fun and games. In some cases, there are literal games. From 1986 to 1996, the Area scheduled a session entitled "Criminous Pursuits." Admission to these sessions was five questions about mystery fiction. The games were great fun, but the sessions died out because it became laborious for people to generate new questions without duplicating questions asked the previous year or without becoming so obscure as to discourage new members of the Area.

Another regular session devoted to the sheer joy of reading mysteries is "Read Any Good Books Lately?" In this session, which is often scheduled over the noon hour, people bring their lunches and talk about the detective fiction that they've read in the last year that they think others would enjoy. The discussion is not limited to books written and published in the last year, because sometimes people will have read older novels that they enjoyed a great deal. The Area Chair for the year or a volunteer will take notes of all the authors and titles that are mentioned, in order to e-mail the list to the members in the coming year. Since the discussion is fast and furious, the recorder has a difficult job.

Part of the reason for the rapid growth in this Area has to do with the people who started it. Some, like Earl Bargainnier, made a point of attending every session, and, when he noticed new presenters, stopped to speak to them and encourage them in their work by complimenting them directly, asking questions about their papers, or making suggestions for ways in which their work could be expanded. Bargainnier died suddenly in 1987 (Browne 50), and the Detective & Mystery Fiction Area immediately instituted an award for the best paper by a first-time presenter in his honor. Others, like Jane Bakerman, took her research and that of others very seriously, and thus the Women's Studies Area created an award in her honor for her work in the study of women writers. George N. Dove was another participant who did a great deal to welcome newcomers and promote the serious study of detective fiction. Upon his retirement, the Area created the Dove Award for major contribution to the study of detective and mystery fiction. There were probably no more than twenty presenters in the Mystery and Detective Fiction Area at the meeting in 1974, but the papers presented and the people there were inspiring to people who had been reading mysteries for pleasure for years.

MOVING FORWARD FROM 1970

The PCA's success over the years has been well-documented in Ray Browne's *Mission Underway: The History of the Popular Culture Association/American Culture Association and the Popular Culture Movement 1967-2001* (2002). The PCA influenced growth in programs in popular culture and journals in popular studies and, between 1970 and 1990, scholarly publications about detective fiction increased more than a hundredfold. But the PCA was not the only influence that increased interest in detective fiction by academics. Another reason for this increase was the development of new academic journals, journals whose missions would allow the publication of articles on detective fiction. Three of these journals are *The Journal of Popular Culture*, *The Armchair Detective*, and *Clues: A Journal of Detection*. Two of these journals were started at the Popular Press in Bowling Green, Ohio, which was associated with the Popular Culture Studies program at Bowling Green State University and the PCA. These three journals account for a significant amount of scholarly publishing about detective fiction in the 1970s and 1980s. Of the 1,200 journal articles about detective fiction published from 1970-1989, 647 were published by these three journals *(MLA International Bibliography)*.

Many scholarly books on the genre were published during this period as well, and not only by the Popular Press. Between 1970 and 1989, ninety-seven books (or book collections) about detective fiction were published. The Popular Press accounted for only thirty-one of these titles. The other sixty-six were published at a range of presses, including the university presses of the University of Illinois, the University of Iowa, Notre Dame, Harvard, and Yale *(MLA International Bibliography)*. Clearly, detective fiction as a legitimate study for scholarly research had arrived!

However, one of the most important developments of the critical study of detective fiction was the fact that graduate students began to write their doctoral dissertations on the subject of detective fiction. Critical theory made its presence known in this period, and a form of fiction whose primary action is interpretation is especially fertile ground for its application. Thus, the fact that forty-five dissertations were written on detective fiction during this period should not be very surprising *(ProQuest Digital Dissertations)*, nor the fact that critic Umberto Eco's first detective novel, *The Name of the Rose*, was published in 1980.

Subjects for critical study of detective fiction in the 1970s and 1980s reflected the newness of the area for academic study and the roots of its newfound respectability. There were many articles giving overviews of a particular author's life and writings, and there were many studies of women who wrote detective fiction and of women detectives themselves. Other studies traced the history of detective fiction as a genre, while others looked for reflections of our cultural attitudes in detective fiction.

The development in the genre itself created other avenues for exploration. One of the most-discussed events in the history of critical work on detective fiction was Sara Paretsky's creation of V. I. Warshawski, the first unabashedly hardboiled female private investigator. Women's roles in detective fiction had changed forever, and so did literary criticism about the genre. Detective fiction in which women are presented as professional detectives demanded comparison with the "traditional" hardboiled novels of Chandler and Hammett.

SECURING THE FUTURE

The study of mystery and detective fiction has continued to grow, reflecting both the new fiction that is written and new scholarly interests. Gender studies have become popular, as scholars explore the significance of masculine and feminine roles in the genre. The appearance of gay and lesbian detectives has also stirred scholarly interest. Ethnic detectives, including African-American and Hispanic detectives, have also been getting a fair share of attention. The numbers have remained strong for scholarly publication on detective fiction; from 1990 to 2002, there were ninety-four dissertations written, 963 articles published, and seventy-four books (or book collections) printed *(MLA International Bibliography)*. The position of detective fiction scholarship is secure, even though one of the two refereed journals specializing in that arena and that helped early scholars earn respectability, promotion, and tenure has ceased to publish. *The Armchair Detective* ceased publication in 1997 after a thirty-year run *(Ulrich's Periodicals Directory)*.

The scholarly study of detective fiction has come a long way since 1960. Work that once had to be done in an academic's elusive spare time can now be the major focus of his/her research. Opportunities for publication in scholarly journals abound, where before they required their own journals. Most important, the critical literature itself has responded to the growing interest of the academy, and has developed in new and engaging ways. The Popular Culture Association and the American Culture Association (http://www2.h-net.msu.edu/~pcaaca/) continue to provide publications that encourage the study of detective fiction and to sponsor conferences where presentations about the subject are welcomed enthusiastically.

REFERENCES

Browne, Ray B. 2002. *Mission Underway: The History of the Popular Culture Association/American Culture Association and the Popular Culture Movement 1967-2001*. Revised and updated ed. Bowling Green, OH: Popular Culture Association/American Culture Association. Original edition, 1989.

MLA International Bibliography 2003. SilverPlatter Information [cited 25 January 2003]. Available from http://web5.silverplatter.com/webspirs/start.ws.

Popular Culture Association and American Culture Association 2003 National PCA/ACA Conference, New Orleans Marriott, April 16-19, 2003 [cited 24 January 2003]. Available from http://www.popularculture.org/Program%20PCA.htm.

ProQuest Digital Dissertations 2003. UMI Company [cited 25 January 2003]. Available from http://wwwlib.umi.com/dissertations.

Ulrich's Periodicals Directory 2003. R.R. Bowker Company [cited 25 January 2003]. Available from http://www.ulrichsweb.com.

Tracking Miriam Grace Monfredo Through Herstory, Librarianship, and Sleuthing

Judith Overmier
Rhonda Harris Taylor

SUMMARY. Librarian Miriam Grace Monfredo's Glynis Tryon historical mystery series portrays a multi-faceted librarian sleuth. The series is a case study of using genre fiction to popularize women's history with its many political and social issues. It also emphasizes the important role of collections of resources in supporting the creative activities of authors. *[Article copies available for a fee from The Haworth Document Delivery Service: 1-800-HAWORTH. E-mail address: <docdelivery@haworthpress.com> Website: <http://www.HaworthPress.com> © 2004 by The Haworth Press, Inc. All rights reserved.]*

KEYWORDS. Miriam Grace Monfredo, Glynis Tryon, women's history, historical mystery series

Judith Overmier, PhD, is Professor Emeritus, University of Oklahoma, 1965 East River Terrace, Minneapolis, MN 55414. Rhonda Harris Taylor, PhD, is Associate Professor, School of Library and Information Studies, University of Oklahoma, 401 West Brooks, Room 120, Norman, OK 73019-6032.

[Haworth co-indexing entry note]: "Tracking Miriam Grace Monfredo Through Herstory, Librarianship, and Sleuthing." Overmier, Judith, and Rhonda Harris Taylor. Co-published simultaneously in *Collection Management* (The Haworth Information Press, an imprint of The Haworth Press, Inc.) Vol. 29, No. 3/4, 2004, pp. 197-209; and: *Managing the Mystery Collection: From Creation to Consumption* (ed: Judith Overmier, and Rhonda Harris Taylor) The Haworth Information Press, an imprint of The Haworth Press, Inc., 2004, pp. 197-209. Single or multiple copies of this article are available for a fee from The Haworth Document Delivery Service [1-800-HAWORTH, 9:00 a.m. - 5:00 p.m. (EST). E-mail address: docdelivery@haworthpress. com].

Available online at http://www.haworthpress.com/web/COL

doi:10.1300/J105v29n03_15

INTRODUCING THE AUTHOR

There have been several mystery series that portray librarians as protagonists (Judith VanGieson's rare book conservator, Claire Reynier; Elizabeth Peters' librarian/romance writer, Jacqueline Kirby; Jo Dereske's public librarian, Helma Zukas; Kate Morgan's Dewey James) and there are librarians who pen mysteries (Barbara Fister; Charles Goodrum; Margaret Yorke). Miriam Grace Monfredo is perhaps unique for being a librarian by training who has written a series with a female librarian detective. The series is also unique in that the librarian protagonist is placed within a nineteenth century setting. That historical context means the series is dependent on the information seeking skills of the author for authenticity in everyday historical details. The important role of history in the series also reiterates that the collective acquisitions efforts of librarians are vital for providing the resources so necessary for supporting authors' creation of new literary works.

In 1990, Monfredo celebrated her fiftieth birthday by completing her first mystery novel, *Seneca Falls Inheritance* (1992). This title initiated a mystery series set in the pre-Civil War period, 1848 to 1859, and through the turbulent Civil War years. Other works in the series include: *North Star Conspiracy* (1993), *Blackwater Spirits* (1995), *Through a Gold Eagle* (1996), *The Stalking-Horse* (1998), *Must the Maiden Die* (1999), *Sisters of Cain* (2000), and *Brothers of Cain* (2001), and *Children of Cain* (2002). This series is notable for its dynamic portrayal of a female librarian protagonist in a genre that has often relied on stereotypes for characterizing librarians. Both the plots and the characterization of the protagonist as crusader are vitalized by the historical series' passionate coverage of women's rights issues and of librarianship's intellectual freedom and access issues. Not surprisingly, the realistic coverage of these two arenas clearly reflects the author's own background and experiences. Indeed, Monfredo has been quoted as saying that her "goal in writing is to play some small role in giving women everywhere a sense of where they have been and what they are capable of achieving" (Nancy Berland). Certainly that goal is particularly relevant in blending a profession that is historically and contemporarily viewed as a woman's profession (librarian) with one that has been viewed as a man's profession (detective).

Monfredo has a bachelor's degree from Nazareth College, a small, woman's educational institution where she majored in sociology and history. The latter subject was one that she detested while in high school and was forced to study in college. However, during her college years,

Monfredo overhead a faculty member talking about women's history, was intrigued, and signed up for his class. That course was the beginning of an educational journey that led her to conclude that "History is the most fascinating thing that I know–it's not just men and wars" (Telephone interview). In 1976, Monfredo brought her knowledge of history to her daughter's Girl Scout troop, teaching them about interesting historical women personages in Western New York. She then began extensive historical research with the goal of writing a nonfiction book on the topic. Fortunately for her readers, that intention culminated in a mystery novel. Monfredo's interest in women's history is coupled with her professional background in the quintessential information field–librarianship. She holds a master's degree in library and information science from SUNY at Geneseo (Telephone interview).

INTRODUCING THE DETECTIVE

Monfredo's first mystery, *Seneca Falls Inheritance*, introduces unconventional nineteenth century heroine Glynis Tryon, librarian of the Seneca Falls, New York library. Tryon, an advocate of women's rights, is thrust into the middle of murders, which she solves utilizing the persistence and detective skills innate to good reference librarians. In her depiction of Glynis Tryon, Monfredo has achieved that memorable, complex, and evolving mixture of traits that constitute a believable, likeable protagonist. That same mixture, of course, gives flesh to the real human beings whose company we enjoy. It is the lack of recognition or appreciation of that complexity, especially in diverse peoples (including women), that breeds the stereotypes against which today's library profession rails. These flat images of librarians appear both in information products (such as books and visual media) and in the assumptions (known within the profession as the "Marian the Librarian" stereotype, as portrayed in the 1957 Meredith Wilson musical and the 1962 movie, *The Music Man*) held by individuals outside of the profession.

In *Seneca Falls Inheritance*, readers meet a thirty-year-old librarian protagonist who has been courageous enough to use a loan to attend Oberlin College, complete an education at "the first four year institution to admit women students" (64), move from the town where her family is centered, and become involved in politics even though she is aware that at least one member of the library board does not approve of that involvement and questions her morals. In contrast, Tryon is shy about, even dreading, asking women to simply sign a petition. In Glynis Tryon, Monfredo has developed a multi-faceted individual, eschewing the simplistic and common characterization of the typical librarian stereotype that was already forming in the nineteenth century. For instance, in *Seneca Falls Inheritance*, when the villain comments to Tryon that she doesn't seem to be a librarian, she inquires what his idea of a librarian is. "'My experience in Boston,' he said, 'has been that there the few female librarians are dry old ladies with steel-framed spectacles, and hair pulled back so tightly their lips scarcely move when they talk. And they wear black, black dresses which button up over their chins'" (129). There are many twenty-first century librarians who would say that image persists today (Marinelli and Baker)!

The literate Glynis Tryon thoroughly thwarts the librarian dress code in the finale to *Through a Gold Eagle* by attending a costume ball as George Sands–dressed in trousers. This incident, amusing to us, was startling to the Seneca Falls cultural community, and like many of the other details of Monredo's novels, has an historical parallel. John Cotton Dana, Director of the Denver Public Library and leader in the emerging library profession in the 1890s, sent his female staff members a picture of a woman in trousers, labeling it the "latest librarian uniforms in the East." His staff, perceiving a challenge, willing to flout the current social conventions, and full of good humor, appeared at the library's weekly book review session wearing "loosely made trousers, some of which were tied at the ankles with red bows" (qtd. in McReynolds, 30).

THE SERIES

The Tryon series thrusts the protagonist into the middle of mysteries that not only involve murder but are woven into social and political issues and important historical events of the time period.

In *Seneca Falls Inheritance*, the accidental drowning deaths of the head of the library board, Friedrich Steicher, and his wife, Caroline, set into motion a conundrum revolving around the issue of inheritance. The arrival of an unexpected female heir, Rose, to challenge the claim of Steicher's son, Karl, is the catalyst for four murders. Mayhem occurs during a critical time for women, as the Women's Rights Convention is being held in 1848 in Seneca Falls. Also critical to the plot is New York's passage in 1848 of the first state legislation that would allow wives to inherit from their husbands.

Set in 1854, six years after the events of *Seneca Falls Inheritance*, Monfredo's second book, *North Star Conspiracy*, takes place four years after the passage of the federal Fugitive Slave Law, and the ramifications of this policy directly impact the lives of friends of Glynis Tryon. Tryon becomes involved in the Underground Railroad as she also solves three murders.

In *Blackwater Spirits*, the year is 1857, and Tryon is investigating a series of murders that are occurring a decade after the vigilante lynching of a young Iroquois. One of Tryon's romantic interests, Jacques Sundown, is accused of the murders. Monfredo highlights the problems of women physicians with the introduction of a new doctor in Seneca Falls, Neva Cardoza, who performs autopsies on victims, but must use a male surrogate to testify about her findings in court.

Monfredo's Tryon series is also a family saga, and later additions to the series feature the unmarried (so far!) and childless Tryon's successors–her nieces and nephew. The first of the series to introduce the nieces is *Through a Gold Eagle*. Set in 1859, it involves Glynis Tryon and her niece Emma Llyr in a mystery that begins with a twenty-dollar gold piece, a "double eagle." Before the mystery of counterfeiting and multiple murders is solved, Tryon finds her life intertwined with the plans of abolitionist John Brown.

The eve of the Civil War provides the backdrop for *The Stalking-Horse*, in which another of Tryon's nieces, Bronwen Llyr, a Pinkerton detective, thwarts an assassination attempt on President Lincoln.

Must the Maiden Die finds Bronwen Llyr arriving in Seneca Falls in a balloon to attend her sister Emma's marriage. Glynis and Bronwen solve the murder of a man whom they discover was smuggling arms to the South and who was sexually abusing his wife and their indentured servant girl.

In *Sisters of Cain*, Bronwen Llyr is an undercover agent for the Special Intelligence Force for Treasury. Kathryn Llyr, the third of Glynis Tryon's nieces, is a nurse for the Union army. Bronwen and Kathryn thwart Southern sabotage plans.

Brothers of Cain introduces Seth Llyr, Glynis Tryon's nephew. He is captured by the Southern forces and sentenced to hang. His sisters Kathryn, nursing in a field hospital, and Bronwen, help Seth escape from a Confederate prison.

Children of Cain is the third of the Cain trilogy, and it is set against the backdrop of the 1862 Peninsula Campaign. In this novel, Bronwen Llyr is not only investigating a murder but is trying to uncover a plot to assassinate President Lincoln. Her sister Kathryn and aunt Glynis Tryon are also featured in the book.

INTRODUCING THE HISTORY

Monfredo's historical mystery series reflects her ability to present broad historical themes and issues of the last half of the nineteenth century. She excels in detailed historical areas related to women's political and social history, such as education, work, and property rights (including control of their own funds and wages). One acknowledgment of Monfredo's effective popularized coverage of the history of women was an invitation for her to be a speaker in Seneca Falls on the 150th anniversary of the first Women's Rights convention (held July 19-20, 1848). Specific women's political and legal rights covered in Monfredo's series include voting, property rights, employment, spousal abuse, and the impact of slavery on the lives of African American and white women.

Monfredo is also especially effective in her coverage of another area often popularly considered to be the purview of women: American libraries, librarianship, and reading. By the nineteenth century, American academic, public, school, and medical libraries had been in existence in one form or another for a number of years, but were in many ways still in their infancy. For instance, Harvard had a library in 1636, and by 1890, even Denver, in the far West, had a public library. By the nineteenth century, there were also attempts at establishing the profession of librarianship, but it was not until 1887 that Melvil Dewey established the School of Library Economy at Columbia College. Prior to that event librarians learned on the job, in apprenticeships, or in training programs. Although many of the recurring issues of the profession were already in place by the time period of Monfredo's series, librarians of that era had no established educational programs, no professional associations, and no professional journals. The American Library Association was not established until 1876, the *Library Journal* began publication that same year, and the first library school (at Columbia College), was not yet founded by Dewey.

Monfredo has captured important aspects of the reality of librarianship in the nineteenth century. Her portrayal of Glynis Tryon serving at the pleasure of a board in *Seneca Falls Inheritance* accurately reflects the way many libraries were administered. The establishment of the Seneca Falls library as a private philanthropy, thanks to the donation of books by a leading citizen, in that instance Friedrich Steicher, was a very common form of establishing or developing such collections. Steicher's collection included typical works, such as all of Jane Austen's publications, and atypical works, such as Emily Bronte's *Jane Eyre*. Steicher was a fan of Edgar Allen Poe and brought the author to town for a live reading, invoking a sense of the thirst for cultural activities that spurred the Chautauqua movement of the nineteenth century.

The Seneca Falls library is a social library, precursor to the current iteration of public libraries. Social libraries varied greatly in size but had in common the collections and the characteristics of being housed in a room or building, having a caretaker to manage and protect them, being open to the public, and enjoying (or not enjoying) the financial support of the users or private benefactors. Thus, the most significant difference between social libraries and the now-familiar public library in the United States is that the latter have an on-going commitment of funding by a governmental entity. Both social and public libraries included the provision of entertaining reading in their goals. Finally, it should not be forgotten that both public and social libraries have benefited from a long history of active support and advocacy by women, both as groups and as individuals.

Like the heroine in the 1990s television series on CBS, "Dr. Quinn, Medicine Woman," Tryon is portrayed as a bright, college educated, dedicated, often-crusading woman who encounters social issues familiar to contemporary readers–the historical backdrops become a frame for viewer/reader cogitation of controversy. On the one hand, Tryon is depicted performing such routine library tasks as receiving gifts of books, cataloging books, shelving books, and answering questions. On the other hand, she is also someone who has taken a stand on the side of what contemporary librarians would recognize as access and intellectual freedom precepts from the current American Library Association "Library of Rights": "(1) Books and other library resources should be provided for the interest, information, and enlightenment of all people of the community the library serves. . . . (2) Libraries should provide materials and information presenting all points of view on current and historical issues" (http://www.ala.org). Tryon is a nineteenth century proponent of free access to information. The Seneca Falls library regularly takes or sends books to readers; Tryon lends library materials to the framers of the documents for the women's rights meetings, which were considered radical gatherings. In another instance, Tryon was aware that the inclusion of such works as *Jane Eyre*, a novel of "love and passion, written by a woman" was going to create a stir. Its presence in the library offended reviewers and readers and one board member, but was very popular. Tryon literally could not keep it on the shelves, so Steicher bought the library a second copy. In contrast, Jane Austen is considered "good literature." Through such details in her narratives, Monfredo manages to invoke the nineteenth century's "passion for fiction which led crowds to gather at the docks in New York in the 1840s, awaiting the arrival of the ship which was to deliver from London the latest installment of Dickens's *Old Curiosity Shop*" (Conway 5).

By *Blackwater Spirits*, Tryon has an assistant, Jonathan Quant, for the library. Quant is a reader of popular fiction and is portrayed reading a "sentimental novel," *Meadow Brook*, by Mary Jane Holmes. This activity bothers Tryon, who notes that this kind of book–not good literature–was being read "while Hawthorne and Melville sat on the library shelves gathering dust" (21). Tryon does not think the library should buy this kind of book. However, Tryon herself is portrayed as reading ladies' magazines, as indicated by her comments about a man's mustache as being similar to a ladies' magazine villain. This controversy about the inclusion of books the readers want versus collecting only the "best" literature existed from the beginning of publicly accessible libraries and still continues. Obviously, popular culture studies scholars and fans, including Monfredo, self-defined reader of Hardy Boys series mysteries (Telephone interview), advocate the inclusion of the "frivolous" into library collections!

Attention to details is critical in historical fiction if one is to avoid the public embarrassment of a memorable faux pas. Monfredo notes, "You walk a tremendous tightrope when writing historical fiction," adding that "it is sometimes what you think you know that gets you into trouble." She recounts an episode in which she awakened suddenly in the middle of the night, knowing that derringers were invented in 1848, but realizing that she was unsure of the month. Such detail would be critical if her book were to include use of the derringer in that year. In the library (where else to verify!) the next morning, Monfredo discovered that derringers were not available for use until November of 1848, and her book was set in July (Telephone interview).

It's been suggested that Monfredo is a "voracious polymath." In an interview, she accompanied this description with a laugh but then admitted that there's nothing that does not interest her, except football (Telephone interview). Such wide-spread interests are to her advantage as Monfredo utilizes her skills as an historical researcher and reference librarian to research the often neglected primary sources that reveal the achievements and challenges faced by women in nineteenth century America. Indicative of her organized approach to information-gathering was a 1992 newspaper profile, which described collections of resources in her study, including reference books and file folders with such titles as "Fashion 1880s" and "Flora, fauna, seasonal, N.Y." (Forbes). Monfredo is careful to provide detailed historical notes at the end of each of her Tryon novels, which provide explanations of individuals, events, places, language, and material culture. These notes are written for the lay reader and serve to popularize the issues and details of history.

From the acknowledgments in the front of each of Monfredo's novels, it is obvious that she is a sleuth in her own right, drawing upon an extensive network of library and museum resources, historical societies, and knowledgeable individuals, including family members. For example, her physician father was also a sailor who designed the boat Cascade that appears in *The Stalking-Horse* and was a consultant about nautical details. For medical details, Monfredo reports that she did research at a medical library, and the portrayal of a recurring character, the female physician, Neva Cardoza, reflects the details of her research. Monfredo's daughter, a museum professional, has been given credit for her assistance with material culture details as well as providing the numismatic theme for *Through a Gold Eagle*. Monfredo's husband, a litigation attorney, has supplied legal and trial expertise (Telephone interview).

Monfredo documents her use of primary materials in such special collections as the Elizabeth Strong Museum Library (Rochester, New York), of which she speaks with great affection, while applauding the richness of its popular culture resources (Telephone interview). Monfredo has also acknowledged her debt to the Edward G. Miner Medical Library (University of Rochester) History of Medicine Division, where her research has paid off in her novels' accuracy of details about Genesee fever, medical education of women, development of hospitals, autopsy methods, and Civil War nursing. For *The Stalking-Horse*, Monfredo visited historic locales in Montgomery, Alabama and read the diaries of Mary Boykin Chestnut who was in Montgomery during the pre-Civil War era (Wilkerson).

All mysteries require attention to plot and character; the precedence of one over the other will continue to generate discussion, but the dexterous integration of the two provides the readability that sells books. The successful writer is distinguished by the deft handling of the challenge of providing the details that make for credible historical fiction while maintaining a pace that interests the readers. Monfredo's historical series, judging by comments from her readers and the reviewers, juggles these varying demands skillfully.

RESEARCH MEETS ROMANCE: HERSTORY

While Monfredo's novels are rich in historical detail, and while she has devoted many hours to verifying those details, her books are also eminently readable. The serious elements of the plot are offset by her melding of the historical detective story with the characteristics of the sprightly romance novel (including Tryon's dilemma of her attraction to two potential suitors), while focusing on a multi-dimensional female protagonist. This model reflects the dichotomy of approaches to women's narrative, including fiction. In *When Memory Speaks: Reflections on Autobiography*, Conway suggests that the Western European tradition of autobiography provides "archetypal life scripts for men and for women which show remarkable persistence over time" (7). For men, "life is an odyssey, a journey through many trials and tests, which the hero must surmount through courage, endurance, cunning and moral strength" (7). In contrast, Conway traces women's life narratives through stages of influences from "visionary encounter with God, a God often viewed in extremely abstract terms" (14) to the "bourgeois pre-occupation with romantic love, marriage, family and property" (13) to the "conventions of the romance [that] require that the heroine be courted, and the dynamic of the plot comes from the way in which the barriers to expressing her response to the hero. . . are progressively removed by fate, destiny or other external force" (14). Contrary to the acceptance of external intervention in the woman's life, Chappel, in her "Romancing the Real: The Use of History in American Popular Romance," notes that in contemporary historical romance fiction, "not only do writers want to write women's history accurately in their novels, but getting the details right is often an ideological practice, a righting of old wrongs which involves placing women at the center of historical occurrences and male-dominated venues where they would have been unlikely to be found at those times in history." This empowerment by re-appropriating their own history is demonstrated in Monfredo's works. In contrast to Conway's sense of the nature of the romance genre of the past, Chappel's conclusion about the contemporary historical romance is that "the history these romance authors wish to establish, histories of the woman-identified discourse of love being taken seriously, histories of women altering outcomes of wars and dynasties, opposes commonly accepted ways of seeing the past and therefore requires a great weight of historical detail to grant it the legitimacy of truth." Certainly Monfredo's continuous emphasis on her commitment to historical accuracy demonstrates this need to have the women's issues raised in her works taken seriously by the reader.

Conway has noted that the one exception to the lack of women's realistic recounting of their own epics in print was the female slave, "who could ignore the social taboos governing speaking about female sexuality by recounting histories of sexual exploitation by white slaveowners," because she was a victim and the strength of her story was "safely contained within the boundaries of racial subordination" (15). However, Monfredo's fiction makes clear the reality that slavery silenced the voices of African American women. In Monfredo's *North Star Conspiracy*, the powerful forces that may drag the young African American, Kiri, back into slavery, lead Tryon to realize that "because their wives wouldn't talk, and the female slaves the men violated *couldn't* talk, in effect, slaveholders . . . could do as they wanted, without anyone calling them to account" (245-46).

Conway also takes note of the nineteenth century autobiography by the woman professional, who "told her story as a philanthropic romance: she seems to have chanced upon the causes which elicit a lifetime commitment from her. She never acknowledges strategizing about how to advance the cause" (15-16). This approach is used in Monfredo's portrayal of Tryon. In spite of her activist approach to solving mysteries and of "standing up to be counted," on issues of social import, Tryon is also someone who is reluctantly recruited by Elizabeth Cady Stanton to survey local women about their participation in a meeting about women's rights. Tryon "did not want to do the asking. She voiced her objection, protesting that she was by nature shy" (12). Numerous rejections lead her to conclude that "this personal approach business was going to be even worse than she'd imagined" (p. 12). Tryon has "chanced upon the causes" and has to grow into activism.

Thus, Monfredo's series reflects the challenge of juxtaposing real issues of women's history with the readability of fiction, of providing the romance desired by readers (who, according to Monfredo, always ask her about Jacques Sundown, one of the potential love interests for Tryon) while maintaining the integrity of characterization to which Monfredo also expresses a commitment (Telephone interview).

CONCLUSION

Monfredo's historical series mysteries featuring Tryon exemplify Monfredo's commitment to striving for an accurate portrayal of women's history in a readable format. Confirmation of Monfredo's success in reaching her goal of "giving women everywhere a sense of where they have been and what they are capable of achieving" by incorporating historical issues in her popular mysteries is that twelve- and thirteen-year-old girls tell her they read them, that college and high school level history courses utilize the books, and that at the Seneca Falls celebration a ninety-three year old woman told Monfredo that she, too, was a reader (Telephone interview).

Ray Browne has reminded us that detectives are historians (Browne, 2000). Monfredo concurs, noting the corollary that "all historians are detectives," and their detecting efforts are dependent on the acquisition and preservation of primary and secondary sources in libraries (Telephone interview).

REFERENCES

Browne, Ray B. and Lawrence A. Kreiser, Jr., eds. *The Detective as Historian: History and Art in Historical Crime Fiction*. Bowling Green, OH: Bowling Green State U Popular Press, 2000.

Chappel, Deborah K. "Romancing the Real: The Use of History in American Popular Romances." Popular Culture Association Conference. Orlando, FL. Apr. 8-11, 1998.

Conway, Jill Ker. *When Memory Speaks: Reflections on Autobiography*. New York: Knopf, 1998.

Marinelli, Staci and Tim Baker. *Image and the Librarian: An Exploration of a Changing Profession*. 2000. 9 Aug. 2003. <http://home.earthlink.net/~cyberresearcher/ImageHomepage.htm>.

McReynolds, Rosalee. "A Heritage Dismissed." *Library Journal*. 1 Nov. 1985: 25-31.

Monfredo, Miriam Grace. *Blackwater Spirits*. New York: Berkley Prime Crime, 1996.

Monfredo, Miriam Grace. *Brothers of Cain*. New York: Berkley Prime Crime, 2001.

Monfredo, Miriam Grace. *Children of Cain*. New York: Berkley Prime Crime, 2002.

Monfredo, Miriam Grace. *Must the Maiden Die*. New York: Berkley Prime Crime, 1999.

Monfredo, Miriam Grace. *North Star Conspiracy*. New York: Berkley Prime Crime, 1995.

Monfredo, Miriam Grace. *Seneca Falls Inheritance*. New York: Berkley Prime Crime, 1994.

Monfredo, Miriam Grace. *Sisters of Cain: A Seneca Falls Civil War Mystery*. New York: Berkley Prime Crime, 2000.

Monfredo, Miriam Grace. *The Stalking-Horse*. New York: Berkley Prime Crime, 1998.

Monfredo, Miriam Grace. Telephone interview. 10 Oct. 1998.

Monfredo, Miriam Grace. *Through a Gold Eagle: A Glynis Tryon Mystery*. New York: Berkley Prime Crime, 1997.

Nancy Berland Public Relations, Oklahoma City, OK. Press release: Miriam Grace Monfredo Champions Women's Rights. n.d.

Wilkerson, M. P. "Author Working on Book Set in Capital City." *Sunday Montgomery Advertiser* 28 April 1996.

Index